e *for* Heartache Sp
ntry and Western mus
...... *divorce:*

... ok for anyone who's ever loved and lost' *Country Music International*

ubtitle only scratches the topsoil of Stephen Walsh's revealing and
..tely funny/bittersweet account of life following cuckoldry . . .
..che Spoken Here could well be Country & Western's *Fever Pitch*'
.endent on Sunday

. unusual and highly original book . . . full of genuine warmth, humour,
..it and optimism' Terence Blacker, *Sunday Times*

. the best, and one of the most underrated travel books of the year . . .
.ry of a haphazard trip around British Country and Western hangouts
. .uthor comes to terms with the death of his marriage . . . Walsh writes
. .lly, and Country music is the perfect setting for a story of lost love'
. .heeler, *Daily Telegraph*

.quirky, beguiling travelogue, Walsh brings to life some fantastic tales of
.nd woe eased by the plangent twang of a steel guitar' *The Big Issue*

.iverting, deadpan account of a regular chap spending a year travelling
.d the British country and western scene, while his own life turns into
. .ry song . . . On the way he builds up a convincing picture of the
.eness of ordinary life in blue-collar Britain' *GQ*

.us and flippant in equal measure and at the right time; as a UK snapshot
.h the lens of a particular musical genre, there won't be much better'
.& Journal

Stephen Walsh was educated by nuns in Edinburgh and Jesuits in Glasgow and can still, when under the influence of the demon drink, sing his way through the Gregorian songbook. He has a wife, four children and a day-job as a Housemaster at Christ's Hospital, Sussex. His previous books include the critically acclaimed Country and Western travelogue *Heartache Spoken Here* (1997).

Faithful Departures
Travels With Catholic Pilgrims

STEPHEN WALSH

VIKING

VIKING

Published by the Penguin Group
Penguin Books Ltd, 27 Wrights Lane, London w8 5tz, England
Penguin Putnam Inc., 375 Hudson Street, New York, New York 10014, USA
Penguin Books Australia Ltd, Ringwood, Victoria, Australia
Penguin Books Canada Ltd, 10 Alcorn Avenue, Toronto, Ontario, Canada m4v 3b2
Penguin Books India (P) Ltd, 11 Community Centre, Panchsheel Park,
New Delhi – 110 017, India
Penguin Books (NZ) Ltd, Cnr Rosedale and Airborne Roads,
Albany, Auckland, New Zealand
Penguin Books (South Africa) (Pty) Ltd, 5 Watkins Street, Denver Ext 4,
Johannesburg 2094, South Africa
Penguin Books Ltd, Registered Offices: Harmondsworth, Middlesex, England

First published in Great Britain by Viking 2001
1

Copyright © Stephen Walsh, 2001
The moral right of the author has been asserted

The publishers wish to thank The Marvell Press for permission to reprint an extract from Philip Larkin's
'Church Going', from Collected Poems (Faber, 1988)

Set 11/14.75pt Monotype Bembo
Phototypeset by Intype London Ltd
Printed in Great Britain by Clays Ltd, St Ives plc

A CIP catalogue record for this book is available from the British Library

ISBN 0–670–87912–6

For my daughter, Olivia
A star of the sea

– It is a curious thing, do you know, Cranly said dispassionately, how your mind is supersaturated with the religion in which you say you disbelieve.

★

– Then, said Cranly, you do not intend to become a protestant?
– I said that I had lost the faith, Stephen answered, but not that I had lost selfrespect.

James Joyce, *A Portrait of the Artist as a Young Man*

Contents

Processional

In my youth my friends and I used to buy mail-order postcards with tart, thought-for-the-day witticisms. *Just Because You're Paranoid Doesn't Mean They're Not Out to Get You. You Don't Have to be Mad to Work Here, but it Helps.* Cheesy mottoes in wacky fonts on primary-colour card – they read like period pieces now, as solidly seventies as serious sideburns. *Apathy Classes Have Been Cancelled Due to Lack of Interest. My Final Decision is Maybe.* And, of course, *Keep the Faith – if You Have Any Left.*

I still have no idea why this last is funny; perhaps it's because pretty much my first memory involves a question of faith. It's an Edinburgh winter. I am seven or eight or nine. This being the 1960s, when children are still allowed out on their own, I take the bus home from school by myself. Every now and then, between bus stop and home, I encounter some Big Boys. (Like 'Black Babies', in whose general name we frequently gave generously, 'Big Boys' is for small Scottish boys of the 1960s a watertight classification.) As my panic steadily mounts, they walk along the other side of the road just to the point at the periphery of my vision at which, relieved, I think they're going to walk on by. But they don't: they turn sharply, cross the road, form a colossal circle around me, and put me on trial for my beliefs.

'You a *Kafflik*?'

Even without the problems of local orthography, this is a difficult question. I know I am a Catholic, and I have the crucifix burned into my forehead to prove it. But the Big Boys are

I

marauding Protestants (they, my education has encouraged me to believe, have 666 etched into theirs, as sure as eggs are eggs and as sure as their womenfolk carry prophylactics in their handbags) out to give any left-footer significantly smaller than themselves a swift right-footed kick up the arse. 'No' should be the safe answer, but it won't save you, the swift right-foot kick being (quite naturally when the nature of the question is religious) the point of the question. Which harsh reality I discover on the sixth or seventh occasion, when I foolishly try to smart-arse them by saying I am an atheist.

The biggest Big Boy answers. 'Aye. But are you a *Kafflik* atheist?'

(Kick.)

So it's Joan of Arc and me – a shared and noble history of being brutally tortured for our Catholic heritage. But *am* I a Kafflik? Or, as a soul brother of another kind might have put it – can I say it loud, I'm a Pape and I'm Proud?

It's still a difficult question, thirty-odd years later. I know that I was brought up as one. As they say (though only when you die), I am fortified by Rites of Holy Church – meaning that I was baptized and taught to confess, that dressed in lamb-white shirt, woolly, shorts and socks I took my First Communion, that – some time later, though still before I'd reached double figures – I was confirmed in the Faith of my Fathers. My primary school teachers were Sisters rather than Misters; my blazers were always green; and I spent much of my youth servicing services – altar-boying and choir-boying and even (once my balls had dropped and I had mastered C, F and G7 on my old Spanish steel-string) playing folk-guitar hymn-accompaniment in a right-on chapel. Yes: I gave them oil in their lamps and kept them burning.

But of course I know other things too, and they're not things those happy-clappy sing-along-ers would necessarily want to *Sing Hosanna!* to. For I know that, as it happened, I turned out to be fundamentally faithless, utterly without that core of credo and conviction they all possessed, and so wasn't left with much to believe in when the poisoned chalice of independent thought arrived, when secular push came to spiritual shove. Somewhere along the line my flame got itself snuffed out; my own oil-lamp, foolish-virginal, ran dry and did not make it to the break of day. When I was a child, I worshipped as a child, but once I'd put away childish ways, and become a Big Boy myself, I was more likely to be found on the other side of the road from that little boy in the green blazer suffering for his sinless-ness. Not kicking anyone's head in over it, of course; not boorishly bigoted nor troublingly troubled; but forever, it seems, walking away.

So am I a Kafflik? Certainly not in terms of faith and belief and observance. When the bough breaks the credo will fall – these adult days I don't practise, and I don't confess, and I don't commune; I kneel for no one. Taught, as I have been, to be honest and true, and not just to bow obediently down before dogma, I cannot honestly, hand on *mea culpa* heart, say that I think there's any real, hand on *bona fide* brain possibility that that round bit of wafer-bread up there on the altar is really the body of Christ, that that quarter-pint of wine in the cup raised above the priest's head is His blood. I'm familiar with that old 'without doubt there's no faith' chestnut (it's kept many like me at their observances over the years) but I suspect this is deeper. When that host is raised and that little tinkling bell is rung there is no answering chime in my insides; for some deep-gut-*nein-danke* reason, I am pathologically unable to inwardly celebrate that daily miracle.

As well as that stark inner reality there's a social problem – the compelling evidence from the Devil's Advocate in the shape of the shape of my life. The Rites I'm fortified by now are not exactly those that the Holy Church recommends for those seeking the narrow heavenward path. If Strait is the Gate, then try fitting through when your baggage includes a messy divorce, some child-bearing out of wedlock, some not getting the little bodkin baptized even after remarrying un-Kafflikly. My existence is not exactly a cocktail of orthodox spiritual virtue. Living in sin, some would call it; I prefer to call it the real (or perhaps the modern) world, but I suspect that camels and eyes of needles probably will come into it somewhere, and that, when the chips are down (whatever I may believe or not believe) the band will be playing *Oh, you'll never get to heaven*, that it's my song.

And rightly so. And yet . . . and yet. If my faith, is dead, why do I never seem to get to the point of completing the bereavement by reaching what the psychiatrists call 'closure'? I can never, it seems, quite manage to put it all behind me, to write it off, to shut it all down in the name of humanism or rationalism or hedonism. Once a Kafflik, I suppose – amongst all the complex screw-ups an ex-Kafflik famously inherits there can be a pride there, a perverse marking-out of borders, a sense of what in-ness or out-ness is, that one can't quite cross with any true conviction. Maybe it's a kind of brainwash, but if it is – well, brainwashed, how would I know? Sad and middle-aged it may be, but I can't help feeling that somewhere along the line the whole shooting-match was good for me, that it gave me a sense of something other than myself to hang bits of my life on; not virtue, exactly – just look at me – but a sense of virtue, a desire to be good, a wish to be truthful; a shape to things, an inheritance; something that means I can't quite wish not to be in that club that won't quite have me as a member.

So sometimes it's hard to be as visibly non-practising as I am. It's partly because there are things you like in anything that has significantly occupied your life. (This occupier has odd joys: truth-telling, Liberation Theology, my nun-aunties, Latin.) It's partly because you are who you are: if you are a Walsh you are Irish or Scottish-Irish or Irish-American or some other shade of diluted emerald green; it means you are one of us, not one of them; you are untannable and heliophobic, have freckles and the genetic pool to contribute to the fashioning of a ginger baby. It's natural to feel a kind of call when you are brought up as I am. There's another kind of heritage in this business, a sense of where you've been and where you come from. Turning my back on my family is what it feels like to turn comprehensively away from Rome; or felt like for a long time until (confusion on confusion) I acquired the spanking, new, real/modern life family I live with now, with our multitude of sins, from which I do not hope in any way, shape or form to turn.

Crystal clear, what? I believe I don't believe, and yet my lack of belief lies just beyond belief. I live in perpetual fear (and when Kaffliks say perpetual, they mean perpetual) of speaking out – of saying too much, or saying too little; of confirming where I stand. Neither flesh nor fowl, neither weft nor woof, neither burdened nor unladen. Neither in, out nor shake it all about; eggs lodged insecurely in several baskets waiting nervously for chickens to come home to roost; one foot, and quite a lot of excess baggage, firmly on the platform from which the Glory Train will depart. And if that's not an example of one prime two-hundred-pound fucked-up ex-Kafflik, then I don't know what is.

Kafflik, fucked-up; fucked-up, Kafflik. A-levels in guilt. It's not the sex outside marriage that makes us feel guilty, it's the sex within. Shame of the body. Fig leaves. Dress to repress. *Did you eat of the fruit of the tree which I forbade you?* There. It didn't take too long to get on to that, did it? But – allegedly – that's the interesting bit, isn't it, to all you faithless lot looking in from the outside? That poor Kafflik boy you shagged way back, who did this or did that funny little thing, who wiped the evidence off with a pure white hanky afterwards – *Jesus wept!* That woman with the statue of the Virgin overlooking her bed, who said a little prayer, who, at the moment of crisis, suddenly called out – *Christ on a bike!* So let's get it over with. Let's deal with the sex bit now, and we can get on to other things. (And isn't *that* the Kafflik in me talking, I hear you say – push it out the way, sweep it under the carpet, get it out of sight and out of mind . . .)

But there is an unavoidable fact: if you belong to my generation or before, being brought up a Kafflik is unlikely to have been positively good for your sex life. An inflexible blanket ban on pre-marital relations, enforced by inflexible and blanketed men in black, engendered nothing so surely as an absence of good quality sex education; and the sound of silence on sexual matters, we all know, is rarely of benefit in the formation of happy emotional bunnies. Kaffliks of my era – those who bloomed in the swinging sixties and the smooth seventies – did not suffer too badly. (Those fear-of-the-priest Graham Greene types, who, somewhere in the fifties dark, balanced their faith and their catechism against their libido and their desires, and ended their affairs – now they had it really bad.) But I think even my lot were brought up to feel – especially as things really began, pre-AIDS, to swing – a sense of otherness about sex, a sense that that sex-thing might exist but was not quite for us. As a result we are likely to be dimly haunted by a feeling that our sentimental education never quite managed to move at the same sexual pace as everyone else's.

Just think about it, especially you lot on the outside, you lot who've been in the habit of having a laugh at our expense; look back in pity. While you were that innocently sinful secular nipper enjoying pre-pubescent swing-park snogs, we whiter-than-white ones were locked in the church hall, busy preparing for First Communion. When your hormones were jiggling you into self-exploration, we Johnny-come-latelys (knowing sin to be a stubborn stain) were strictly hands-off. By the time you had (quite naturally) moved on to real relationships and the exchange of working parts, we were still considering whether a sin of impurity was worse when undertaken 'with oneself' or 'with another'. Is it so surprising if, padding across your bedroom floor in our bare feet, we were inexperienced or neurotic? Since birth, we had been on an intellectual diet which fed us the notion that sexual transactions were acceptable only under the eye of a peculiarly exact and unchallengeable set of criteria featuring rings and sacraments and a contraception policy celebrated worldwide for its dismal inefficacy.

Look: no doubt Buddhists in the Burmese badlands suffer sexual hang-ups; all early sex is five to four against, and the Kafflik bit is in all probability just icing. But when I consider what I knew as a thirteen- or a fourteen- or even a fifteen-year-old, and compare it with what was known by my non-Kafflik friends, or is known by my non-Kafflik children, certain things do surprise me. Part of it is anatomical: a certain aura of shame and concealment meant that certain facts (and certain helpful opinions) were simply not laid on my table. Part of it is positively weird: I remember being told in my early teens that in the best marriages the marital bed was occupied not just by husband and wife, but by Jesus Christ too. (Thus the merely physical enjoyed metamorphosis into something more significant.) Now as a small child I found it confusing to be told that God was every-where, and I often turned round quickly to see if I could catch sight of Him lurking behind trees; that notion was disturbing enough. The idea that the bearded one would be somehow *there* when you finally came to get down on it . . . the flash-forward was a bit of a mind-blower.

Things fall apart, but mostly they just change very slowly.

Things are, I am sure, better now, with Kafflik educators more realistic, with Kafflik parents more knowledgeable and careful; the world is a better place, whatever the hardliners think, and Kafflik children of the future will be less unlike their contemporaries than we Kafflik children of the past. Even I, who have had bad moments as a result of being brought up in a world of unworldly purity, have, with a little help from my friends, escaped into modernity. But it does seem to me that my childhood has a certain typicality of not so much time and place but of atmosphere; and before I travel any further in this vale of tears, I intend to look again at how the religion of my family helped shape me. Partly to understand it, of course, to enjoy a long slow peer down the belly-button; and partly to make a bolster, to create an ability to pass on to my ginger baby a feeling that what she does with her body and in her bed is nobody's business but her own.

(Oh, and, of course, the business of any of the saints or angels who happen to be looking guardianly on at the time.)

Some of this book, therefore, is an exploration of the personal past of sorts; an attempt, by looking back, to understand how and why what happened in my head happened. But it must be said, especially to those who doubt our complexities, that there are a million more legacies of a Kafflik childhood than sex-life peculiarity; the Kafflik mindset is a whole network of underground caves and potholes, even in the case of those of us who've had to find our way out. A certain liking for the moral high ground is one legacy, of course; a certain sense of being built for superiority, of being chosen, is another; a certain condescendingly sympathetic spite for those of other persuasions is another. A fourth, I think, is the urge to travel Kafflikly. Throughout my fickle, fevered, faithless adulthood, for reasons not entirely clear – though I'm sure I'm not alone – I have consistently narked my fellow travellers on life's journey with my zombie-like hauntings of the holy places of the world.

It's been an irritating tendency. The more diverting the holiday destination, the more I have had to spoil it with a perverse yen to touch religious base. The leafy by-roads of Northern Spain turned into a detour to Loyola, birthplace of arch-Jesuit St Ignatius. The evocatively fog-bound spin round the flatlands of East Anglia hijacked to earn a few hours at England's own Shrine of Our Lady at Walsingham. The crisp winter days in Kraków truncated to witness the grotesque, incense-clad exposition of the Black Madonna of Częstochowa. So on, so forth. A plethora of postcards on the pin-board. A series of brochure destinations botched. Pretty Puglia becomes those chalky-soft sandstone churches. Marvellous Matabeleland becomes vibrant mission wall-paintings. Even Tacky Torremolinos – on the Curvaceous Costa del Sol – becomes (in the hills above the sweaty-sinful city) Spanish village chapels, one after the other explored and devoured, along with their naves and chancels, their mosaics and friezes, their altar-pieces and their tombstones.

I can't fully account for it, this faithless churchgoing, this unconnected wandering in and out, this baffled show of love among the ruins. Philip Larkin thought he knew what he was up to when, bicycle-clipped, he stood and gawped at the naves of English country churches:

> It pleases me to stand in silence here;
>
> A serious house on serious earth it is,
> In whose blent air all our compulsions meet,
> Are recognized, and robed as destinies.
> And that much never can be obsolete,
> Since someone will forever be surprising
> A hunger in himself to be more serious, . . .

Well, maybe: the cathedral at Le Mans, for instance, which I broke into while they were about to renovate, and no one was there; to stand solo and gasp at Gothic as it should have been, with no seats, no chairs, no impediments between earth and heaven, but just a great, gasping space of air and angels, was surprising, was for a moment transforming. But it seems a bit over-noble for me; seems to give too much spine to the invertebrate nature of my meanderings. In truth I think at times it's been just a habit, in either sense of the word; a sort of fix, yes, but also a semi-atavistic, semi-pathetic instinct to toe the party line, to come home from the beach at Biarritz and instead of announcing a welter of worldly joys to start talking about the more sober pleasures of nearby Lourdes.

The reasons for wanting to do it again now, in this book – and to do it deliberately, and on a rather grander scale than these bits and pieces from the past – seem a little clearer. As I turn the corner of forty and begin to see that wide, poplar-lined Cemetery Road opening up before me; as a new millennium begins and God only knows what rough beast slouches towards Bethlehem to be born; as my life continues to resist the great, pre-established shape-and-form destiny-template that was placed on it by the accident of my birth, I feel an urge to have another look at all these Kafflik matters. To travel to some of the great places of the Kafflik world in the company of fellow pilgrims, the better to talk and think, to examine what lies in the past, to search for some kind of answers to some kind of questions, to search above all for some kind of closure, seems like a kind of grand notion, and is what this book is, I hope, mostly about.

Pilgrimage, anyone?

PILGRIMAGE: A journey made to a sacred place as an act of religious devotion.

For that most inoffensively multi-faith version, you need only a middle-sized *OED*. It won't do for me, of course, and anyway, I prefer the more venial, Kafflik version, found in the less well-known *VCE*. *Virtue's Catholic Encyclopædia* has graced my bottom shelf as top-drawer ammunition in the struggle against the devil and all his works for many a long year.

PILGRIMAGE: A journey to some sanctuary or holy place, to pray there for grace, to obtain some spiritual or temporal favour from God, to fulfil a vow, or as an act of thanksgiving or of penance for sins.

There's something much more Kafflik about that. That notion of receiving as well as giving, that sense that there should be no pain without gain, that stress on the last word. It still doesn't do for me and my shapeless ways. But the motivations – to pray, to keep a promise, to say thank you, to say sorry, to ask for something – are clear as the light through a cathedral rose-window, and Kafflik pilgrims have been travelling in hope of fulfilling them for nineteen centuries.

Yes – pilgrimage has always been the essence of Kafflik travel, and what a long, strange trip it's been. Think of the early days, the first few centuries AD, when it was still possible to buy splinters of the holy cross on any street corner, when it was all PILGRIMS DO IT IN BARE FEET and searching for St James's jawbones. Consider the dark, and then the rather lighter ages, when every Tom, Dick and Harry (and even good King Macbeth, who hit Rome in around 1050) would go walkabout. Ponder the Crusaders getting themselves barred from the Saracen's Head and getting Jerusalem listed on the Dark Age equivalent of the Home Office website. Contemplate Chaucer's time, the salad days, when Rome, Jerusalem, Canterbury and Santiago de Compostela became places and names central to European culture, when pilgrimage, earthly and heavenly all at once, began to sit plumb on the knife edge between purpose and poppycock. And dwell on the last flourish before Luther and his cronies, appalled at indulgence collectors behaving as if the soul was a swipe-card and pilgrimage sites simply supermarkets where you collected your reward points, came to sweep it all away.

Yes: certain roads were well-trodden, and certain clichés well-established in the years leading up to that great shake-up and the regrettable invention of Protestants. Our idea of a pilgrim comes chiefly from these times. The hair shirt. Shanks' pony. The simple staff-and-water-bottle ensemble. The shells and the palms and the bells. The idea of seeking help along the road. The thieves in waiting along the ancient routes. The souvenir sellers. The solitude (sometimes); the caring and sharing (sometimes). The tales and songs en route. The road slowly becoming a Pilgrim's Progress, a metaphor for the journey of life, with its sloughs and troughs, as the soul makes its journey towards its God and tries to cast off the stain of original sin. The arrival and the soul's rest. The whole kit 'n' caboodle, in other words, of Sir Walter Raleigh's 'Passionate Pilgrim':

> Give me my scallop-shell of quiet,
> My staff of faith to walk upon,
> My scrip of joy, immortal diet,
> My bottle of salvation,
> My gown of glory, hope's true gage:
> And thus I'll take my pilgrimage.

Of course not so many take hope's true gauge, their pilgrimage, in this day and age; it's no longer all the rage, for 'to be a pilgrim' is not quite so central to our idea of ourselves as it once was. But such travelling still happens. The great medieval sites, places Raleigh saw, are still busy. Rome, with St Peter's at its panting heart, still receives as many religious as secular visitors. The ancient routes through Spain to Santiago de Compostela still attract walkers and bikers and others in the mood for a bit of high church retro. (I have some neighbours who are saving the whole thing – the English pilgrim route all the way from the ferry to northern France – for their retirement.) My own parents, not great peregrinators by any means, and somewhat advanced into the vale of years, went to Jerusalem with seven busloads of Glaswegians just last year.

But there's a madder music now – Marianism, or Mary-worship – which has changed the face of Kafflik pilgrimage in these our times. The Blessed Virgin Mary's attractively modern habit of appearing in different parts of the earth from time to time – normally, conveniently, to unlettered rural folk in war-torn areas ripe for a bit of development – has added a whole tranche of new (that is, nineteenth- and twentieth-century) sites for Kaffliks to make their journeys to. If the tales of Chaucer's pilgrims ring with the great names of the past – Rome, Jerusalem, Santiago and Canterbury – then the tales of the modern age pilgrimage ring just as clearly with the great names of today – Lourdes, Fatima, Medjugorje and Knock. They're names, too, which ring loudly in these travels, in the little stories from the new Pilgrims' Ways this book contains.

As poetry is the new rock 'n' roll, travel is the new religion; it's kind of appropriate that the trade in religious travel, fuelled by these new and urgent sites, is so busy. (You can see the draw, the unique selling point: this is tourism with added value, holiday with self-improvement thrown in, like a spiritual tennis camp or an intensive week-long celestial driving school.) A glance through the small ads in the *Catholic Herald* and the *Universe* and the *Catholic Times* and the *Scottish Catholic Observer* reveals a whole host of opportunities to boldly go on a religious journey, and most of what's on offer takes you to these 'new' places. The language of the advertisers – 'Spes Travel', 'Pax Travel', 'St Catherine's Pilgrims', the 'Rosary Apostolate' – is both familiar and unfamiliar; part bulletin-board, part adman's copy, part pious advocacy.

TOURS OF **ENCOUNTER** AND **SPIRITUAL ENRICHMENT**.
MEDJUGORJE – WEEKLY DEPARTURES FROM GLASGOW.
CELEBRATE THE JUBILEE: THE PILGRIMS' ROUTES TO ROME, JERUSALEM, SANTIAGO de COMPOSTELA.
CZESTOCHOWA: SEE THE BLACK MADONNA!!!!!
IF YOU ARE SEEKING *'THE CHRISTIAN EXPERIENCE OF A LIFETIME'*, THEN WHY NOT TALK TO CHRISTIAN TOURS?
FATIMA – 5, 6 & 7 DAYS BY LUXURY COACH. ABTA BONDED: *WHY SETTLE FOR LESS???*
THREE DAYS AT BRUGES (**PRECIOUS BLOOD**!!!).
CHRISTMAS IN LOURDES. HOLY MASS AT GROTTO ON CHRISTMAS DAY . . . *FREE WINE WITH MEALS*!!!
TRUE CATHOLIC PILGRIMAGES TO THE HOLY LAND, WINTER BUDGET DEPARTURES – JUST £399 . . .

These highly dodgy bits of copy, I blush to announce at this stage, are the sources of the journeys that make up the bulk of this book; these are the sort of ads I answered as I went in search of my faithful departures. Partly because I am not a virtuous man; I would have felt a fraud walking the great paths, stealing grandiosity from those on a different sort of pilgrimage altogether. Partly because I am a worldly man; however many rugged individuals set off along those old roads, most modern pilgrimage is a matter of planes and trains and automobiles, of hotels and full-board arrangements; it's my world, this modern world, and I can't pretend to be anything other than a traveller who prefers the next best thing to being at home. And partly, and most importantly, because I wanted to travel not only with others, but with a range of others; wanted to catch a snapshot not just of the virtuous who, deep-spiritually, travel to Taizé, or deep-mortifyingly, walk the *Camino*, the path to Santiago. I know I admire these things; I know I admire my neighbours, my parents, their faith. But the world of the mass-migrators, the true faithful who endure the true pain of coach-seat sores; they seemed (perversely) like the ones for me, the ones who could show me, if not the truth and the life, then at least the way.

And out of these semi-negatives, I think, come great positives. Those who pay £299 to fly out for a full-board five days at Fatima including excursions and free wine with meals are making an important journey, are at turning-points in their existences, are seeking outward signs of inward graces, have pressing questions to put to the Great Architect of the Universe just as much as the hair-shirt mob do. If to be a serious pilgrim is to be solitary, to enduringly walk, to fight wind and weather, then I have to confess that this is not a book about serious pilgriming. But if being a pilgrim has its essence in the idea that by travelling to some far-off place one can acquire some grace with your God by worship and wonder and contemplation, then most of those who journey in these pages undoubtedly qualify, just as much as a self-improving self-mortifying traveller does. And these, of course, need no long history of others travelling the same route to validate the sense of worth their journey offers; they belong wholeheartedly in the modern world, just as my life does.

So: to go to places that are central to Kafflik religiosity, and see what happens there in the company of those who know better than me what miracles can be worked upon the world – this is surely a worthwhile thing. And there is more. I hope I – yes, even I, who, by a simple absence of something mysterious near my heart, is doomed to stand outside the worship and the wonder – can find some kind of grace too, some kind of reconciliation, some kind of closure, as I make my future-looking pilgrimage through the past, as, looking for a path forward, I look back at the Kafflik things that have so filled my life with their language and presence and ideas. I don't mean a reconciliation in the sacramental, or even in a mildly deep sense; I'm confident about what I do and do not believe. But it remains the case that whatever the Kafflik Church thinks of me – me, the divorcé, the mortal sinner, the failed renouncer of the devil and his works – its culture and its people and its places together constitute the place from which I come; however much they may want to turn their backs on me – me, the infidel, the non-believer, the mocker – at some level I remain one of them. You can choose your friends, as the saying goes, but not your family.

The Kafflik life is full of mystery, of mysteries joyous, glorious and sorrowful; and here's another one, one I'd like to solve. Life in this religion gives one tribal feelings, without a doubt; yet (unlike the Jews, say) Kaffliks don't call themselves a tribe; the stress on the endless observance of ritual, the notion of communion and excommunication, means they tend to say that if you don't believe then you don't belong. It seems wrong. Why is it that there is no place – or where is the place, apart from dark, neurosis-driven corners? – for the doctrinally-no-culturally-yes school of Kaffliks? There are enough of us about, you know, wandering the globe as exiles, formed by a faith without having any of it, full of exclusion and paranoia, full also of pride and an admiration which must always be at a distance, which perhaps takes strange forms, like a desire to travel Kafflikly.

I can't claim, then, as most pilgrims do, to be seeking to find out the nature of the thing that made me; but I would like to know what I am now, would like to know what all the things that made me make me. I too have definitions to coin, have questions to answer, as I pass through this world at the start of a new century. Things which have to do with the distance/ proximity conundrum, things to do with belonging, things to do with the slippery meaning of that slippery word, *family.* Are you in or out if you're neither in nor out? Can you be a Kafflik atheist, with or without a multitude of sins? Can your final decision be maybe? And have you any chance of keeping the faith if you haven't any left?

I
Baptisms

St Joseph of Cupertino (The Flying Friar)
Feast: September 18
Patron Saint of Air Travellers
Joseph had visions and ecstasies from a young age; his family called him
'The Gaper'. When enraptured he could carry a thirty-six-foot cross
like a piece of straw, and was known to float in the air several feet above
the ground.

There are two flights floating out of Speke Airport at nine o'clock on the morning I go to Lourdes. One is the official flight of the Liverpool Archdiocesan Pilgrimage; the other is a tourist flight bound for Palma. And the moment I enter the departure lounge, I can pick out precisely who's going where.

For Palma: the slim, bonkable mothers in bright orange and acid-lime-green; the fathers in chubby-leg khakis blowing smoke into half-quaffed-straight-glass-seven-a.m. lager; the sinuous teenage girls in the shortest of shorts and the boobiest of tubes; the bristling boys, all set, all cock and no trousers; the children in red or blue football shirts manically slapping each other with huge foam feet in the play area; the three lads in their Wigan rugby league shirts and their bright-patterned shorts from budget shops, their Bootle Bermudas.

For Lourdes: the plethora of priests, ancient and modern, fat and thin, smoking and non-smoking, jolly ('Hi Des! how you doin'!') and flight-fearfully miserable; the old ladies with their tight, smiling, Irish faces, in practical drip-dry fabric skirts and blouses; the men with the craggy faces of St Vincent de Paul

Society collectors outside a Sunday mass; the curiously retro bald *hombre* with his shirt collar pulled horizontally out over his jacket and a pair of horn-rimmed specs that make him a dead ringer for (and who better to describe the scene?) Philip Larkin.

For Palma, in other words, a planeload of Peter Pans, perpetually youthful; for Lourdes, a veterans' side that maybe ought to have hung up its fairy-wings years ago. For Palma, the dreamers of nothing more resonant than the burning heat of the Balearic sun; for Lourdes the contemplatives of altogether more final incendiary moments. For Palma, suitcases with tickets saying *Going Places*. For Lourdes, those that say *Cosmos*. (Well, they should have, these journeyers from here to Eternity; but the big boys of the travel trade, like Cosmos, don't trouble themselves with pilgrim travel, and instead we've labels from a two-bit outfit somewhere in Kent.)

But who am I to sniff at the veniality and worldliness of others? Here I am taking the tour-company charter-plane, when most of the fifteen-hundred-and-odd Scouse pilgrims on this annual beano are doing the decent thing and going by coach (hours), then ferry (hours), then train (hours), all the while working their passage by serving the ill of the diocese who have been Specially Selected (it's not me that makes it sound like a junk-mail offer) to be 'Official Sick Pilgrims'. The real pilgrimage, the hard-work-your-passage one, starts by the Mersey at six one morning and doesn't reach the Pyrenean foothills until nine the next, with nothing supplied on the French side, the brochure warns, but bread rolls. But man – or, at least, men like me – cannot live by bread rolls alone, so I book the flight.

The Palma departure is called first. To a chorus of *get your shoes on* and *chhoooom on* most of the colour disappears from the waiting room. The fathers swill the dregs of their beers back. The women rearrange their fleshy breasts in their meshy vests. The kids toss aside their giant foam feet, and the reds and blues and greens and pinks head off for their seventeen-day sultry séjour of sun, sand and sex. Those of us who are left have only six days to look forward to, and there may be sun, down there in the southernmost quarter of France, but that's about it, even for the Bermuda and rugby-shirt trio who, it turns out, are with us.

They're seminarians it seems; and the only young people on board. The Palma lot (seminarians of a different sort) having safely ascended into heaven, the call comes for Lourdes passengers requiring special assistance. For once it's not just people with children in pushchairs who come forward. Even with the majority of the sick taking the land-and-sea route, half the flight could do with a leg up from the stewardesses. Wheelchairs and Zimmers are pushed to the gates and geriatrics winched unceremoniously into the aircraft. Those of sounder mind and body follow in due course; they have a disturbing resemblance to half my family. Bringing up the rear, me, a couple of steps behind everyone, not sure what I'm doing here, or even where I'm going.

Some might say it's a perfectly pilgrim state of mind.

St Francis Xavier
Feast: December 3
Patron Saint of Tourists
(also of Plague Victims and Argentinian Pelota Players)
St Francis (1506–52) travelled widely in the Far East, calming storms, speaking in tongues, raising the dead and evangelizing. He is reputed to have converted more than 40,000 Indians and Japanese.

It's a rather more chaste scene in the waiting room at Gatwick, with little in the way of sins-of-the-flesh potential; the Medjugorje Peace Pilgrims do not have the room to themselves either, but they manage to make a faithful phalanx in amongst the crowd of Croats. The key to I'm-in-with-the-In-Crowd identity, one understands immediately, is to have been there before, and most of the break-the-ice-ical conversation concerns multiple visitation to Medjugorje, a multiply visited shrine deep in what was once Yugoslavia and is now (in the ball-busting way of these Balkan border disputes) in a Croatian-settled section in the Herzegovinian part of Bosnia-Herzegovina.

'Five times before,' boasts Nora, one of two sisters at the hub of things; they're both Irish, though Nora has the green card she needs to live in Manhattan, while Angela (three times before) requires only a passport to Pimlico. But my seven trumps your five: here's Cecilia, a ruddy, feisty-looking woman, busily, perhaps busy-bodily picking up Mary-Ann, a tense-looking waif-stray over from some lost corner of the Yukon, and taking her under her experienced wing. 'Seven times before,' Cecilia tells her, which seems to reassure Mary-Ann. Cecilia has lost James, her son, and goes on about it. (Somewhat insensitively, as it turns out, since all he's done is refuse to travel to the airport with her; he's on his way, whereas Mary-Ann, it seems, has recently lost her husband in a more final sense and where *he's* on his way to is a matter of some preoccupation.)

Various Serbo-Croat sorts look on curiously as the rest of the group start to arrive. It's an oddball bunch, most from round London. There are a couple of Hispanic types, an Indian man, a (separate) old Indian lady with a folding campstool and a Maori-looking mother-and-children team. Of the rest, most are Irish or Italian somewhere along the line; the names that are called are Ferranti and Lynch, di Giacomo and Hickey. And each who gets near enough to be identified quickly hears either of Angela's three or Nora's five or Cecilia's seven; each is immediately drawn into immediate friendship, into a disparate alliance of experience and innocence in which the conversation bubbles through histories both personal and geographical.

'Oh, we were there from the very beginning.'

My life has been turned upside down by all this . . .

'One toilet there was, for the whole village of Medjugorje.'

I know I have to go through this, that it's the most natural thing in the world . . .

'There wasn't a single shop or a single hotel. You'd to stay in people's houses.'

But I don't know if it's going to take me a week or a month or a year . . .

'We'd mass every day, of course, even back then, but then Fr. Jozo was imprisoned by the Communists.'

So I suppose you could say I'm looking for some answers . . .

The travellers are more disparate than those going to Lourdes; there's not that cosy parish feel. Yet there are lots of Irish, lots of old people, lots of women. They eye me a little suspiciously as I earwig, because I've not got my badge on, and on organized pilgrimages badges are important; Badges R Us and Badgeless R Them. But as we're called for the flight Cecilia is in front of me in the queue, and she sees the tour-company logo on my bright yellow ticket wallet. She delivers me my own version of the speech I've already heard.

'Your first time?' At least she waits for a grunt of assent. 'I've been seven times before. I've my son with me today, or I will have by the grace of God; he's checked in now, they've told me, I asked the stewardess. Insisted on coming out here by himself. It's *his* first time – at the age of thirty. Can you imagine? He's made it at last.' (It's not clear if she means on the plane or on the trip.) 'I suppose you could say that I encouraged him to come. But let me tell you something – nobody, and I mean *nobody*, comes to Medjugorje without a purpose. I don't know why you've come, and maybe you don't know why you've come, but I *know* you haven't come without a purpose.'

I smile congenially and don't get into purposes for the time being; this, remember, is coming from a sexagenarian Irish lady, fuzzily going a little thin on top, and wearing the slackest of slacks. I let her speak on: 'You see, Our Lady's gathering troops for her army, you know, and *you're* one of them . . .'

St John the Baptist (John the Forerunner)
Feast: June 24
Patron Saint of Motorways
(also Bird-Dealers, Lambs and the Monastic Life)
Dressed in a camel's-hair tunic and living on locusts and wild honey,
John travelled widely. Envious of his eloquence, Herod kept his head
long after it had been presented on a platter. He would rant at the
decomposing face and stab its tongue repeatedly.

Friday, 3.30 p.m. I leave home once again, pilgrim staff in hand; or, at any rate, holdall, rucksack and laptop – the wherewithal of the worldly pilgrim. And what a wherewithal to get where I'm going; at the station the fast train has gone and though there's another choo-choo on its way, it's a slow train coming. Weary-windowed, I make the long, tedious trail through the southlands (Redhill, Coulsdon, Purley, Croydon) to London Victoria Station, by which time I've finished my book, and with only seventeen hours or so of the outward journey to go. I have so far on these travels avoided too much travel-toil, but this is payback time. First, a sweaty rush-hour Underground through Euston and Finsbury Park, then the above-ground landscape going slowly bagel shop and Caribbean Day Centre before I even meet up with the party that's coaching it overnight for what's described in my documentation as a 'refreshing weekend itinary' at the Shrine of Our Lady at Knock in County Mayo.

On the way I have the distinct feeling of a sharpening of my eyes – I'm beginning to see Kaffliks everywhere. On the Tube, for instance, that weirdo in the beret and the raincoat – when I see the faxes and papers he carries are from the Kafflik Family History Society it only confirms, it doesn't surprise. And shouldn't I suspect the worst as far as that old lady with the twin-set and the fixed, dogmatic expression goes? For all I know she might be my tour operator, Sister Pius, 'International Student Chaplain' by title, geriatric nun with a desk and an incredibly primitive booking system by occupation. My contact with her has had a slightly anxiety-inducing quality. The first time I ring her she doesn't have the tour documents to hand, though she guesses at the dates and takes what, Dickensian, she calls 'my particklers'. The second time she has the documents but not my particklers; I give them again and send her fifty pounds. When I ring several weeks later to check if the cheque's arrived she hums and haws – to a chorus of clicks from her abacus and the scraping of nib on slate, by the sound of things – and asks for my particklers.

Within reach of the starting-point outside the good sister's flat I sit down on a wall at the corner of Seven Sisters Road to see who's making their way towards the coach. I have envisaged a specially selected Sister Pius-sound-alike group of middle-aged Irishwomen, rosaries fiercely to hand, and pretty much nobody else, but, after a quarter of an hour, no one I've seen fits that description. I see Sri Lankans, Eurasians, Filipinos; a Chinese man with a Sacred Heart on his lapel; a minuscule spiky-haired half-Indian; and any number of members of the North London Rainbow Coalition, each carrying dodgily volu-minous luggage, chained trunk-like impedimenta that look suitable for a year's storage in someone's garage, not two nights and three days on a bus. The fat West Indian mamas who are passing by with suitcases could be on their way to Knock; but they could – we're on the fringes of a rough-looking council estate, where Sister P, I suppose, does some of her ministry – be on their way to the launderette.

27

At the door of the coach there's a tubby Mr Jobsworth driver called Martin who's looking a bit flustered, and – at last, the expected – an ex-ginger grey-hair called Peter or Pat or Danny who's holding Sister Pius's carefully handwritten rosters. He points me to a seat near the front, inviting me to 'take a pew'. 'Are yiz a good singer? We need some good singers,' he says, his voice a ringer for Robert Shaw's in *Jaws*. Temporarily off my guard, I flippantly suggest that I have a certain forte in Country and Western. 'Ha,' he laughs, shortly. 'But how are yiz on "The Lourdes Hymn"?' I don't have to answer, thanks to a certain hubbub of chaos and confusion: a black woman is begging, please, petrol paid, any indignity endured, for a lift home to Stamford Hill to get some more clothes, while a Sinhalese man, his wife and two small kids are all cross-purposedly searching for a lost video machine they left on their suitcase when the taxi dropped them off.

Sister Pius, meanwhile, is making the most unholy scramble out of incoherently reading a register of tongue-twisting names, from which she only barely, but often, breaks off to pronounce, on the subject of the lost video, that 'if it's not round this side it's round the other, and that if it's not round the other then it's probably on this'. Ten minutes later, three other people are simultaneously reading the register in a stumblebum game of Chinese Whispers – one holding the list, one holding the mike, one a sort of adjoining door between them – while the other forty of us – *en masse* – search the bus for the missing item. Imagine an overcrowded coach in which all passengers opt to stand in the aisle simultaneously and you have some idea. 'It might be in the luggage compartment,' suggests someone, originally, after some twenty minutes of this, but it isn't found, and we resume our seats like a football crowd after a goal is scored, none of us quite sure if we are in the place where we started.

The woman who went to Stamford Hill re-arrives, twenty-five minutes after the scheduled departure time. Having been dressed for the beach before – it's early June – she is now dressed for a polar winter and appears to have added several attachments to her hair since we last saw her. 'Sorry, everyone,' she calls, jovially. 'Just so long as you're not late for heaven,' calls a shrill West Indian falsetto from behind me. 'Or you'll have to plead with Saint Peter to let you in.' The respondent's tone is semi-genial, in a frosty way, as if to imply that the latecomer had better hope that no one on the bus will have had a word in St Peter's shell-like. The woman sits herself down with a sigh, and, with a substantially more sizeable sigh of troubled responsibility from Jobsworth, Sister Pius's Redeye Roadshow finally gets itself rolling.

The night is dark and I am far from home – not. By the time we have turned one corner from the leafy North London street where we started, Sister Pius is already at the coach-driver's mike, arranging a round of applause for him and for Fr. Jude, our on-board spiritual director who sits in the courier's seat. The formalities over, she calls out, 'Now, then. What would we like to sing?' Jobsworth, cheering up considerably, says he does a good 'Mustang Sally', but Sister Pius doesn't give him the chance to finish the sentence before she's begun, in a wheedling whimper (which nonetheless rips out the woofers of the bus's speaker system):

'All over the world
The Spirit is moving . . .'

(Which is just as well – here in the last ructions of the rush-hour, the bus hardly is.)

' . . . All over the world
There's a mighty revelation
As the prophets said it would be . . .'

The singing, I regret to report, does not take off straight away,
so Sister Pius – who must be seventy-five if she's a day, and
stands no more than four foot eight – gets up in the aisle, waving
her wizened hands and making the people in the front seats give
it vigorous voice. Luckily I have, in the confusion of the search
for the video-player, been bounced to the back, to the bad boys'
seats, where I am sitting beside Edmund, a lone-groover black
guy with a holdall on his knee. He is dressed in the spivvy
manner of a minicab driver (blue patterned shirt, smart jacket,
slacky trousers, pointy black shoes, loads of jewellery and mobile
phone) but in fact he's off the road; he took a trip to France five
months ago, 'tasted some wine', was pulled over somewhere
between Dover and the A2 and banned for a year. And in any
case, he tells me, he was a train-driver until the reorganization
of the southern region left him jobless.

When Sister Pius totters and teeters her way to our end,
waving her arms octopally, like a Hindu statue, trying to get us
to sing too, I feel a little embarrassed, perhaps even a little
obliged, but Edmund is calm: 'I come down to the back of the
bus to relax, sister. That's why you find me back here. Don't be
thinking you can *force* me to sing.' The Swing-Out Sister is cross;
as she wheezes and sneezes her way back up the bus, her asthmatic
last-breath puffiness sounding like an audition for a bit-part in
a hospital drama, he adds to me: 'To me a pilgrimage is a different sort of travel – a different level of travel altogether. Here we
are together, making the road our home; we can't just be forced to
take part in these things. There has to be an element of personal
liberty. Y'unnustand?' I unnustand; and – seeing Sister Pius's
dagger stare, thrown over her shoulder – let him go for a scapegoat.

Fr. Jude is handed the microphone by Sister Pius and he chimes in with an opening prayer. It's a message of welcome, rather than the establishment of a profound theme; he's doing this business on the hoof, it seems, not quite sure what he might expect to encounter: 'We are sure to have many blessings together, and we ask Mary to be with us every step of the way . . . I like to think we're here not because we chose but because He chose us to spend this time together.' Edmund, no rebel really, uh-huhs in thorough assent. Sister Pius has at least half the bus on her side now, as the hymns re-start and continue (even if those of us at the back remain a stiff-necked people) as we pass the car dealers and the insurance brokers and the pizza restaurants of the workaday world:

'Oh Lord my God
When I in awesome wonder
Consider all the worlds
Thy hand has made . . .'

An hour later, we're still stuck in traffic, are still a thousand miles from nowhere. But there is an entertainment. Fr. Jude's introductory discourse (still going on) is punctuated by so many half-familiar hymns one after the other that for me it turns into a seventies-disco-style celestial beat-the-intro competition, as my fellow passengers – at least those in rows A to G – make their way through the traditional hymn book. (They're building the city of God on rock and roll, I suppose.) I play with my history as a chanter. *Now thank we all our –* . (I beat the intro in two on that one.) *Lord of all –* . (Two, again.) *For all the saints –* . (I beat that intro in one, of course.) *Jesus my Lord my God My –* . (Three.) And all performed in that comical way of breathless-singing-without-commas that we mastered while at school and effortlessly carried into adult life: *Come Holy Ghost Creator Come*

From Thy Bright Heavenly Throne Come Take Possession of Our Hearts and Make Them All Thy Own . . .

Another hour later, and Sister Pius is still prowling the aisle of the bus, and Fr. Jude is still introducing our pilgrimage and chiming away at his prayers; we have some 'Our Father's, some 'Glory Be's. I, in pilgrimage mood now, at this third time of asking, am entirely reflective, though not perhaps in the ways normally prescribed. 'Ponder the last things you had to thank God for,' he says. I think of the end of my last marriage. 'The Lord reminds us He is a healer of those who need a healing touch. Commend to Him all those who need a healing touch . . .' That'll be the ex-wife, then. 'Be still, and ponder something that no longer has power over us . . .' Not her again. 'Find the areas we are secure in, and hold on to them . . .' The hymn is 'So Sing My Soul', and my soul does so, rejoicing for the new shape of its life, Kafflik or not.

It does not rejoice for the rosary, which Fr. Jude now starts; one side of the bus leading, the other following. By the Third Sorrowful Mystery Edmund's aftershave is beginning to strike a severe, agent orange-type blow at my neurons. Looking around the bus – anywhere away from the smell – I see Jobsworth is on his mobile phone, ostensibly calling base to enquire about the state of the motorway traffic, but laughing a lot for someone who's receiving an auto-route report; his conversation about directions has changed to some sort of jocularity, and I have to say I'd be tempted to laugh at us myself as we sink into this river of darkness, were it not for the fact that my voluntary presence means I have concrete boots on. The sister pushes on with her singing; I hear a kind of hush, the sound of the spirit 'falling afresh on me'.

★

St Neot (The Pygmy Saint)
Feast: May 1
Patron Saint of Small People (and Fish)
Some accounts of St Neot, a ninth-century monk of Glastonbury, say
that he was only fifteen inches high, which may explain why he was
followed by 'a small band of apostles'. When not performing animal-
related miracles, Neot spent much of the day up to his neck in wells.

Whatever the virtues of going to Lourdes by air, we are not travelling in style. There's not much legroom; there are septuagenarians by every escape hatch; and we're on the sort of charter plane which has a spare-part tail unreassuringly painted in a different colour from the fuselage. And while I'm grateful that fate and the agent have allocated me the last available seat on the plane, I am (as it were) praying that fate hasn't given me the seat simply to cream me off. Is it a lack of faith that leads me to haplessly fantasize about the ultimate irony – of going to Lourdes healthy and, thanks to a crash or a fire or a freak auto-wreck, coming home a cripple?

It always affects me this way, flying, when there's a new baby at home to remind me, as it's the function of babies to do, that I am dust and unto dust I shall return. One or two others look to be in the same state. Most of the pilgrim punters have the look of infrequent flyers; they climb aboard, their duty-free clinking, and soon some non-priests get on, too. And while not quite going so far as to clutch their rosaries as they go, the pilgrim party do cheer the plane off the ground and sit white-knuckled as we speed airily through the low Liverpool cloud. I look around at them as the plane eases to level above the Mersey sandbanks and they begin to relax. It's a clear day, and on a clear day you can see for ever. When you're flying, the faces begin to seem to say, you feel a little closer to God. There's a warmth there, a purpose that's plain to see; I wish I had their confidence.

My next-door passenger is a minuscule, curly-permed blue-rinser from Southport. She asks me if I'll help her with her seatbelt. I do, and she thanks me. Then she decides she wants to take her jacket off, so she asks if I'll help her with her seatbelt. I do, and she thanks me. I try to make conversation: has she been to Lourdes before? Yes. Did she fly then, forty years ago? Yes. Is she looking forward to it now? *Oh*, yes.

Distraction comes as one of the priests – a thin, nervous one called Fr. Gerry – hands out the pilgrimage handbooks. If this was a football match then this would be the official programme, a hundred-page commemorative special featuring texts, schedule, prayers and readings, and for my neighbour it's the perfect excuse to avoid the unwanted intimacy of further dialogue. She reads the prayers in it for twenty minutes or so until the breakfast comes; she decides she'd like to pop to the loo, so she asks if I'll help her with her seatbelt. I do, and she thanks me.

So far so bad: this isn't quite the churchly chit-chat, the peregrinative pot-pourri, the soulful spiritual solace I had in mind on this search for the truth of my existence. But once the croissant and the jam and the strange mélange of brie and ham begin to spread their well-being through her veins, her tight, nervous jaw loosens and she begins to speak. She asks if I have a family. I tell her, without going into too many of the canonical implications. She returns the favour, with all implications supplied. Eight children, six boys and two girls; and that total arrived at only if you leave out the horrors her calm eyes mark only calmly: stillborn twins, and a girl who died at five months. Trials of faith, I suggest, and she nods, without ever suggesting that her rigorous faith has deserted her.

Down below, the neatly Domesdayed fields of England have given way to the higgledy-piggledy fields of France. I show her these out of the window; she shows me what parts of her family are with her, sitting together in a six-seat group just behind us.

Along with her parish curate, one of her daughters and one of her sons. Her daughter is in her late thirties, I'd say, is blonde and jollyish; while her son (she tells me he's forty-two, and I don't guess, for he looks younger) is a cropped-haired big man rendered brain-damaged after a car accident five years before. I glance over as she talks, and he now and then looks possessively over at us, intruding just enough to give us a sense of what she suffers; for he won't tolerate being looked after by anyone but her, she says. His brothers and sisters would, but can't; bone of my bone, flesh of my flesh – only mother will do; and he has no wife, for his fiancée, having found it hard to love a man whose spiritual legs were bent and paralysed, took her love to town long ago.

The plane begins to descend. I get nervous again, and with my eyes closed contemplate an afterlife in which I try to reach through the heavens, trying to touch, but not being able to, my love, my children, my ginger baby, knowing that, were I Demeter, I would have to go into Hades to look for Proserpine; that, were I Orpheus, I would not be able not to turn my head. Panic, in other words. The woman asks me to fasten her seatbelt. I do, and she thanks me, and we share some mints; a funny sort of closeness has somehow come about. Behind us, as the clouds outside become canyons in the Pyrenean air, her son begins to feel the descent and gets excited.

He nudges her. 'Down! DOWN!' he shouts. His eyes are wild, are manic with excitement. Indulgent, admirably calm, she nods. 'Down! DOWN!' he shouts again, to no one in particular. The chubby young curate smiles a little awkwardly, but the grey-haired woman opposite him winks. He nudges my neighbour again. 'Down! DOWN!' She nods again, with just the same precision, the same echo of his rhythm. 'Down! DOWN! FAST!' he shouts, and his face is animated, as if he's suddenly going to leap up out of his seat and run up and down the aisles with his hands outstretched *brrm-brrrming* like a primary school playground aeronaut. His mother reaches out a hand, and effortlessly half-stills him until the plane taxis to the terminal. 'AGAIN!' he shouts, Teletubby-like, and the children on board laugh and sigh with relief.

She asks me to take her seatbelt off: I do, and she thanks me, but this time she's voluble. 'It's the loveliest bit of the whole holiday,' she says, by way of what she imagines is goodbye, 'the flying.' But as we queue to get out she keeps talking, like we've got somewhere: how he was in the building trade, how his car left the road, how he lay in intensive care for months on end, how he emerged crumpled and damaged, and how she would never have known, thirty years back, when her mother paid for her to come, all of £65, just for the run, if you know what she means, that now she would be returning, and that now she would be hoping against hope for – literally – a miracle. Down the steps to solid ground I find myself earnestly imploring the architects of the universe to give her one.

In the baggage hall of Tarbes Airport – first stop Lourdes – a pair of priests, one fat and white, one thin and black, smile at me. It's the odd couple – Fr. Des-how-you-doin' and his assistant, who I later learn is from Wallasey out of Ghana. Odder still is Fr. Gerry, the nervous-looking programme-seller, who steps forward out of the airport shadows to make sure I'm not lured into complacency by this show of geniality, to make sure I'm au fait with the level of *sheer organization* that goes into such an enterprise as the Liverpool Week. He's caught up with what I'm doing here, and it's obvious that he feels ill-at-ease with such a maverick meanderer, such an unparochial pilgrim in the party. What harm I could do to the order of divine intervention I do not know, but he clearly hopes to blind me, if not with science, then at least with statistics. He recites them like a darts compère calling the scores, peppering them with exclamation marks.

Two hundred and fifty! pilgrims flying in with me on this charter flight.

Twelve hundred! others arriving by 'Jumbulance' (mighty sick-carrying road vehicles) and by train, by other agents, under their own steam. And among them –

One hundred and fifty! 'official sick' – sick people chosen by the diocese to be pampered by the pilgrims and lodged in the Lourdes hospitals. Among them, too, those who will staff the hospitals for the week, such as –

Three hundred! youth helpers who need physical as well as spiritual feeding and watering; and –

A hundred and fifty! handmaids, females in white robes, proud to be the handmaids of the Lord; and no less than –

Fifty! 'brancs', or brancardiers, the male corporal workers of mercy, the wheelchair-pushers and general dogsbodies who, like the handmaids, give up the price of the holiday and their week to help the sick and dying.

'You have to know these things,' he says, with threatening smoothness, with almost extreme unction, 'and *admire* –'

Half an hour later I sit in the transfer bus, ready to admire. And sit. And sit. And sit. Again, it's Zimmers at six o'clock, and loading each wagon takes quite a time. The bus fills with *thirty!* or *forty!* of the *two hundred and fifty!* I am the youngest by *twenty!* years, and I am no spring chicken. A handmaid sits beside me: a sixty-year-old with a grey Rhine maiden haircut, bad to no teeth and poor hearing. She's a veteran and no mistake: great pilgrimage tales grate on my ears as she recites the highlights of her twenty tours of hospital duty. I drift off into a reverie of home as she tells me the famous landing-in-a-thunderstorm drama of '86, not to mention the celebrated broken dishwasher saga of '75, amidst a litany of other tragical-comical-historical-pastoral experiences.

Oh well, I reflect: they also serve who only stand and make a big deal of serving. And some are quieter. As I check in and get the key for my cell at the Hotel Roissy, I chat idly with Roger, a balding man in jeans and a T-shirt. He has a bright, open, intelligent face; the cut of a middle-class gait. His aged mother Margaret (pushed sweatily in a wheelchair) is with him, along with Margaret, a family friend. Rog starts to tell me something about his being here, and for the first time I feel a little human warmth, but Margaret, the friend, accidentally cuts across, asking if he'll have a beer. He doesn't reply so much as simply gush appreciatively, his slaked throat emitting a flood of relief.

He doesn't finish his sentence, since he has his key in his hand. I line up obediently for mine, which is dished out coldly by a madamish madame in smooth chenille and slick slacks. In Lourdes even the fifty-quid-a-night places are on the stern side.

St Polycarp of Smyrna
Feast: February 23
Invoked Against Earache
Polycarp (69–155) was burned alive in the stadium at Smyrna, where he was bishop. He refused to be nailed to the pyre, arguing that God would give him the strength to stand tall, and the flames, instead of consuming him, made an encircling dome. When his killers came to finish him off with daggers, there arose from his baked but not burned flesh a smell of incense and sweet gum.

Having been outed as a member-in-mufti of Our Lady's Light Infantry there seems no reason not to wear my Medjugorje badge; I put it on. Encouraged, consolidated, Three-Time

Angela chats with me on the plane. We talk a lot as we rise over middle Europe: she's sharp and bright; sixty, I'd say; acute, a little troubled, and speaks in a nervous rush of something like kindness, though there's a proselytizing wish to inform there, too. The stages of the journey are marked by her breathless, considerate wish to fill the empty vessel of my soul, to give me the things I need for divine love.

So over the Channel, it's true-life tales of the wonders of Medjugorje. For instance: 'There was a certain Methodist preacher,' she says, making him sound like the Ancient Mariner, typically experiential, 'who was told about the place, went to visit, and was awestruck. Simply *awestruck*. He came back from the place, arrived home wavering about all the articles of his faith on which he'd based his ministry,' she says. 'Yet he couldn't quite make up his mind to convert; his mind was so full of objections to the Catholic faith, from all his training and his upbringing, from everything he had been taught to think. Seven years, it took him . . .' Seven years, that is, to process and finally dispense with his objections before taking up professional left-foot-kicking.

Over the Alps it's tales of the apocalyptic prophecies of someone called Mary-Jane Even. For instance: 'Even to me,' she says, 'who's well-read in these things . . . even to me they're very, very frightening. I'm not sure I could show them to most of the people on this plane. I'm not saying they're not devout; not saying they wouldn't know how to react, how to make sure their lives were in order. But –' The but is that she offers to post them to me if I'm interested; I'm clearly, in her eyes, in need of a short sharp shock, some extreme unction. Ms Even, it seems, writes 'scary books' foretelling the end of the world, and includes in them auguries that in note-form sound like Mormon-style averrals that anything that's happening in the world presages the end of it – global warming, tidal waves, the slaughter of cattle, the running-over of pet cats; but which in Angela's telling sound frightening, sincere.

Over Northern Italy Even's predictions reach their deepest, darkest point (and one the Mormons never trouble themselves with) – the impending break-up of the One True Church. And here's where at least some of Angela's troubled air comes from. On the one hand she's nicely rebellious ('Of course the Church has got to change with the times, I've been saying this for years'), on the other, John Paul II is for her the Last True Pope ('I have this worry that the next Pope will change things – will change big things about the way we do things'). And the thought of women up there on the altar, or married priests – for these are the things on the progressive agenda of anyone with a lick of sense, no matter how darkly certain agencies can conspire in reactionary foot-dragging – these things are things her liberal, and, it's clear, honest soul is just not ready to deal with yet.

Over the Adriatic she becomes more quiet, more personal. I'm surprised by her capacity to come clean, to become personal. For instance: 'What you would call a classic Irish childhood,' she says, 'is what I had', and she goes on to describe it. Born rural, boarded off to school, struck down by tuberculosis, or polio, or brucellosis, or something caught from cows; a resultant childhood disability, meaning lots of time in the land of counterpane spent reading *Lives of the Saints*; the possession of – by the time she arrived in London as a limping eighteen-year-old – what she calls 'a simple faith'. But 'the bright lights and the big city dazzled me, I'd admit, and I couldn't see the wood for the trees; after a while I came to believe it incredible that any intelligent person could believe this stuff that I'd been brought up on'.

And over Croatia, some tales of the years that followed her decision to walk out into the wilderness, the long years that stretch out in the memory, and that ended when she had a troubled conversion at a charismatic renewal session, and everything that had sat in the back of her mind, unfulfilled, began to draw itself out, began to make a bit of sense again; how wood became wood again, and not trees. And her especial for instance: how, following some sort of an inner calling, she had enjoyed some kind of (I'm to discover it's a big word for these Medjugorje people, which means something more than the simple transfer of loyalties the Methodist indulges in) 'conversion'; and, as coherent and true as the mountains down below, how she started to come to Medjugorje, to make her regular filling-station-style stop-offs there, every two or three years.

At Split we take a bus, for three hours plus along the Dalmatian coast. (Long enough to recall the tale of St Blaise, patron of Dalmatia, who walked on the waters and invited his persecutors to do the same. They, of course, drowned, even if their associates subsequently cut Blaise up with wool-combs.) Then it's up into the forbidding mountains, and across into Bosnia-Herzegovina, which is where the shrine of Medjugorje, this most Croatian creation, is situated. Cecilia, Recruiting-Sergeant for the Virgin's Volunteers, sits opposite; her son James – the lost sheep – is next to me. He's non-pilgrim-like in his looks; a good-looking, dashing thirty, he sips Glenfiddich from a miniature bottle, and once it's clear I'm no ordinary pilgrim either he slips me one under cover of the chair-back; as the bus slips along a Eurotraveller-friendly tourist coast of *chambres* and *zimmer* and *camere*, of tents and caravans and motorhomes, of girls in shorts and men with bellies red from sun and beer, of many cool-of-the-evening strolling families and the odd water-polo match floodlit in a harbourside against the black sky, we sip and talk *sotto voce* of jobs and callings, girlfriends and partners, of (his) life in London.

En route Cecilia passes us worthier supplies. Sandwiches,

plum tomatoes, a banana: she even pushes one into the hands of an elegant, ice-cool Croat courier, whose poised gymnastic presence and calmly clipped sangfroid at the bus mike is severely threatened by the sudden arrival of slices of pork pie and potted-meat sandwiches in best Yorkshire silver paper. Cecilia, like Angela, seems to be no fool. On discovering my mission her questions are searching and acute, and her advice about keeping an open mind is almost minatory in its pert, poised, precision. Have I been to Lourdes? (Yes.) Have I been to Fatima? (No. Sorry.) Nodding, stern, clocking, she hopes I'm not just looking for the bad, because *untruths* – she booms the word, and half the bus stands to attention – have been written about Medjugorje.

She takes a long look at her son and catches sight of my bottle. 'He's got you on it now, has he?' she says; she's not stentorian, in fact, even though she starts to sing-song a long parabolic parable about two young men who were attached to a pilgrim group but were travelling without a true sense of what they were doing there, and who irreverently set out for a wild night on the town in Medjugorje. 'They were thinking wine, women and song,' she says, 'but as they rolled along the sacred streets the Virgin herself appeared *in person* to them to tick them off. Well, let me tell you, their drunkenness and high spirits disappeared in an instant, and the next day they were up early to begin a Novena of prayer to Our Lady of Medjugorje.' And, no doubt, to sign up for a long-service stint as NCOs in the Virgin's Volunteers.

I look suitably impressed and say what matters; that I am a searcher of sorts, and in that sense a proper pilgrim, however I come there, and that she should respect that. Her look makes it clear that having found the One True Path, good and proper is the only thing that's really acceptable, but that searching will do to be going along with, especially if it's the kind of searching that will lead on without too much more wandering to the aforementioned path; and the bananas and the ham rolls keep coming. I take them as a sign of approval until, from behind, Mary-Ann offers me a lump from a huge, consoling bar of Dairy Milk (of such a size that only the bereaved could justify buying) and she has a little pop at me: 'Don't give *him* chocolate – he's an agnostic.' I cast my mind back, assure myself I never used that word; James tips me a wink, and I understand why he made his own way to the airport.

Further exchanges are impossible, as a brother appears from the back of the bus and, as we drive through the night, he begins to say the rosary in full. The key to the Sorrowful Mysteries, he says in one of his interim meditations, is that we must learn to crucify our own natures. I feel the pain of three nails: the bus journey, the prayers, the singing. The agnostics aboard are doomed to silence, and the whisky dries up too. As we leave the coast road the whole bus – except us – sings to the disappearing Adriatic:

'Mother of God
Star of the Sea
Pray for the wanderer
Pray for me.'

Eventually the rosary comes to an end, and our svelte Slav courier teaches us a few quasi-jovial words of Guidebook Croatian. Then, with a job-done sigh, she puts on a tape for the rest of the journey, in the manner of a parent retiring out of earshot of further enquiries about when the journey will end.

Funnybones it ain't: a smooth-talking friar with Victor Meldrew adenoids occupies the airwaves, telling the story of Medjugorje pithily and economically. How, in the place where we're heading, at 6.45 on the 24th June 1981, several children

43

saw apparitions of the Virgin Mary on a bare Yugoslav hillside; how they were naturally frightened and confused; how news spread quickly through the gorges of Medjugorje; how, 'guided by an inner call', the children returned to the place later in the day; how the apparition offered them the name, rank and serial number of Our Lady, Queen of Peace and Commander-in-Chief of the military corps on board our bus; how other villagers saw MIR, the Croat word for peace, etched vastly on the sky; and how visions, apparitions and Virginal messages have continued to occur to this day.

And there's more: 'Mary has promised to reveal ten secrets,' the tape says, 'at predetermined times, to each of the six children. Two have had all ten, the others nine; Ivan, Marija, Vicka and Iakov still receive them.' So on the 25th day of each month, a message is given to the world via Marija, one of the children; or is it Vicka? Information has a way of becoming redundant; the names confuse, even if the friar doesn't. The messages, we're told clearly, 'all have a theme of peace. Peace to our world and peace to our hearts.' World-issue-myopic, he makes no mention of the fact that for the last six or seven years the country we are in, and the others that together made up the former Yugoslavia, have been tearing each other limb from bloody limb; what's discussed instead is the bish-bash between the Franciscans, who run the shrine of Medjugorje, and the local bishop, who has his doubts about the authenticity of the visions and the desirability of what has followed in their wake. By way of a touché we're told that John Paul II has issued a *nihil obstat*, of an informal sort, to the doings and cooings in the place; so there we are.

The mountain road begins to make a winding stair and the courier says an evening prayer that is touched with agonized Croat tongue-twisting. *Terr-rust in the Lor-id that he may cleans-ey your hearts*, she says. As we climb we begin to see visual evidence of war we're being implicitly implored to ignore: piles of rock from mashed buildings litter the rough grass verges. *Mary – tank you for helping us to cleans-ey our-i-selves. As our mother you don't care how soil-ied we may have become.* The road signs, we see, are pock-marked with bullet-holes. *We pray especially for the person you may have quarrell-ed with.* That's her story and she's sticking to it. Our course through the night has more of this, and then the litanies (including Anthony of Padua, patron of travel hostesses, whose eloquence the very fish would come up to admire) before Slavenka or Zlata or Danjela or whoever she is sings us the 'Song of Medjugorje', or of Mir, or of Croatia, or whatever it is. Call it a haunting Slavonic air, or call it incomprehensible tosh: it's still beautiful to hear her working in her own language.

'When I came two years ago,' says Cecilia, who is talking of the sixth of her seven goes at this pilgrimage, 'the Yugoslav War was at its height' (she means the war over Bosnia, not that over Kosovo) 'and they –' (she doesn't specify whether she means Croats, Serbs or Bosnian Muslims) ' – were shelling the road. On the way back we had to leave Medjugorje at four in the morning, and the driver had to drive without lights.' She's had the grace to withhold this information until we've reached our destination safely; the road we've just travelled has borne a striking resemblance to those Riviera highways you usually see Roger Moore or Sean Connery racing an open-topped head-scarfed bimbo along, and the mind boggles at the thought of Cecilia and her rosary-gripping chums pegging along it in a battered sanctions busting tourist-bus running on empty while shells fall from on high.

At Pansion Tomas they're still up, though it's gone midnight, and they've made a heavy supper for us, which we all lay into with gusto. Mary-Ann, the woman from the Yukon who's lost her husband, shares half a bottle of Herzegovinian white with me; think sub-Algerian, or think watered-down sherry with added antifreeze, and you're more or less there, but in the thick midnight heat it slips down well enough once the epiglottis stops convulsing. Mary-Ann is, it seems, the not-so-merry widow, and she's trying, but failing, not to look like a troubled soul; there's a desperation about her that's not difficult to recognize, not so much in the furrow of the brow but in the second of hesitation before everything she says. She tells me the tale of how she came with this particular group: having come over to England from Canada to pay a courtesy call to her late husband's mother, down in the Cotswolds somewhere, she suddenly felt 'impelled' to make the journey here.

That 'inner calling' again: her mother-in-law, for one reason or another, did not approve. Nor would she approve of us, after supper, at half-one in the morning – which is, I suppose, adventurous for some of the sexagenarians I am travelling with, but the call is fierce and strong – wandering down en masse to the Church of St James, the epicentre of the spiritual earthquake this place is marked up as. The main drag of Medjugorje is developing, the old hands say: where once there was nothing but dirt and dust, there are *diskont* stores, mini-markets, sports shops, Fanta machines. Nora the Irish New Yorker shows us where the tobacco fields were the last time she came; now they're sprawling building sites where new pensions and restaurants are going up in good time and best breeze-block. Mouthfuls of consonants make up most of the names, of course, but there's a Glasgow Restaurant and a Paddy Travel Agent and (a biblical best) *Dalila's* Hairdressing Salon, before we move into the rosary and winking-Jesus heavy-sell sector; it's a developing industry, by all accounts.

The shops are shut, of course. 'Peace,' says Cecilia. 'Peace is what you find here, if nothing else.' It hardly seems a test of the place as the clock strikes two, and we are more or less alone.

The church is closed too, of course, but there's a little white statue of the Virgin on the forecourt where pretty Croatian girls and handsome Viennese boys are saying the rosary together, locked in some kind of spiritual holiday romance. Some of us wander round the back, where the white, double-spired church has been extended with a PVC conservatory that Everest Double Glazing might have put up; and then to the side. Nora, woman of the spirit, is interested in finding the loos; I'm put out when, once I've found them, she has no use for them. No, she's looking for the old ones, so that she can offer another I've-been-here-before hardship tale.

'They had a guy there,' says Nora, 'a *communist*, who used to charge you a *quarter* for a *single strip of toilet paper.*' Her face crumples in a Baudelairean, *où sont les cruddy public conveniences d'antan?* way when the new lavs appear before her, all white and spanking and new, their marble walls polished smooth with dustcloth dollars from stateside Croats in exile. On the way back she pauses in front of a shop. 'Shoes,' she exults, as if this is the biggest surge in the earthquake of all. 'I just can't believe they're selling *shoes* in Medjugorje.' It seems a somewhat specialist point of view, but one that says we're all glad – in our own ways – to have come here.

St Frances of Rome
Feast: March 9
Invoked to Encourage Safe Driving
Frances is author of 'Ninety-Seven Visions', accounts of dreams of the
punishments of Hell. When she went out at night a guardian angel
only she could see made a headlight-like illumination of the path ahead.

Friday, 9.30 p.m. *Sometimes the road is long, my energy is spent.* We may have reached Lourdes, we may have reached Medjugorje. But on Sister Pius's bus we've reached . . . the Motorway. *Then*

Lord I think of you and I am given strength . . . We've trailed our way through the outskirts of London (*Woe to the bloody city! It is full of lies and robbery!* is the feeling) and are now only just working our way up the motorway in a three-lane tail-to-tail slow-oozing jam that runs past Luton and Milton Keynes and Bedford. Edmund shares some sandwiches and crisps and biscuits from his Kwik-Save bag with me, talking about how it's all about 'going together', about being 'travelling companions, y'unnustand'. He has a sense of idealism, some pilgrim spirit, which is nice, and fair, and wondrous, and it takes me a minute to realize he's not talking out of context; he's working to smooth the furrow on my brow. We shake hands formally, for some reason; maybe we introduce ourselves to each other again. I decline sweet-looking white tea from his flask, sip my Coca-Cola, and listen to something from the front which reminds me in no uncertain terms that I am a Banished Child of Eve, there at the back of the bus.

The rosary ends, at last, and, freed from the shackles of the drummed-in rhythm of the decades, Edmund and I talk our battered lives for a bit. He is divorced too, as it turns out, maybe twice: it's hard to discern all the sense in his mutter over the noise of the engines. Certainly one wife has gone in the journey to his forty-eighth year, and, if I get it right, another live-in-sinner went the same way, all of which has made him philosophical: 'It's all greed in the modern world, y'unnustand. People so busy filling up one pocket. Then the other pocket isn't full and they don't want to know about it, y'unnustand? Materialism, you see.' I don't really, but it makes more sense than the Sri Lankan couple who, with their two kids, occupy the back seats.

This lot are as far from that as possible, and as far from Edmund's modern world. When Sister Pius comes down, the mother says, talking of her two minuscule children: 'Did you hear them saying the rosary, Sister?' and when the sister has gone the mother, a tense, pious-looking woman with a scabby face, tells me a story about how her son, who looks about five, had all his friends from primary school over to the house for a 'rosary party'. It's hardly sex, drugs and rock 'n' roll: I think of St Anne, mother of Mary, patron of Kafflik mothers, handing her daughter over to the service of the temple when she was just three. Out in the dark there, meanwhile, our bus wheels move on, dragging us at a rate of fifteen miles an hour towards our uncertain destination. If pilgrimage is about the travelling and not about the arriving, I reflect, then this must be the purest pilgrimage of all.

'Once upon a time and a very good time it was there was a moocow coming down along the road and this moocow that was down along the road met a nicens little boy named baby tuckoo . . .'

So appears, for the first time, the character of Stephen Dedalus, in James Joyce's craftily crafted, thoroughly themed memories of an Irish Catholic childhood in A Portrait of the Artist as a Young Man. *But here is another Stephen, a travelling Stephen seeking out his memories of a Kafflik childhood in another country. What can he recall? Nothing in his book can be as finely tuned as Joyce's, of course; he cannot claim to be assembling so stupendously significant an exit from home, from family and from religion as Stephen Dedalus is. But even in his more secular age, in his less intensely Kafflik country, he remembers feeling a sense of being who he is, a sense that, whatever else he might be, he is a Kafflik first and foremost, and living in a world almost entirely made up of Kaffliks. A surrounding, an encircling of influence of Holy Mother Church. Not a cruel world by any means, not an irrational world, even, particularly. But a feeling that in the Lord's own house will he dwell for ever and ever . . .*

Stephen's family: *he is born the third child of five. Though middle-*

class second-generation petit-bourgeois himself, the whiff of the peat-bog is not far away – he is the son of a man who is one of the nine children of an English-Irishman and an Irishwoman, and the son of a woman who is one of the six children of a Scottish-Irishman and a Scottish-Irishwoman. All four of his grandparents – most of them first generation born on this side of the water – have, like their parents and their grandparents on that side of the water before them, been devout and pious cradle-to-gravers, and both of his parents, having been suitably cradled, are – barring a wreck on the highway featuring unprecedented spiritual carnage – odds-on to be suitably graved too.

His mother's side is comparatively relaxed; that is to say that although all five of her fellow-siblings are or have been devout, are or have been faultless Sunday worshippers, all are or have been out there in the world, as workers, as marry-ers, as breeders of the next generation. His father's side is not unworldly, of course not; but of the nine children of his father's house, three girls emerge into adulthood as name-changed nuns, and two boys (handily pre-labelled James Ignatius and Francis Xavier) as priests. He himself is not the son of a preacher man, but it needs to be said: five of his childhood aunts and uncles, like the bride, wear black.

Stephen's house : *is therefore sometimes full of priests and nuns. Is certainly full of crucifixes in his early days, if not in every room then something like it. He thinks he remembers a holy water font by the door, a small brass cup beneath a white alabaster Mary, but it's vague, perhaps temporary. And of course, not so unusual in a certain day and age; a holy house, but not untypical. Of the rest he must suspect, speculate. There is a picture in the Edinburgh house; he is standing between two russety, tweedy sofas, dingy maroon or beige, antimacassar-less (do you take this for an olde worlde residence, lacking modernity?) carrying a big, pale picture-book called* Our Mother Mary.

There must be other books; there are certainly prayers; that is the way of things; there is a hoped-for rhythm, a worked-on routine. Prayers upon rising in the morning. When he comes into his parents' room in the mornings there is his father, pyjamaed, bare-footed, first-thing-kneeling by the side of his bed, an example. Grace before meals. At breakfast (Bless us O Lord and these thy gifts), *at lunchtime* (which we are about to receive from Thy bounty), *at suppertime* (through Christ our Lord Amen). *Prayers in the evening, kneeling by the side of his own bed, in imitation:* Bless my father and my mother, my brothers and my sister, my aunties and my uncles, and everyone I can't think of, including the starving people of Africa . . . *For this is a time when we just help people; helping them to help themselves is not heard of.*

Stephen's school: *has a green blazer, a gold crucifix on the baize breast-pocket, a Latin slogan. He wears cap and sandals, and shorts, even in the deadest of East Coast winters. There is reading, writing and arithmetic; and there are more prayers. Prayers at mass on Friday in the Church of the Holy Cross.* Our Father, who art in heaven. (*None of the 'which art'; none of 'the kingdom, the power and the glory'; those are Anglican exoticisms, remember, Protestant mumbo-jumbo; English.) Prayers in assembly, with the stern-suited Headmaster. (He prays for the strength to belt the wicked later; or so the little street-song goes.) Prayers on posters on the classroom wall.* Hail Mary, full of grace, the Lord is with thee. *Prayers in the morning with the register. Prayers before leaving for lunch. Prayers on the blackboards in the rooms of Sister Mary Dominic and the maternal nuns who teach him (no sour-faced orphanage bitches here).* Glory be to the Father, and to the Son. *When someone dies, prayers:* And let perpetual light shine upon her, may she rest in peace, Amen. *And even, occasionally, a thoughtful prayer, the noble words of which might lilt and rise with meaning, like those of St Ignatius:*

> Dearest Jesus
> Teach me to be generous,
> To serve Thee as Thou deservest,
> To give and not to count the cost,

To fight and not to heed the wounds,
To toil and not to seek for rest,
To labour and to seek for no reward
Save that of knowing that I do Thy holy will.

Stephen's school playground: *the city is not exactly a Kafflik hotbed, being dour, East Coast, cold and Calvinist in orientation. (Over on the West Coast of Scotland things are considerably hotter, considerably more vicious, considerably more logged and bogged in the patterns of the past.) But even in the Athens of the North the division is never far beneath the surface: you have Us and Them, Kaffliks and Prodestants. There is never any doubt that Stephen will follow Hibs, will learn to despise Hearts and their Gorgie slums where they root in the buckets for something to eat and find a dead rat and think it's a treat; he will be a Tim or a Fenian bastard, while the other side will remain Billy Boys and Orange bastards. A snatch of song comes sailing out of the rainy air of the primary school bike-sheds, and its lilting, rising meaning has less nobility than the Ignatian intonation:*

> I was going down Gorgie
> With my razor and chain
> Along came an Orangeman
> And called me a name
> So I kicked him in the ba's
> And I kicked him in the head
> And now that Orangeman is dead.
> With a na na na na na na na . . .

And the wild rose blossoms on the little green place.

Meanwhile, at home, Stephen is marked out for duties, is recruited. Task. Service. Obedience. At seven or eight years old he is making his way to St Columba's on a Sunday to serve eight o'clock mass. The Big Boys (Kafflik branch), who include his Big Brother, control the servers' list, and they bag the later services which come complete not only with sleep-in, but also (the early mass is low worship) the chance to set the incense going in the thurible — a match set to the black cake of charcoal — to get the smell, to manufacture the happy rhythm of the canister clinking on the chain; the Big Fun of altar-serving. So Stephen gets up in a quiet house (his father is often around, but works, and reads, and goes later in the day, perhaps to read the lesson). He splashes water on his face, walks hungrily through the smell of baking rolls, dresses in black cassock and white surplice (bathetically retaining his cheap supermarket trainers — the great god Adidas has yet to appear on earth) and kneels on the purple altar-carpet.

It's a toss of a coin. The young priest is fine. The old one, the parish priest, the canon: not fine. He is a Scottish-Irish tyrant of the old style; tall until you meet him in later life, when you find he's five foot three and bald on top. He is brisk, dominant, fierce in his fiefdom; like a corrupt rotten-borough member wallowing his way through the trough of life while never failing to preserve the good name of the parish and keeping his local friends. Essentially the situation is this: if the Canon has managed to play his nine holes of golf on Prestonfield Links between six and seven-thirty he is all smiles on a Sunday, and the acolyte can proceed, albeit with caution, to pour the water and the wine, to busily offer the white linen-cloth to wipe the rim of the chalice. But if something has detained him, has kept him from sending his little white ball scurrying on the rich damp Scottish greens and fairways — fog, perhaps, or some poor soul needing the Last Rites in the night — then he takes revenge on the hapless surpliced server, on the cat within reach of the boot.

Not for him a quiet word of private reproach in the silence of the vestry if the water and the wine don't come in good time, if the low chime of the gong doesn't come quick enough to match the quickly-lifted host; no, on golf-less days he tensely screams across the altar, wretched, even in the middle of mass. For Christ's sake, boy! he shouts, even at the crucial second, even at the precise moment of the enactment of

Christ's supreme sacrifice, with the quiet congregation on their knees and hushed, waiting only for the bell to tell them to raise their eyes to the uplifted host. Get those bloody cruets over here! *And Stephen, a blusher thereafter, learns how to do it here, learns early how to flush with shame.* And quick! *As he leaves the church, homeward, picking the flea from his ear, Stephen sees the Canon standing on the church steps, shaking hands, hail-fellow-well-metting, fixing up an invitation foursome at Gullane in the week.*

II
Communions

St Roch
Feast: August 16
Patron Saint of Bachelors, Diseased Cattle, Surgeons, Dog-Lovers and Tile-Makers
Invoked by People with Knee Problems
Roch spent his life tending the sick until he contracted the plague from a patient. He walked into a forest to die, but was befriended by a dog who, each day, brought Roch a fresh roll from his master's table.

As soon as we hit the Lourdes ground we're up and running – there's barely enough time, as they say in Glasgow, to change your knickers before the first event, a Mass of Welcome. I dump my bags and wander down the road and along to the Boulevard de la Grotte. This Boulevard is as it sounds to English ears – a narrow, enclosed, traffic-driven, shop-fitted fug of diesel-fumes and taxi-horns – but it leads to the clear, still air of the Domaine, which is the patch of land at the centre of Lourdes, at the centre of which a few miraculous events apparently took place a hundred and odd years back, creating this centre of signs and wonders.

Whatever it was in 1858, when St Bernadette claimed she saw the Virgin here, the Domaine is now a perfectly appointed pilgrim site. Built around the Grotto and the sacred spring by the banks of the River Gave are churches, chapels and basilicas of different shapes and sizes; a selection of crypts, baths and holy water taps; hospital-type lodgings for the sick, Miraculous Cures exhibitions for the well, and offices set in stone for the admin people; keeno youth centres and oddball evangelical HQs full of people in big glasses; the headquarters of Third World charities, the headquarters of the Legion of Mary, the Lost Property Bureau. And here, gathering now, today – in addition to the usual madding mob of those who come here looking if not for a miracle then at least for a message, are a couple of thousand seekers from Liverpool, filling the air with their plosives and their fricatives and their loud laughter.

Although the Liverpool thousands are spread far and wide in Lourdes – in hotels, in guest houses, in youth hostels – the sick they've brought (the 'Official Sick') are camping in the Accueil St Frai, which is, as brochure-speak has it, 'convenient for the Grotto'. For this half-hour there's manic movement going on around the Accueil as the helpers – the handmaids and the brancs and the youths and any other hands which happen to be on deck – seek to organize the sick and the dying into chairs and beds-on-wheels to take them to the Basilica for mass. It's a tumult, a maelstrom, and at the heart of all of it is Vin, a still point in a turning world, a five-foot-five-inch bundle of energy and a veteran of thirty-five Lourdes pilgrimages. A spare part myself, I watch him, envious of his mastery and his company, as he chivvies here and hails well-met fellows there.

He introduces me to one or two others, all of them happy to hello but too busy to linger; all of them have offices to attend to, and it's dizzyingly efficient, this turning world. There's Tony the Treasurer, a tall thin man, a little dandruffy, who wears a snowed-on suit and tie as his badge of office; he's guiding the Chief Branc-elect, similarly besuited and betied but a baldie, who takes over next year when Vin becomes a deacon. Knowing I'm from outside (the city, I mean, rather than the faith) Vin insists I put on the badges of this particular pilgrimage experience. Throughout the rest of the week I will be pestered by pilgrims of many lands demanding that I swap them the chaste

Our Lady of Liverpool I bashfully, and with no little self-consciousness, pin to my chest. 'There,' he says, smiling his work to see, 'you're one of us now.'

If the peace of Lourdes is what people come for, then they shouldn't be where I'm standing: the atmosphere becomes positively mental as the massed ranks of the youth section – hundreds of them, in yellow polo-shirts as their basic wear, but with their own shorts and socks and trainers, like a pub football team – turn up from their hostel to push the sick in their chairs and beds to the mass. One of the brancardiers takes the mickey. In the middle of the hubbub and the huddle – and it is chaos – he sits himself in a wheelchair and wheedlingly asks a nubile sixteen-year-old (the best-looking one for miles around, unincidentally) to wheel him to the toilet. She has presumably been told that her chief duty is to help everyone needful for these six days or so, that it is hers not to reason why, so they disappear into the hospital building, he po-facedly pathetic in the chair, she, with a placid Madonna smile of function at the back. When they return, a minute or two later, it's to a chorus of raucous laughter; he's upright, pushing the wheelchair with her in it, the smile on the face of the tiger. 'Take up thy bed and walk, eh!' he shouts, Scousily.

The little red-headed girl blushes, and the youth section looks collectively affronted at the parody of their efforts, but the other brancardiers, getting their hands round her shoulder (no doubt copping a little feel of her slender teenage frame as they do it, and I can't say my flesh is anything but weakened by the sight of her) assure her that they were 'only kidding' and encourage her to get her own back. And she probably will. For just as the sick pilgrims are sick, so are the youth section youthful. The two come together outside the Accueil to make a long procession to the St Bernadette Church. Two youths are allotted to each wheelchair, and it's an odd sight, for the youth catch the eye, just as the sick do, in the way they reflect the variety of the things of this world. As they pass, pushing and pulling, they have only their rude, and visible, health to link them: lank-haired, fat bodies, frizzy hair-piles, plumpsters in turquoise shorts, sweating teenagers with their Wonderbras showing; slim babes in Adidas shorts, willowy redheads full of colleen-good-looks, studious Why-Miss-Jones-You're-Beautiful speckies, Alice-banders in expensive sandals; and all sorts of lush, sun-glassed long-hairs that make me feel my age. They have nothing to fear but their acne.

But what they push, now . . . it's painful to watch, let alone relate, even though (like the heap of shoes in Auschwitz, say) you've seen the image before in every documentary about and every photograph of Lourdes. The sick who pilgrim here every summer represent an almost indescribable array of illnesses and ailments, ranging from the covert to the oh-too-overt. Amidst the Liverpudlian parade, cancers and strokes are of course hardly discernible, except for the odd testimony in the shape of a chemo-bald hairstyle; but the thoroughly ancient sit stretchered on their mobile bunks, some not even able to be held upright; Death's door is open and the moving finger points, not just at these, but at others too, at those who sit exhausted and wasted with the weariness from fighting unknown and unseen and unimaginable diseases. And it grows worse: the blind, the deaf, the dumb follow on behind, with disability to add to their infirmity. The mentally handicapped cases come, too, and the others – a whole line of the shrill-voiced, the slumped, the (God forgive me) slack-gobbed, tongue-out, head-down, cross-eyed, thrawn-necked, cerebral-palsied, spina-bifidated. And each sits in his own old-fashioned bath chair with squeaky wheels, marked out for official, special treatment; getting it.

I'm racked with an envy as useless as my uselessness as the healthy ones push the sick ones past: even if there's pleasure for some in helping, in offering the clearly corporal work of mercy, it's still the case that I'm nothing but an alien, a non-helper, an idle hand the devil probably has work for. It puts me on the back foot, the purpose with which the helpers seem to stride ahead, seem to face down, by action and endeavour, the little voice that must ask the inevitable question about how any gentle God could make such signs and wonders as they push before them. Reticent, useless, I contemplate not entering the church at all. In the end I go in late, and hesitantly, and I sit right up towards the back of the great, concrete football stadium of a basilica. From there I watch as the priests call the brancs and the handmaids and the youth to pass up past the ghastly organ with the gold fitments to the altar with marble pillars; as they make their way forward to have their sick-helping hands blessed.

They come back all dignified, all those hands that were on the girl's shoulders and bum and (the ever-so edge of her) breasts, and the faces above the hands are ennobled, uplifted; I watch in a shake, never so unsure, almost certain I shouldn't have come; my hands are as unhelpful as the fake badge that sits over my faithless heart. The reading is, of course, *Take up thy bed and walk*, dealt with in a rather more serious way than before, though we're warned now, by the Archbishop, kicking off the week, that we should take it no more literally than the brancs did earlier. And this being the welcome, he rehearses the story of Lourdes, of Bernadette's eighteen visions at the Grotto, of her sightings of and conversations with the Virgin Mary; and explains why these people, the sick and the well, the young and the old, the helpers and the holidaymakers, the questers and the dumbstruck, those who sit at the front and the pale white figure at the back, are here in fulfilment of the Blessed Lady's personal request that we come to Lourdes to seek the cure of the miracle of holy waters.

I go outside a little early – leaving mass before the close is a habit from adolescence I can't quite break – and outside the church I stand on the balcony of the fire exit – above myself as ever – as the pilgrims egress. I have a bird's eye view. The nice bald man, Rog, now in T-shirt and Pumas, pushes out his ancient mother: she's chattering, wittering about the loveliness of things to Rog and Margaret. The lady from Southport's daughter pushes out the Teletubby son; he too is upright. Fr. Des-how-you-doin' emerges, as does his aloof Ghanaian curate, as do thirty other priests who, on the concourse, greet old friends and join parish clusters. Tony the Treasurer and his acolyte are there, too, in visible organizational colloquy. The handmaids stand around in gentle clusters of their own, wearing white for purity, and the brancs, enviably mechanically minded, begin busily to assemble and lead off the wheelchair caravan.

Soon, only two twelve-year-old lads remain, and they're standing next to me way up high. They are discussing moral issues: is it right or wrong to gob on a priest? The priest in question is heading the Italian delegation, which is waiting on the brutalist concrete concourse, ready to file in now that the Liverpool mob has filed out. (You need a tight ship on this sea of miracles.) He has a shiny pate that would make a tempting target for expectoration, that's for sure; a great gleaming beacon of shiny target-worthiness. We look around, the three of us, in odd conglomeration. The Italian youth have the dark, almost black beauty of southern Italians; the two Liverpool lads are suddenly hushed in their admiration, for the handmaids are dusky Puglian nurses who giggle with their tall, handsome flag-bearers. There are other elegances: their second priest's shirt is elegantly cut in an Armani off-denim blue, and their sick people have slicked-back hair.

★

Loose-ended – and thoroughly shamed – by the sight of so many workers of corporal mercy toiling away, I decide to drift out and find some reading; I pick up a couple of works on the story of Bernadette. Of course they are pious pieces: nineteenth-century hagiography is controlled by Victorian mores, and what that sanitizing era did for folk-song it did for saints' lives too. (Give me the madder music of the early martyrs any day. Saint Agatha, for example, who had her breasts cut off to punish her over-vigorous defence of her virginity; who is represented in icons as carrying her removed baloolahs on a tray, which circumstances caused later viewers, stuck for a way of adequately explaining away these mysteriously rotund items so smooth, so resplendent, so beautifully bell-shaped, to appoint her Patron Saint of Campanologists.)

But we're in Lourdes, so the song is the song of Bernadette, not Agatha. And what's clear is that the place had been little but a Sleepy Hollow of a place before whatever celestial element it was that appeared to her and made the place into Busy Town. So who was Bernadette? A few unembroidered facts, if the guidebooks are to be believed: daughter of François Soubirous, a miller, blind in one eye and entirely blind in his drifting from domestic disaster to domestic disaster, who eventually abandons his mill and takes refuge in a *cachot* (a former police lock-up cum workhouse), who is so poor that one of his sons is had up by the parish priest for eating candlewax off the church floor, who – as with all these prodigal types – has his unprotected whanger out too often, and has nine children with his Louise, of whom five survive early childhood, of whom the eldest is Bernadette. Other salient facts, as gleaned from pages and pages of turgid tourist tosh: born 1844, sent away to wet-nurse at Bartres 1844–5, survived cholera 1855, contracts (if you can contract) asthma, gets TB 1856, is sent back to her wet-nurse to 'recuperate', i.e., spend long days alone in sheep-tending and in other equally dismal agricultural pursuits, before, in 1858, returning to Lourdes to prepare for First Communion. Whereupon she begins to have visions of the Virgin Mary.

A little more detail, maybe? Here's the pious version. Bernadette returns to live at the *cachot* on 21 January 1858 and on the 11th of February, gathering firewood by the stream, she hears the surprise uprise of a whistling gust of wind, which nonetheless and strange to say does not sway the trees. She removes her *chaussettes*, ready to cross the stream as scheduled, and hears another gust. Looking over to the Grotto – to the remote and half-hidden cave which as yet shows no sign of being anyone's Domaine – she sees a lady in white, with a white veil, a blue waistband and a yellow rose on each foot. The lady, she reports, takes the rosary, which is wrapped around her wrist and makes the Sign of the Cross.

Defying maternal bollockings and paternal threats she returns the next week. (The 'inner calling' card is played – it's the usual excuse for saintly disobedience, the hagiography writer's version of *God Works in Mysterious Ways*.) She goes to the Grotto bearing a little bottle of holy water, kneels down and begins to pray. Within seconds, the vision reappears and, sprinkled with the water, remains. The other girls who have come panic, run and reveal themselves to be idle shilly-shallyers, not worthy of the Virgin's call, but Bernadette is ecstatic – literally – and is unable to move, so much so that a local yokel has to be called to remove her fixed foot. Another bollocking proves ineffectual; within a few days she is back at the Grotto to see the silent movie become a talkie all of a sudden, with the Virgin letting her in on the fact that she will get more happiness in the next world than in this.

And so on and so forth: eighteen apparitions it runs to, and the Lourdes bookstalls are full of syrupy descriptions, each more saccharine than the last. In short, the story is as follows: the Lady returns over and over again, with crowds of rubbernecks from near and later from far gradually growing larger and larger. Sometimes the vision is silent, sometimes she comes over all evangelical – political, as all Mary-visions seem to feel inclined to do at least once in their lifetime. At some stage this one gives the habit-forming suggestion that Bernadette should drink from a spring; so begins the custom of ingesting H_2O from Lourdes. (Bernadette was, in the same vision, instructed to eat grass by the side of what was to become the shrine, but for some reason this instruction has not survived so well.)

Other highlights, as the visions proceed: Bernadette is arrested on public order offences, as she displays devotion in a variety of ecstatic ways; the Lady gives her message to priests ('Tell the priests to have a chapel built here.'). Fr. Péyramale, the local one, doesn't want to get the organ restoration fund out, however. Cynical, he offers the Virgin a deal – in a *tell her to make me a cambric shirt* scenario, he says he'll do it if the Lady names herself and makes the rosebush at the Grotto bloom in the middle of winter. The flower never arrives – it is February into March – but the vision does, on the umpteenth visit, on the Feast of the Annunciation, announce herself to be the Immaculate Conception. 'Those were her last words to me. Her eyes were blue,' Bernadette apparently comments, before Blessed Lady turns Fat Lady to sing a final hymn and turn Lady in White into Little White Dot.

So much for the cheesy version. What about the cynical one? Look at this biography by another kind of reckoning and what do you get? An inner melody playing to a tune that goes something like this. A father's chronic failure to put food on the table. The premature familial responsibility of an eldest child, part-parent to candle-wax eaters. Incomprehending pubescence. Chronic solitude. The company of sheep. Repressive religion. Bundle that lot into the machine and what will come out in the wash? Visions, that's what you might suspect. But don't go breathing the word *hysteria* in Lourdes, for fear that you'll get your lights punched out by a hotelier or a shop owner – for one or two pious Catholics, maybe even including some of the latter-day Soubirouses, incidentally, are doing very well, thank you very much, trading on the family name and the Faithful's piety . . .

Later, and in spite of the bare white bulb in my room, I fall asleep over one of the guidebooks and have a strange dream. There are lines and lines of wheelchaired ones, as far as the eye can see, which is far, as they are all wearing yellow polo-shirts; and every one is pushed by a strange centaur-like creature; the plain, humble face of Bernadette Soubirous atop the expensively clothed body of Madame L'Hotelier. And, at the back, me, useless and spineless, a creature void of form.

St Peter Chrysologus
Feast: July 30
Patron Saint of Orators and Rhetoricians
As Archbishop of Ravenna, Chrysologus ('golden word') made only shortish homilies, but delivered them with such energy and enthusiasm that he could render his listeners literally breathless.

If only dreaming were possible, I would take any dream, here tonight in Medjugorje. But however favourable to venial appetites the place may have become in these post-Communist days of wine and toilet paper, Pansion Tomas does not stretch to air-conditioning, so I lie lathered in sweat for the best part of my first night there. I eventually doze for a few minutes and when I wake (I am clockless and watchless, without temporal orientation – clearly deep-spiritual) I don't know if the cups on the tables downstairs are the breakfast or the noonday settings. It turns out it's six a.m., so I walk the streets for an hour. The shopkeepers are hosing down their bits of pavement and the front windows of their shiny new mini-markets, and the early-bird taxis – Mercedes every one, in the beiges and browns of the late eighties – roar up and down the street.

Back at the ranch, the up-and-about fellow-pilgrim breakfast chat is intense. Some faces are familiar now, some new. I meet Valerie, Irish-Canadian, pursuer of another inner calling – abroad, in England, she felt a sudden desire to come – who complains about the pillows, the heat of the night, the crick in her neck. 'You come here to make sacrifices, I suppose,' she finally says, embracing staff-and-sandal humility. I meet again Mary-Ann, the Yukon Yee-haw, who tells us joshingly about summers and winters there, with, as Woody Allen used to joke, 'Night and Day' sung twenty-four hours at a stretch. I meet Errin, a Tongan New Zealander, who signs up readily to Mary-Ann's newly formed Medjugorje Bereavement Support Group; she has, it emerges, a list of fifty names of souls in Purgatory on whose behalf she intends to get to intentional work. And I meet again Angela from the plane, who tells me Knock's nothing compared to here, though Lough Derg (where, by the sound of things, you go for three days, walk barefoot, are not allowed to sleep and are allowed only dry toast and black tea) is quite something.

In the full light of day the sense that this is a place that has taken a sudden progressive leap forward takes on more substance: the streets and shops are busy, and the spread of pilgrim business, of shops and cafés and bars, makes the place feel like a proto-Lourdes, ready to follow in the master's footsteps, though there's a pleasanter, airier feel. Every field near the centre is slowly being turned into *pension* accommodation; celebratedly, the early pilgrim visitors to Medjugorje stayed in locals' houses, and now the houses are growing and multiplying; the shops, now open, are brandishing for greedy pilgrim appetites the old tick-tackery of holy knick-knackery, with prices in Polish, Czech and Irish as well as the more gilt-edged currencies of travel – the dollar, the pound and the Deutschmark. (God, it seems, has yet to recognize the Euro.)

The holy buildings of the place – the basilicas and the chapels and the offices of the pilgrim bureaucracy – have come on, too, and in more ways than the lavatories. The word on some streets is that during the recent Serb–Croat conflict in Bosnia some donations to the shrine did not arrive – they were 'diverted', as they say (the Croat state had a war effort needing funding, after all). But now that a peace of sorts prevails the money is going where it's supposed to, to the church. I see a marble yard, established and fenced, with a stock ready and willing to pave a proper Lourdes-style precinct. There are rich arrays of flowers around the Virgin's marble feet; and built on marble slabbery, amidst verdant shrubbery, there's a set of eighteen outdoor confessional booths (made, it appears, of the creosoted trellis-work you get in a B&Q shop) where once, in the days before multi-toiletry, pilgrims queued to confess to an alfresco Franciscan on a dust-floor footstool.

We're here for mass – English mass at ten, that is. (The Croats have the eight and the Germans nine, with Italians and Poles to follow on from us. The poor old Japanese don't get in until the afternoon, but I don't suppose there are many of them in this corner of the world.) Clustering by the front door I see some of our party – Nora, Angela, Mary-Ann. Cecilia is there, craning her neck with her airport anxiety, but the sad truth is that James hasn't made it up. I wonder aloud whether a few more bottles of the Glenfiddich were consumed in the quiet of his room, and find myself thoroughly rebuked for the unworthy thought. 'We'll just have to leave Our Blessed Mother to sort him out,' says Cecilia; and otherwise, she points out with a kind of rallying satisfaction, it's a full house.

The fact that the church is icy-cool is an incentive, for me at least, but here also is a mother-and-child theme that woos the mass of the Marian meanderers. An American priest, a Vietnam vet military chaplain with a voice like a gravel pit, tells his pulpit tale; how his mother once gave him an earful for not ringing home every day on a seven-day U-Haul migration from New York to San Francisco. Some of the world's worst-dressed people – a Kafflik tour party from Birmingham, Alabama – hoot with laughter at the image of the big man in hock to the little lady, and the metaphorical message is driven home with a pious anecdote of a dying friar who didn't just call home, but went there, and with an appeal that we should all become little children. Then a living friar stands up next and tells us – by way of a prologue to his feast day, which falls tomorrow – about Saint Iakov, whom we know better as Santiago, or as St James the Apostle, and who's standing on the altar there as a ten-foot statue complete with mantle, shell, staff and sandals; everything but the rucksack.

All life is a pilgrimage, the friar says, striking a tone of some beauty, *and it doesn't end until this earthly journey does, when we stand before Our Lord.* We exit, making our own little journey, making for the shade of the trees. All life is a pilgrimage; Danjela, our newly introduced dry-land courier, tells us how to make a petition to our Blessed Mother, how to have a mass said for a private intention, and how to get hold of a ticket (gold-dust, apparently) for a benefit concert by a singer (confusingly) called Danjela who sang for Croatia in the most recent Eurovision Song Contest. It's an offer one can hardly refuse. Somehow – thinking of our bus-ride courier, and what she might do with 'Boom Bang a Bang' – I manage.

Fearing evermore the heat of the Adriatic sun, I retire to bed for an hour in the Yugoslav afternoon. Later I drift out to hear a talk by a certain Fr. Branimir in a big air-conditioned barn –

the result of a donation from Chicago or Des Moines – that passes for a conference hall. Branimir is a louche, good-looking man, a suave Slav in Franciscan habit and sandals; while Slavenka, a suavette Slavette, stands by like a conjuror's lovely assistant, to interpret. Slavenka is the butt of a few saturnine jokes, as is England's underperformance in international football, when compared with the Croats; and the pious are a little scandalized as he advises the pilgrims that if they feel sleepy they should simply fall asleep; or as Slavenka puts it in her poetic Slav way: 'Father says – if you fell sleepy, just fell asleep.'

Of course we have had our introduction to this place already, without leaving the coach, but even so this is all beginning to feel like Ossenburger, the undertaker-patron of Holden Caulfield's school in *The Catcher in the Rye*, who began his speech to the schoolboys before him with a few jokes 'just to show what a regular guy he was'. But Branimir is brighter than that. His personal opinion, he says, is that Our Lady came to Medjugorje because of the war; but – to some disappointment, especially from the American mob, who seem to want talk of signs and visions, of miracles and marvels – this is practically the last mention the apparitions get; he seems determined to keep our pilgrim feet on the ground. 'Father says She vanted us to pray for peace,' Slavenka says in her he-said-she-said manner, 'and She vanted us wery much to place ourselves in hands of God. Bet-lehem happened again here at Medjugorje so that ve could all learn the praying for peace.'

But peace, he argues, is something we won't have unless God comes back into our lives; I sit and take it. 'Father says only ten per cents of Romans go to church. Only three per cents of Germans go to church; only ten per cents of Parisians in Catholic France are bap-tized. Father says in Wienna, fifty thousand came to see the Pope, but Father says they were Czechs and Slovenians, not Austrians, who have also drifted avay from the vun true path.' Only the Poles of Warsaw, which of course she calls Varsav, are excepted; and of course, the Croats. 'Father says in Croatia, the church-going runs at ninety per cents. Father says,' she adds seamlessly, without a single batted eyelid that might suggest non sequitur, 'the crisis in the world is wery big: that's vhy ve have to conwert ourselves.'

Slav metaphors abound in what follows, a series of pithy tales and parables. 'Father says three men carry crosses across the countryside and vun, finding it too wery heavy, cuts a bit off. When he reaches the gorge, guess what? He just can't cross.' Slavenka laughs, tickled; Branimir, the tale's origin, has a face from a game of poker. 'Father says another man, in a troubled time of his life, is valking across a beach and sees only vun set of footprints in sand. Father says he asks God vhy God has not valked beside him and the man is told that the vun set of footprints vere not his; they vere *His*.' Slavenka laughs, tickled; Branimir has a face from a game of poker. 'Father says carrying a cross in this life is good. Only by carrying a cross in this life can vun make it to heaven.' And finally, triumphantly, and slightly mysteriously: 'Father says we should try to be wictim, even in our own family.' She smiles, meaningfully; Branimir has a face from a game of poker.

The patron of playing-card makers, Bernadine of Siena, who drove a card manufacturer out of business with eloquent anti-gambling sermons, is also the patron of Public Relations Officers, and Branimir, taking questions, displays a PRO's skill. After a bit of this and that, a group of pious Americans fight back and try to get him to talk about the apparitions by pretending they're asking a doctrinal question: 'What does the Lady have to say about the souls in Purgatory?' Slavenka says off her own bat that we're just to pray, that those are our instructions. Branimir puts the questioner down swiftly: 'I'm only interested in heaven,' he says, in English. 'But look,' he says, then goes Croat again, trying to calm them down, and Slavenka translates: 'Our Lady appeared in Lourdes in the morning, in Fatima in the afternoon, in Medjugorje in the evening. Father says she wants to be with us all the day . . . and Father says I'm telling you: the vorld is horrible vith wiolence, so don't go anyvhere without your Mother . . .'

Afterwards, several of the pilgrim party repair to Lukas's Bar, just across the road from the church, where we sit under a canvas awning. The talk, though still provisional with hesitancy, preserves its innate hierarchy: Cecilia and Nora, experienced travellers, are allowed to pronounce on what will happen to the rest of us as the week goes on, while the rest of us are not fit to touch the hem of their garments. Mary-Ann, flush with new friendship, buys a drink for all of us: for me, for James the rebel son (now back in synch with the party), for Valerie the Moaner, for Errin the Tongan; but also for Lawrence, a sweet-natured South Indian from Ealing; and for Errin's son, a big little boy with a Polynesian-Aussie rugby frame and a man-of-the-house manner. We all line up to receive drinks and Cecilia/Nora's wisdom, which comes in the form of a series of toasts.

For me, a beer and an assurance that Our Lady must have brought me here for a purpose.

For Valerie, a beer and the assurance that she'll find the peace she's looking for.

For Errin, a Coke and the sure knowledge that her petitions will be answered.

For James, a beer and a double reminder – that tomorrow is St James's Day, and that the end is nigh.

For Mary-Ann, who's most vocal about her needs, a beer and a reminder that the sign she's waiting for will come.

Mary-Ann, already picked up by the togetherness she has already found here, picks up the reins: 'You know, sometimes I think' – she looks at all of us – 'that there are miracles going on all around us and that we don't even see them.'

'You know what your problem is,' says James, who has clearly discussed her situation with her. (And which of us hasn't? She is rich with openness on the subject of her loss.) 'You need a miracle to show you that your husband's at peace, that you needn't worry about him, but you're waiting for the Hollywood version – the big pyrotechnic miracle in the sky.'

'Well,' says Mary-Ann, 'you should know. You're the director.' (It turns out James makes pop videos and TV adverts for a living.) 'But maybe Dick' – her late husband – 'can arrange it, wherever he is. After all, he was an electrician when he was alive.'

'Oh, really?' someone says.

'Yes,' says Mary-Ann. 'In fact, they used to call him Electric Dick.'

It's greatly to the credit of the spiritual depth and the sympathy for those in the company who have suffered bereavement that the conversation carries on without interruption, clarification, explanation, or hysterical laughter. And the afternoon does roll on nicely in a welter of tea and cakes and ices; no moment has to be brought to a crisis just yet, and even I, badgeless, am made to feel as one, and at one, in the warmth of the sunset and the kindness of strangers.

St Brigid of Ireland
Feast: February 1
Patron Saint of Sailors
(also Fugitives, Dairy-Workers and Children of Unmarried Parents)
Brigid – the Queen of the South – was dubbed 'The Mary of the Gael'
after a certain bishop, having seen the Virgin Mary in a vision and
Brigid in the flesh, pronounced them identical. When visitors were

expected at her abbey she could entice her cows to give milk three times a day.

Friday, 11.30 p.m. *Feed me now and evermore.* The opening services have passed in Lourdes and Medjugorje; on Sister Pius's bus it's a service station, and that seems like a relief, since, four hours in, we've finally reached a distance worthy of a stop. Sister P has another go at her register, before retiring, defeated, and simply asking that we note who is sitting next to us. Antioch, Armour, Vela, de Flores, Onuweke, Ouwandoulu, de Souza, Morgan: this bus is a reflection of something much more various than my Kilburn-Irish presuppositions. Inside, by the Burger King – the *refugios* for pilgrims in these, our worldly times – I talk with a Filipino, a Madeiran, a Goan, a Nigerian and a half-Indian Irishman; all born elsewhere, but all living within spitting distance of the Seven Sisters Road (Wood Green, Tottenham, Willesden) and all joined by a faith that spread through the world out from Rome via missionaries to a hundred lands, to the places where their families, wheresoever they were, experienced it and from wheresoever they were, imported it to these parts, where, presumably, they filled with a new devoutness the parish churches that were slowly emptying of the grand old English, who were among those sending it out in the first place. It somehow impresses in its universality, its embracingness; kafflik, with a small 'k'.

We climb back aboard. I diligently check, and Edmund is certainly there, half of his corpulent centre flying in the airspace over my seat; he talks ex-in-laws, Lourdes, and his terrible bookie habit, before our in-coach entertainment programme starts. Sister Pius has produced from her bag of tricks a video entitled *Pray, Hope and Don't Worry – a Celebration of Padre Pio.* I watch, for want of other idleness; Edmund says with some enthusiasm that he too is inclined to do so, that this is 'very important, y'unnustand'. The opening, however, is a montage of images designed to get my goat: John Paul II praying at San Giovanni Rotondo, late-life home of 'the twentieth century's greatest mystic', a man, the commentator says, 'surely destined to join Saint Francis in the company of the Saints'. I scan the bus and see that everyone is watching, intense, rapt. I turn to Edmund to tell him so; and find that he is asleep.

I keep a vigil. It's the usual tale of a life less ordinary, which culminates in the stigmata, of course – but you knew that Padre Pio famously bore the marks of Christ's wounds in his later life. Earlier, we unnustand and are less likely to know, at home in Puglia or Basilicata, or in one of those other provinces at which Christ stopped, proto-Padre Pio had experienced, at just five years old, ecstasies, visions and what are called 'assaults from the devil'; had felt, still five, the (cold? warm? dread? dead?) hand of God on his forehead, assuring him that his barely-out-of-nappies offer to dedicate his life to Christ was accepted in the highest of high places. Pio had eleven quiet years until, at sixteen, a distraught mother had thrown her handicapped kid on to an altar in front of him, intemperately urging God to kill or cure, and Pio had brought about a cure. At eighteen, a seminarian, he had further ecstasies, further fevers, further frets, and when the devil had stepped up his assaults to GBH level, Pio had been sent home from the sophisticated north to spend some time in isolation back in the backwaters; such direct manifestations of disturbance, however divinely inspired, tend to be unwelcome. Far from shutting him up, as was intended, this merely brought the best out of him; he began to bleed.

An Italian priest, a friend of Pio, tells the story: how, at thirty-one, Pio saw a vision of the crucifix dripping blood and turned, in comic cartoon fashion, doubletakingly, to look at his own limbs: 'He ree-aleyesd hees hands, hees feets and hees sayde were pissed.' As is the way in these tales, the Vatican panicked and further isolated him, banning him from saying mass even in Squiddley Bottom until their investigations were completed. Ten years it took, but no one could say he didn't spend his time wisely, getting up at 2.30, going to the church at four, spending twelve to eighteen hours a day in the confessional, indulging in pious anecdote-creating events: telling a distressed woman to look in a well where she saw the face of her long-ago-aborted baby, reading the mind and exposing the hidden sin of an Englishman who (reading between the lines of a story he tells himself) had shagged some woman in a park while a young soldier home on leave from the Second War, and had left the offence undisclosed not only to his maker but also to his later wife and family; a reconciliation, an honesty had been achieved.

And of course, he also spent his time using and exploiting his other gifts, the gifts of the spirit for which he was famous even after the bans were rescinded – healing, language, perfume and bilocation. During the Second World War, it's said, he had reported prophetically on the fate of soldiers, not merely by having knowledge which he could impart to anxious relatives, but by actually appearing at the front, allowing him to bring home first-hand news on a more personal basis. Later, it is reported, he was frequently seen by believers in different parts of the globe, which was a mite strange, since he never, in what remained of his life, left his home at San Giovanni Rotondo; there he hung out with his hands bound and his feet hidden as the believers flocked and were herded in to see him. Yet he was sighted in Rome, in Paris, in New York, and in Oswaldtwistle, near Accrington; an old woman received communion from him in Spain; a squadron leader in the United States Air Force saw him in the sky just in time for him to avert a planned raid that would have razed San Giovanni to the ground.

When Pio died – wearied from the wounds and 'from the physical assaults that, throughout his life, the devil made on him, which at times outbalanced even the strength received from Mary, the Mother of God' – the video does too, suddenly, and boldly, cutting into another programme, about 'one of the twentieth century's greatest mystics' (the phrase, apparently, was not copyrighted on Pio's behalf), Sister Faustina of the Precious Blood. I fall asleep in my chair reflecting on the fact that, to many people in the world outside, Kafflikism is a mainstream, conservative faith. Staid, traditional, establishment. Lacking sufficiently in the charismatic, Big End spiritualism of the newer religions. Full of strait-laced, unfeeling curs, stained with sin, the banished, sin-obsessed, priest-oppressed children of Eve. So how come this bus is full of people clapping the fusing, tracking-distorted, electrically-interfered-with faces of Pio and Faustina?

Saturday morning, 2.30. *For those in peril on the sea* – when I awake we are almost at Holyhead, the ferryport in Anglesey from where we are to sail to Ireland. As we pass the dark chip shops and cafés, the detritus of people passing through, a waiting population, the video is still on its burbling loop: something about Sister Faustina and how the angels used to wake her promptly at six in the morning so she could pray; an alarm clock you can't set to snooze, by the sound of things. There's more, too, of that bilocation business, and I wonder idly if Sister Pius makes her money by appearing elsewhere, perhaps on another coach; maybe she is teetering and tottering up some other bus somewhere else in the world, just as she is on this one. And I drift off into some obscure aspects of the subject, wondering whether BO-sufferers who have the gift of bilocation smell in more than one place at a time.

She speaks to me. 'Did you enjoy the vigil?' I think she says, and, mindful of my gaffe re the hymn singing, I reply yes, for vigils sound like the sort of thing I ought to have been participating in, while I was all too clearly lying in my chair with drool dribbling from the corners of my fly-catching lips. Somewhere along the way she sees I'm confused and translates for me; 'vigil' is London-Irish for 'video', and my rites and observances are, as it happens, reasonably up to date.

Sister Pius waddles back to the front as we pull into the Irish Ferries queue. She gives us a talk that is rich in spirituality, or the spirituality of tourism at any rate: when and where we'll get our next meal, where on the boat is the best place for a cup of tea, what the best bargains are in the duty-free shop. Edmund is attentive-agog: he's looking out for people to trade allowances with. I, clearly, look like a dipso – he doesn't ask me whether I can buy spirits in his name. The more virtuous-looking pilgrims are victims of his advances between now and our catching of the 3.45 a.m. boat; he will need a trolley by the time he climbs back on board the bus. Aboard ship, I spend an hour circulating and yapping before I decide that whoever it was in the Bible who slept for Israel had the right idea; I fall asleep, my own new-bought bottle of whisky my pillow:

> When I lay me down to sleep
> I pray the Lord my duty-free to keep.

'There was a cold night smell in the chapel. But it was a holy smell . . .

Visit, we beseech Thee, O Lord, this habitation, and drive away from it all the snares of the enemy . . .'

The snares of the enemy – or the Enemy, as he is properly known, except in Joyce's eccentric punctuation – are not a significant factor in travelling Stephen's life; except for those of the Big Boys, those Barbarians at the Gates, he has no assaults to deal with, and suffers no physical attacks at the hands of Lucifer or his agents; none that he is aware of (though who knows what dangers lurk for those who stray from the paths of righteousness?); there is not really any need to be aware of anything at all. This type of childhood, even if the days of the Catechism are more or less gone – it only exists in the stentorian voices of the older priests who bewail its disappearance and occasionally, as devotees of the discredited way of doing things always will, sneak it in at the back door – is a training, an acquisition of a rhythm and a routine, an inculcation, a preparation, an indoctrination; a procurement of the wherewithal to be (should the mood take you, as by rights it should, if you have walked the right path) suitably aware at a later date.

But whatever the regimentation, green-blazer God must have a certain something, a certain kindness about him: 'A priest or a sailor', this Stephen writes, when he is first asked – by Sister Mary Dominic, or by Miss Giulidori, or by some other Bride of Christ or Kafflik spinster – what he intends to do with his adult life. Add to the altar-serving the secondment, at eight or nine, from the green-blazer school choir to the white-cassocked under-the-eye-of-the-Archbishop Cathedral one, and you have the grounding for a serious lifetime career in such finery. This is serious, this chanting: there is a uniform (a small wooden crucifix hung on the chest over the long cotton robe), even a little pay-packet for two long rehearsals a week (though the stipend involves some fear, some quaking: twice the fee for a mass forfeited when a rehearsal is missed), and there are high, incense-packed services at eleven or eleven-thirty on a Sunday, full of grandeur and beauty. The plainsong Latin still courses his mind: the Te Deum, *solemn and cool; the* Salve Regina, *glorifyingly light; the* Kyrie, *its diphthong syllables climbing the peaks and exploring the valleys, the* Gloria In Excelsis Deo *and the* Agnus Dei, *reaching up into the crook of each arch of the building; the whole Gregorian kit and caboodle plucked and played from dusty little books with flat tortoiseshell covers and with yellowed pages rich with the square notes of the old notation. Serious, yes, disciplined, yes, but straightforward too; without tension, without strain; without effort, beyond the rehearsing and the cold journeys on maroon and white buses. Nothing substantial enough to make in any way*

*difficult the idealizing, male-voice crooning of those key-words at the
centre of these and any other masses:* Credo In Unum Deum, *I
Believe in One God . . .*

At home, meanwhile, he has a shelf full of children's versions of
Lives of the Saints, *and he thrills to them, as his older brother has
done before him and his younger brothers will after. Well, why not,
when St Jean de Brébeuf has his entrails removed and eaten by the
Huron Indians while they are still quivering with life? Or when St
Cyril is burned to death by the Governor of Wherever-it-Is for turning
his back on the ancient ways of his pagan family? Or when St Charles
Borromeo, who as a youth has enjoyed the luxury of velvet top-clothes
and silk underclothes, is shot by the crazed Brother Farina within the
very walls of the Cathedral of Milan? The sissy-girlie-Mary ones his
sister likes (St Theresa, St Bernadette, St Agnes) he can do without
(he does not know now about St Catherine, and how when the cancers
in her patients' breasts ran pus she used to drink it as self-mortification)
for martyrs are the thing. Sebastian, fastened to a post by a hail of
arrows. Alban, who made his executioner's eyes fall out. Januarius,
whose blood still bubbles when exposed to the air in Naples. All
those other characters from* Saints Especially For Boys: *Stephen the
protomartyr, after whom he is named, falling under a hail of stones
thrown by a mob of the unrighteous.*

*Priests visit the house endlessly. Stephen sees the golf-course guru
walking up the path from time to time; he proves more genial with a
glass of whisky than with the Blood of Christ in his hand. Who else
approaches? A more intellectual sort: Fr. Anthony, the chaplain of the
university, a Dominican with a broad-span slap-pate but a shock of
white hair pushed behind his head in the style of Hulk Hogan, who
tells tales of prisoners he deals with in his work in Saughton jail, how,
when other helpers fail and comforts flee, he wrestles with them in order
to relieve their banged-up frustrations; tales which forever make the
phrase 'muscular Christianity' a positive in Stephen's mind. When he
comes to tea, which he seems to do most long childhood Sundays, with*

best crockery brought to the table in the best parlour manner, he removes his own white cassock and lets Stephen go for three falls or a submission against him. This is for fun, not for training to fight Satan, not as extreme survival measures when the snares of the Enemy await.

And the uncles, of course; they approach, too, James Ignatius and Francis Xavier, Jesuits both; avuncular visitations are frequent and frequently feature the setting up of candles and cloth in the front room. Pre-lunch gins are drained (we're no puritans in this Church, and both have a preference for big doubles, a limited liking for cakes and ale), fags are stubbed out (one is B&H, the other Senior Service or Capstan Full Strength), and, with children called in from football in the street, the family circle gathers around a makeshift altar. A sort of static crackles its way down the years – the swish of Terylene, the cheap priestly garb of the early seventies, in the sitting-room; the sound of black cloth and masses. They aren't wrestlers, these priests and their sister-nuns, who drink less gin but also show from time to time; but they are holy people, kind, devout and active, teachers, social workers, missionaries, writers. The sisters carry on with their work; the fathers are kind. They never impose, and Stephen rarely connects; the words from the altar (this is a preparation, remember, a little experience) make little sense.

Except once. There is a moment of clarity that provides perhaps the first moment of anything he can think of as coherence in this world in which he is being up-brought. It comes when he is nine or ten or eleven, about to pass from one world of hell-warnings to another. He is walking with his uncle, and mentions to him some part of the teaching at his school, something he has brought home of a God Damns All Sinners variety; perhaps he is answering a question about the importance of being good, or of telling the truth. Somewhere in the dialogue that follows, his uncle, in black suit and dog-collar, tells him that he is not sure that hell exists; and that if there is a hell, he believes there is no one there but the devil; and possibly not even he, the Enemy, is there, since no matter how persistently people stray, he says, the God he believes in – the only God he can bring himself to believe in – still *forgives. This time, last time, every time. And Stephen — perhaps spineless, perhaps inspired — nods in agreement. And might still nod in agreement now, if you asked him.*

III
Holy Orders

St Hervé (or Harvey)
Feast: June 17
Patron Saint of the Blind
Hervé was working his fields one day when a wolf devoured the donkey
he was using to draw his plough. He preached to the wolf, and persuaded
it to go under the yoke and finish the job it had so rudely interrupted.

The Hotel Roissy, my Lourdes base, has an elevator made by a German firm called Schindler; it's Schindler's Lift. It's there I first fall in with a group of handmaids; I squeeze my way in amongst them as they make their way down to a lunch they've earned much more significantly than I have. There's lots of white flesh, all of it draped in the white cloth of their half-nun, half-nursie uniform. There's warm, feisty Frieda, and soft-spoken Connie, and soft-spoken Connie's softer-spoken niece. There's Carol, who could pass for one of my Lancashire cousins with her page-boy haircut and her pleasant, plain face. When we come to dine there's Cheryl, sat at the end of the table, with frizzy hair and big glasses, who's along with her mother, Win, opposite; and it only takes five minutes to find out that Win is not only the cream of the Roissy crop; she is also the Mother of all Handmaids.

The facts of the matter are simple: she is a tightly open-faced warm-rich smiling woman of fifty who comes from Wigan or Warrington or one of those periLiverpudlian places. But to watch her operate is to watch, in action, the principle of all things to all women. A nurse at home and a carer there, she's a nurse here and a carer here too; it's clear, as she smiles with energy, that this is the busman's holiday *par excellence*. But more: when the fortunes of those who work with her are flagging, she is the one who raises their spirits, offering to her fellow-workers ('it's a hobby of mine') aromatherapy to make sure they stay on their feet. Anything that involves looking after others is grist to her mill: she's a doer of deeds, an apparently irrepressible woman who smiles with energy. In terms of her week, in spite of a bad back – 'sometimes my vertebrae pluck like the strings on a guitar,' she says – she is spending the whole week working at the baths, lowering infirm pilgrims into the holy waters.

She also has an eagle eye, that cool sense of the importance of things; she susses me out, quickly; too quickly. 'Are you a Catholic?' she says, in answer to an innocent question about what she gets out of her week. I am about to avoid the question – on this my first journey I am hesitant – but she does it for me, as if she doesn't need to think too far down that line but just wants to mark some territory, and it's marked without the answer: she has me cased. 'Why do I come back year after year? To be near Our Lady,' she replies, assured, and needing to communicate. 'If you love someone, you want to be near them – it's as simple as that. That's the best analogy I can give you.' She pours herself some zucchini from the lilywhite gratin dish in front of her. 'It's all a matter of faith,' she says, eyeing me narrowly. 'It makes me sad that so few can find it. Whether you catch it, or whether you learn it, I don't know. But it still makes me sad that so many of the younger people don't bother.' It's subtly engineered so that I don't know if she counts me among them; I struggle to contain that little hint of betrayal that lives inside me whenever I realize that I can't, whenever I disappoint people like her.

Margaret, Win's co-worker, having eaten already on the other side of the room, comes over and perches at our table. She's a buxom woman who would have been good-looking in her youth and, though fifty and big, she's flirty, in a pious kind of a way. She looks me up and down – a stranger at the table.

'Hello, sister,' she says to Win, keeping her eyes on me.

'Hello, sister,' says Win, keeping her eyes on her plate. 'What kind of day have you had?'

'Not bad, sister. Mustn't grumble.'

'No, sister,' says Win earnestly. 'We mustn't grumble.'

'You can't, can you, sister? It makes you glad for what you've got when you see what I've seen today.'

She means down at the baths of course, where they've all been working, where the sick are lowered into the spring water in search of curing; what she's seen is the queue of ailments pushed by youth who will have passed through her big, capable hands today. She introduces herself to me, and we chat for a minute or two. I tell her – waving expansively to draw in Win and Cheryl and all the rest of them – how glad I am that I've got some friends.

'It's her you ought to thank,' says Margaret. For a moment I try to puzzle out who exactly it is I should be thanking – I look at Win, and Carol, even Cheryl in turn – before I realize we are talking Ladies of an altogether more Blessed Virgin variety. 'Yes, *Her*,' says Margaret, capitalizing it. 'She brought you here, and she knows what she's doing. Our Lady brought you to Lourdes and if she did that she did it for a specific purpose; there's something she wants of you. And Our Lady must have wanted you to meet these ladies; must have wanted you to make their friendship. Who knows? Maybe she wants them to speak through you. You have to understand – she controls everything.'

She asks me if I was at early mass this morning. I tell her (for the sake of argument) that I slept in. 'Oh, shame,' she says, then, with a little more emphasis, '*Shame*. It was lovely.' Temporarily off my guard – and too lippy for my own good – I foolishly suggest that maybe Our Lady made me sleep in for a purpose. A *defensor fidei*, she shows me her beefy forearm, and I lip up, for forearmed is forewarned, as they say, and I begin to earnestly outline the beauties of the Mass of Welcome, of the Blessing of the Hands. Margaret, and honour, seem to be satisfied, and the forearm goes away.

Win smiles, but her face is distracted, as if she's puzzling over what I *am* here for; she has a long look at me. With a certain steeliness, she begins to let me know how often she's been, and what I should see if I'm really going to enjoy the week; and by *enjoy* she means something other than *nice weather, nice food, wish you were here*. She talks about the activities of the day, and, even though they all know what they're talking about, has the decency to explain everything ponderously: the Grotto, the Baths, the Torchlight Procession. This time it is my turn to raise an eyebrow. For in a whole new way I feel I know nothing.

'Oh, you should go to the Torchlight Procession, you know. That's the centre of this place. That's where you'll find what's special . . .'

So that Lourdes evening, I go to find what's special: as instructed by Win, I torchlightedly process. It is, as she suggests, a central event in the Lourdes day, an eveningly occasion that occurs after the hotels have fed and watered their people. (All the meals in the Lourdes hotels happen at exactly the same time; they're synchronized to suit the demands of baths, services, processions; so no one misses anything, except the faithless, except voluntarily.) The Procession started almost as soon as pilgrimage to Lourdes did. In the nineteenth century, by all accounts, it was a near-hysterical thing, with the latest *merveilles*, the miracle cures and their beneficiaries, announced and witnessed. Now, in this age where the idea of miracle is not to be taken quite so literally, things are a little more restrained, a little more calm. Yet, outside the Roissy, a crowd is beginning to accumulate.

It starts here and at several other places away from the Domaine, several corners of the town; and paths run down to the Domaine, various yet unanimous, like the roads to Compostela. The crowd thickens as you move down towards the Grotto, and as I arrive there there are several thousand people there, just milling, just waiting by the banks of the Gave and at the Crowned Virgin's statue, lined up along the Basilica walls. Then, slightly absurdly, thirty deep and each carrying a candle in a sort of paper-doily-cum-waxy-windshield, they begin to take a slow half-mile turn around an oval running track-shaped path which will bring them back to where they started, to the steps in front of the Basilica. Throughout the whole combobulation the Rosary is said; not just a few decades, but the Joyful Mysteries, the Sorrowful Mysteries, the Glorious Mysteries, the whole mish and mash uttered (and amplified the half-mile along the Domaine) in at least four languages, depending on what crowd's in this week, with each Mystery punctuated by massive mass singing of the chorus of the Lourdes hymn – *Ave, Ave, Ave Maria.*

Amazed, I stand and watch, my back hard up against the fence around the statue; I become Mr Velcro as the crowds begin to roll, and as others crowd up to fill any spaces left behind. There's an incredible number now, descending from the lodgings and the hostels and the auberges all over the town. They carry banners and they're from everywhere.

Matera. Kortrijk. Warrington. Messina.

Squads of folks, young and old.

Hexham. Nijmegen. Trieste. Tarragona.

(Though mainly old.)

Dublin. Bari. Tallaght. Tallinn.
Priests and people, nuns and novices.
Hildesheim. Szczecin. Wiry. Bayern.
All colours and creeds.
Gozo. Zurich. Galway. Innsbruck.
(Except for the creeds bit, of course.)
Speyer. Limburg. Freiburg. Luxembourg.
And more.
Valence. Dunkeld. Nola. Salford.
And more.
Lucana. Monte Cassino. Metz. Grenoble.
And more.
Vendée. Tamoule. Barcelona. Nancy.

Bringing up the rear, a line of one-day pilgrims of all nationalities: Caucasians of all nations, of course, but also Laotians, Vietnamese, Indonesians, Papua New Guineans, Solomon Islanders . . .

And, of course, somewhere in the middle of all that lot, Liverpool, clustered together in its little parish. I watch them pass: the excited aviator, Roger, pushing his mum, Tony the Treasurer, Frs. Gerry, Des-how-you-doin' and Ghana, Win, Carol, and Margaret with her wrestler's forearms; all begin the walk within a few yards of each other, each person carrying his candle wrapped in a silly paper doily, many not really knowing each other, a travelling coincidence that's anything but frail.

And as the crowd builds – or as it never seems to stop – it does bring a lump, there's no doubt, a call; along roll those vague thoughts on the universality of such things, of the scale of the history and the geography that makes these people gather; that wish for belonging comes again, and challenges that other voice that insists on your right to stand outside. As you watch you can't help pondering the word faithful, not so much as a personal thing – for you can always slink off that pin – but as *the* faithful, as the family of those to whom one once belonged; *ecclesiam catolicam et apostolicam*, as it was when I sang it in Latin as a nine-year-old, the Kafflik and Apostolic Church. For amongst them are not just the old but the young as well, not just men or priests but women and nuns as well, not just the hale and the hearty but the sick and the dying as well, integrated and inside and uplifted, a little parish within the parish, each lifting his or her candle as the *Ave* comes, sung on to the warm night air; and as they pass, people – and not just the Mediterranean types, not just the hysterical Latins, but all sorts of cold-looking Slavs and Aryans – actually weep at the Virgin's statue, actually stop and break down at the feeling of it all.

I am almost inclined to walk, to join that journey. But of course just as I might have done, there's a break: the hyper-efficient brancs come and begin to push the weeping people along, for it turns out it's not permitted to stop by the Virgin's statue; here in this haven of spirituality we can't have any kind of spirituality that would stop the traffic. A bigger, wider, tighter ship needs to sail and we can't have little barques of individualism clogging up the clear blue waters. I straightaway feel sick at heart, and begin to see different things, to hear different voices as I look upon this great, seething mass. Baggy remarks can be heard back where the crowd assembles, about how the Italians always jump the queue, that the Poles are terrible, and as for the Spaniards . . . so much for universality, for Catholicity, for my vague thoughts of joining in this communion. As Charlie Brown's friend Linus used to say in *Peanuts* – I love humanity, it's people I can't stand.

Turning round, using the Crowned Virgin as a wheel, I see the scene from another angle. (As I revolve I remember St Catherine, stretched out on her turning spikes, imagine life and limb of those here today damaged by wheel-burst's flying splinters.) At the end of the walk, of the cycle, I watch the brancs take over the process of shepherding the sick to the front, and what, one feels, should be a sea of humanity, a unique melding of the well and the sick, the good and the bad, the world and his wife – the parish big-time – becomes a display of pointing and directing, dividing up those in line from those not in line, dividing the healthy from the sick, dividing the Official Sick from the unofficial sick; for who knows how many of those of us who walk upright have tumours in our bodies? Aware of the divisions, the great crocodile swinging its tail around begins to look like a trick of scale. Sure, the Italians are magnificent in their crisp, starched uniforms, and the Spaniards look fine in their Boy Scout gear, those little soldiers in the Onward Christian army. But it seems like a trick of the eye, a trick of the tail. Experimenting, I refuse to move from the Virgin, play a fixed-foot routine when the brancs come round again to move on vagabonds hanging round the statue, and get scowled at.

As night falls we're on the Fourth Sorrowful Mystery. *Let us pray for those who do not believe in the happiness of eternal life*, the celebrant says. I feel anything but reproached. Seeking an ever more accurate, more objective, more detached view, I climb up the ramp of the walkway up to the verandah of the Basilica, and begin to watch from above. It seems safer there, just a mass of candles, moving and swaying like parody rock-fans. Yes: from above it's easier to handle, that pull this way or that. The illuminated castle sits above the town to the right, making this look like any chateau-ed French rampart, and to my left a pickpocket works his way along the line until I inadvertently glare at him and he makes a sudden change of direction. Now it's just three or four thousand candles moving slowly around the Crowned Virgin in a *Grand Old Duke of York* manoeuvre, and an unkindness of sick people – two or three hundred strong – brought to the front and made into a phalanx. The *Ave Maria-*

punctuated rosary drones on, seemingly unable to touch me in any of its four languages.

It's true – I can find no stirring on the inside. Yes, I wish my cynical children could have been there to see what the universal crowd is like, to see where they have come from, to have a sense of what the moment is like as the hubbub dies. But when I get back to the hotel and find Win, bright-eyed, asking me if I felt a sense of place here, a sense of moment, I have to answer honestly: that I could feel that people felt a sense of place, but that I could not sense it myself. And as if she had never said any such thing about the procession she says, in a flash: 'Oh, you should go to the Grotto. Late at night, you know. If you want to feel something. That's the centre of this place. That's where you'll find what's special.'

My next set of orders having come, I go to find what's special: as instructed, it's the Grotto late at night, in search of the promised peace. But when I get there, as any regular Lourdes lollard would know, it's not at all quiet; even at eleven-thirty there are at least a few hundred people, possibly a couple of thousand; quiet compared to two p.m. sure – those seeking a cure for narcolepsy at least will be safely tucked up in their beds – but still busy, bustling. Here, at what elsewhere would be the dead of night, there's still a queue to get in. It's just the same in the town, where the promenade goes on well past dark; well past the time of processions, drinkers and smokers congregate in the Little Flower café and the Stella Maris Hotel, which has a sign advertising Stella Artois.

No, eleven o'clock is not late enough for stillness: there's the hubbub of voices of many nations all through the town and right down to the Grotto, where it's dark and eerie and loud until –

Shhhhhh!

Temporarily amnesiac about whether it's a stream or a spring that pops out of the Grotto ground, I'm confused: the hushing noise sounds as if Old Faithful's about to blow. And it turns out that this is not just a rock; this is a rock with a PA system that every thirty seconds or so issues a stern warning to the Neapolitans and the Liverpudlians and all the other *Lourdespilger*, telling them to shut their noise. The scene *is* generally calm: the message does seem to get through. Around the Grotto are benches filled with *tricoteuses*, and in front are many, many silent people, on their knees. I kneel for no one, so instead I join the queue of people waiting to file into the Grotto; into (as they would call it had they snappier PR execs working on the case) the cave by the Gave. (The motto works in either pronunciation: that's the beauty of it.)

Shhhhhh!

It's a long line I wait in. We pass racks of candles set up temptingly, like sweeties by a supermarket cash-line (St Ambrose, the Honey-Tongued Doctor, converter of St Augustine and patron of those who deal in tallow, could hardly approve) and come eventually to the silence and peace of the cave. In this crowd of devotees I at first feel nervous, fraudulent, disinclined; feel obliged to play conspicuous; to adopt a detached body language as far as possible from the mimed hysteria of the Spaniards and the Portuguese who are apparently transfixed by the experience of touching the sacred rock. They walk round it, their hands running along the rock, taking every last second they have to touch it, most of them muttering under their breath; some clutch rosaries, some kneel for a few seconds, for as long as they can, until the moral (and physical) pressure from behind begins to tell. I don't do these things. Instead I file out, cynical, overtaking, swaggering, casual. But then I see, next to his mother's chair, my Roissy-mate Roger, bent over, on his bare knees.

Shhhhhhhh!

I'm inwardly silent, struck by something other than a speaker telling me to be so. I'm struck by Roger's manner – his knuckles are white over the edge of his mother's chrome handles, so deeply is he in – and feel shoddy, feel like I have no right to take what's going so heavily so lightly. In some kind of perverse act of repentance, some strange gesture of a kind of decency to him and others, I return to the start of the queue to take another turn, to have another look, to see what he's looking at. This time, less embarrassed, more justified as a sinner, I take my time, try to savour whatever savour there is. And at slow pace it is different: I hear the hush come over the place, feel it perceptibly separate itself from the dark world outside.

Shhhhhhhh!

The oddest thing is that wall: I feel it properly as I walk through this time, granity and outcroppy at the edges, then smooth under the touch as you reach the deep inside, where you suddenly catch a sense of the hundred and thirty years of days of minutes of seconds of hands that have stroked and caressed it; some, of course, seeking a miracle for themselves or for another. I look up to see the wire of crutches hanging above the cave mouth, the evidence of something, and for a spell I am lost in the silence of the place – in the silence you do feel something even if you're an infidel, and you feel that it's something that must be frightening if you're not, and which is strong enough to make an infidel feel that it must be extraordinary to have faith. I feel it momentarily in my knees and in my groin – a tingle, a deep gnaw – and for a few heady seconds it fills my brain, too, with its hint of conviction.

Shhhhhhhh!

Be still, my soul: a thought of home, of reason, sends that thought scurrying; and, anyway, when you emerge from that silence and return to that madding crowd, that madding

PA telling you to be quiet, you lose touch with whatever contact there was. When I walk out, I see that Roger and his mother and Margaret have gone, and, unwilling to return to my cell, I walk the banks of the river. Clustered at every path-light along the banks of the Gave are Bible-bashers, rosary-makers, prayer-readers, intention-placers, votive-offerers. I feel utterly alone, and wish I was at home. I head for the Bar des Brancardiers (ironic, given my failure to bear a stretcher or do anything else useful) where I drink a couple of Pelforth Bruns and am entertained by four boys from Salford who are spending the night dressed as scarecrows, with mop-heads and sticks along their shoulders. I think of Roger, on his knees there, wondering what hidden ailment means he has had to bring his mother to this place; what secret terror makes him pray so earnestly.

Next morning, in the Roissy lobby, I chew the fat with him for a bit. He is finding his mother hard work, and so he's taking an hour or two off; a bit of respite care for the carer. Margaret, the family friend, has taken her out for 'a bit of shopping, a cuppa. It's marvellous to have her here,' he says, of his mother, 'but it can get a bit trying from time to time. You don't want to knock it – she has that, well, that simple faith, and it's maybe the case that we can all learn lessons from that. But it can get tiring if you don't share quite the same form of belief that she has.'

The tone gives him away: he's a primary school head, he says, so we talk performance charts and league tables and Literacy Hours. We talk about our own experience of schooling; I recite some tales of Jesuit sophistry, some stories of dry-as-dust doctrine. 'Well it's all changed now,' he tells me; and then says, 'I'm not actually allowed, by the diocese, to arrange for a mass to be said in my school. I'm not saying I don't: the parish priest is a friend of mine, and I think children should hear mass. But the diocese has moved away from organized worship in schools: they say that what worshipping children do they can do on Sundays at home. You might feel tempted to feel that it's strange, but there is some sense in it: they are saying that everyone must find his own path to God. As I say, I let the priest come and say mass: I lead them up that path, if you like, because as far as I'm concerned I'm a Catholic and I want them to share that; I want them to share my faith. But it's not strictly according to the rules so to do.'

Eventually I pry a little, trying to winkle out from him what's wrong with his mother, but no hint that I drop can penetrate whatever kind of thick skin he's holding over the bandage. In the end I drop it: my prurience is not enough to defeat his resistance, and we sit and guzzle our Stella Artois, talking of the place. Intelligent, he is not sure what to make of the institutions of Lourdes or the sorts of piety that are practised here, but in the end, he seems to say, he is not inclined to feel censorious; he has his mother's chair to push and that is that. Like Win and the rest his works of mercy are corporal and – likeably – enough to be getting on with.

Later, I have tea with Win and Carol and Cheryl: the rest are out, are coming in later. (They won't miss their tea, of course.) Win is in naughty mood, with her jobs done for the day. She laughs at Cheryl for the smoking ('Fagash Lil') and she lightly tosses Carol on the fire for her eating. 'The thing about her,' she says, 'is that she doesn't like any strong flavours. Garlic, spice, pepper. Now I –' she deals herself another pile of whatever garlicky, spicy, peppery vegetable we're enjoying – 'Now I love it. But Carol – she only likes the French food when it's chips, or beef. Or sausage.' I ask about the day, and the answer's the same as ever: the baths; hard labour; a feeling of a job well done.

'It's a privilege to work at the holy spring: the closest place on earth to Our Lady,' says Carol, her face serene in the way of Bernadette Soubirous.

'The closest place on earth to God,' says Winnie, not disagreeing.

What strikes you as you look at them is their ordinariness. Carol has a plain white T-shirt, a bobbed haircut with a fringe. Winnie has cream gear, tight grey hair and specs. Cheryl will look like Winnie in about twenty years, although for the moment she's more phlegmatic. And much of their storytelling is ordinary – the jokes about Carol's husband, the yarns of Win's. And in the same ordinary vein they tell tales of the pilgrims they have lowered into the water today. A woman with terminal liver disease. A woman with cancer of the bowel. A woman with Crohn's disease. A woman with one leg. A land-mine victim from Yugoslavia.

'Are they looking to be cured?' I ask. 'Do you think?'

'Some I suppose,' says Carol. Her eyes don't narrow: it means she's thinking. Yes. No. Not really.

Winnie is more decisive. 'But sister,' she says, though she's really talking to me. 'People get the wrong idea about miracles. About healing.' This from a healer. 'People make this mistake of thinking that what miracles are all about is making the blind see, making the deaf hear, making the lame walk. And I'm not saying that that wouldn't be miraculous, and I'm not saying it's never happened. Of course it has, and it will happen again. But most miracles are not about that. Most miracles nowadays are about hope and about faith. Most miracles are about changing the person on the inside. About changing their heart.'

'Yes,' says Carol, her eyes narrowing now that she's certain, now that Winnie has made her wonder: 'Often we have people who actually die on the train back to Liverpool. Cancer patients, people like that. And while I wouldn't say they're dying happy, exactly – yet you're pleased to have had them because of what happens to them –'

'I'll give you an example from this morning,' says Win. 'There was this woman of eighty-five came in today, from somewhere up in the north-east – Durham, somewhere like that.' (Because, of course, Newcastle, where the coals come from, is here, along with Seville, where the oranges come from, and Amsterdam, where the tulips come from, and Dresden, for china.) 'And when she came in the door she was absolutely petrified: she was trembling. And we helped her into the water. And I tell you, Our Lady was near as that old lady went in; and when she came out she was transformed, utterly transformed; her whole face was transformed; she was changed. And you know what she said to Carol and me? She said, "I'll never be afraid again." And to me,' she closes, 'that was a miracle.'

Win describes the baths to me. Just down from the Grotto; filled daily with water from the sacred spring; at one time, in the nineteenth century, advertised as a purveyor of miracle cures, now more generally offered as the end of pilgrimage, an adrenalin-rush bit of piety that brings you closer to those you came to see. (Nowadays it's not the chemicals that ring the changes; it's poverty, prayer and penance that bring them.) 'It's cold, the water,' says Win, 'but you can't be cold when you come out: you're just buzzing,' and she tells me I must go. 'Oh, you should go to the baths,' she says, unfazed by any sense that she is leading me up the garden path with her repetitions. 'The sacred spring baths. That's the centre of this place. That's where you'll find what's special.'

St Vincent of Saragossa (Vincent the Deacon)
Feast: January 22
Patron Saint of Wine Growers
Imprisoned in third-century Valencia, Vincent refused to renounce his

faith. Pierced with iron hooks, roasted on a huge grid-iron and thrown on a cell-floor strewn with broken pottery, he nonetheless converted his gaoler.

Of course we are now (back at the Pansion Tomas in Medjugorje) a sort of little family, with our meals and our drinks and our groupishness. But there is a real family, too, amongst us. For a day and half now, through airport and bus-shelter as well as through thick and thin, I've been watching the Bishop family doing their stuff, and I swear I have never seen a family smoke so many cigarettes so constantly and relentlessly as they do. Of Laurie, the eight-year-old daughter of Sally-Ann, I make an honourable exception (though what she does in the privacy of her own room is up to her); but Sally-Ann (Laurie's single mum, twenty-six-ish), Paul (pallid young blade, twenty-ish) and Sheila (craggy mother/grandmother, fifty-ish) are rarely off the patio (where the invisible Tomas drives his smokers into the air-conditioned night) without a duty-free Superking or a gold-wrapped B&H to hand. An odorous, smoky haze and a tobacco scent hangs round them like it hangs around schoolkids coming down the stairs of a bus.

They're a slightly bizarre group. Sheila is vivacious and lively, ageing perhaps, but energetic, not pious to look at though unsettling to talk to; in talk she's an odd mixture of the devotedly devout and the wickedly worldly, and one wonders what she might have been like if she'd stayed in Ireland and God hadn't given her so much to deal with. Sally-Ann, with Laurie and Paul, is, as James with Cecilia, along with her mother chiefly for her mother's purposes; Sheila wants a last familial week together before Paul goes off to the university. Paul himself has a rather stately, self-consciously educated voice and funny, off-red hair. His skin is pale, tinged with the off-pallor of someone who doesn't go out much, and I've yet to see him go anywhere since we touched base at Tomas's place. Sally-Ann is otherwise. She is feisty, healthy-looking, vibrant, sexy, with a little tattoo of a devil on her bare right shoulder.

We end up having dinner together in the Pansion, and at the end of the meal the night's supply of Herzegovinian wine, largely unused by the other pilgrims, who are saving themselves for an evening benediction or an exposition, is taken out on to the patio to finish off. When it's gone – all six litres, washed down with a few hundred fags – the duty-free Baileys comes out from their room; and soon we're embarked on a most unholy session in the late Friday sun. Sheila, fag in mouth, talks shocks to life, death and divorce, unmarried Catholic girls who have tattoos and babies at nineteen. Sally-Ann, fag in mouth, talks child-care and child-rearing and husband-care and husband-steering; Paul, fag in mouth, talks law degrees (he's going to Derby, though he clearly feels that in a world with any justice he would be off somewhere with less red brick and more ivy) and strange years off involved in Internet projects in some of the stranger states of the USA; in the strangely biblical lands of Utah, of Oregon, of Illinois. Soon I (a renounced smoker of some years' standing) have a fag in my mouth too (St Peregrine, I learn later, looks after the cancer victim) and I assent to some rather unholy orders to meet a bit later at Lukas's Bar to talk the problems of the world over a little further.

Angela passes, troubled, on her way for a walk. At first I wonder if it's my fag, or my glass, or my sitting close in between Sally-Ann and Paul, with Laurie on my knee. In fact it's not me; she and her sister Nora, she tells me, have a relationship that's not without its burdens. Nora, the Manhattanite, is intolerant and demanding and needs space and has money; the Londoner Angela is quieter, and more reflective, has her own insistences but comes on Nora's ticket. Angela says she has struggled spiritually today; the new built-up feel of the place that Nora keeps boasting about, she says, is depriving her of the peace she wants, and you can see she's troubled by so many people coming and appearing to want miracles. For miracles, she doesn't say, are not unlike credit; better not to ask for them, for a refusal often offends. Sheila makes her sit down and cheers her up, though; she tells her a tale of her mother, just before she died, being given a set of rosary beads made of rosewood or dogwood and which spontaneously released a perfume just at the moment when her mother passed away. And Angela, whatever her hard London edge, finds the story alluring and comparable with other things she may have heard.

Sheila then invites Angela, in a Herzegovinian wine sort of way, to join us for the somewhat wild and not altogether pilgrim-like night that follows. Angela, of course, declines; she has bigger fish to fry down at the church. For James, who joins us, for Sally-Ann, for Paul and for me it's simple: we have a ridiculous six or seven or eight beers at Lukas's. The justification is a conspiracy of sorts, for Sally-Ann and Paul and, most vocally, James, spend most of the evening chewing the fat about how to keep pious parents sweet. I would be an expert in some company, but they have their own Ph.D.s in the subject, and it's not long before the inevitable conclusion to any such discussion – that there's simply nothing you can do, that you choose your friends but you don't choose your family's religion, that such institutions are there to be endured, not enjoyed – is rolled out, and rolls out – the discussion having occasionally been of a manner tired and emotional – on a tide of slurred slur.

What happens later more or less proves that there is no God. While we drunken bums get home without incident, poor old Nora Batty, on her way back from church and the nine o'clock service, having no intention of stopping by at Lukas's Bar at all, drops by just to say hello, takes a tumble off a kerb and appears at the bar with her face covered with blood and her handbag, clutched to her side throughout the excursion so far, gone in the taxi she has alighted from. James staggers up, finds Cecilia, who has some experience as a nurse, it seems, and is thus able to perform suitably corporal works of mercy; James, meanwhile, nobly (but probably not in a straight line) runs off to alert the first-aid team, who because of their choice of Mediterranean cross-symbol are absurdly known as the Maltesers; and when he returns he still has the puff to locate the taxi driver, who reports that the bag went home with one of Nora's mates and is safe and well. They all go off, bloody and bruised, to search for it.

When the old folk disappear – well, what with the excitement and all – we go on to another bar. Sally-Ann tells, in a woild Plymouth accent, woild tales of noights out in the towyin. James (he's an open and zestful conversationalist) flirts with Sally-Ann relentlessly, up to and including the point at which we end up back at the Pansion steps, fags in mouths each, filling our glasses to the uppermost with the lower half of the Baileys on ice. I get hazy, Sally-Ann gets dazy; James gets lary and Paul – incredibly – tries to get scary. Clearly a nocturnal beast, he decides that he wants to show off some kick-boxing moves. In celebration of the first signs that his body has an athletic capability I re-christen him The Ginger Ninja.

Sally-Ann tells us more tales for an hour. She runs through her father (at home, but absent in spirit), her mother, her own troubled history with men and (while Paul kicks a football about outside, slipping and sliding on the lurching gravel in the gripping dark) her troubles with her brother. I listen blurredly; James listens keenly; we both watch disappointedly as, finished, Sally-Ann goes off to bed, leaving us to the dregs and the darkness. (One of the pious in the party may have had a private prayer-word with St Mary of Egypt, who gave up courtesanning in favour of forty-seven years in the desert, and is thus invoked against sexual temptation.) As she goes, she seems to feel we need some gloss, for she says, tiredly, slurring, as she watches her brother fly-kicking the empty air: 'We ought to be called the Simpsons, you know. Welcome to the world of our dysfunctional family.'

Next Medjugorje morning we get disapproving looks for a bit but if there's one place we're guaranteed forgiveness it's here, and we duly get it; at least after a frosty half-hour or so. I have a hangover bad enough to make me feel I'm walking a line: temptation on one side, quest on the other. And it makes me wonder whether this hasn't always been my problem: a restless veering between the spiritual and the corporal, with the corporal – even in such company as I was last night – appearing to have the upper hand whenever push comes to shove. I must have been a spineless adolescent, I reflect, a feather for every debauched wind that blew; wherever I choose to try to spread the blame.

I don't get up until eleven, and even that's a struggle: it's Coca-Cola, can after Croatian can of it, until two or three in the afternoon. (I read a little paperback Dictionary of Saints I've picked up for an hour, and, discovering that Benedict is patron of the poisoned, wish I had his legendary power to bless the cup and draw its sting.) Sometime in the morning I go up to the church to watch, in the heat and the dust, half a dozen local yokels celebrate the feast-day by picking up the ten foot statue of St James from the parish church and carrying it out to what's called 'the field'; in fact it's a wood. The service that follows is in Croat; I sit, bleary, in the red dust, unable to make any kind of sensible connection. Faced with incomprehensibility, I concentrate instead on listening to the surreal deafening shrieks of the crickets and the grasshoppers before the men carry Saint Iakov back to the church in their unhysterical way. There are no banknotes pinned to the hem of his garment, no grim images of snakes or skeletons; the Croatian way — like the way they bomb their bridges — is calm and collected.

Outside, Cecilia meets me. She's a little disapproving (and can't help mentioning it) of the idea that I was unsteady on my feet when she last saw me, but I point out that it wasn't *my* friends who were falling over in the gutters of the streets, and with a sort of fair-cop laugh she forgives me. In any case, it's not me but her son she's worried about; when you pay for your son to come on a Holy Willie tour I don't suppose you expect the first night to see him pissing it up with a drinking partner and a tattooed trollop. I'm feeling regretful, feeling that I've sided with the wrong team; I'm glad there's no sign of James, or of Sally-Ann, and Cecilia and I go to have lunch together, joining a long table at Café Columbus, where Angela and Lawrence the Indian bloke and Nora and Cecilia's best friend Eileen and Vicky, an Hispanic-looking Londoner, are already in residence.

We chat harmlessly and order some lunch. Cecilia tells Catholic jokes in a cack-handed sort of way. (A man goes to Lourdes and is pushed through the healing waters in his wheelchair. When he comes out the chair has four new tyres. Boom-boom; the old ones are the best, and it's the way she tells them.) After a bit they all turn on me, the stranger at their table. Eileen wants to know my place in the hierarchy: have I been before? No? Then what's brought me here? I explain, curtly but genially. Cecilia asks me questions about misrepresentation that are at least partly designed to warn the others that I might be, if not the Devil's Advocate, then at least a junior on his legal team. I say that I think myself honest in terms of representing what people say to me, and that deeper down I'm open, a seeker, but Cecilia is shrewd and not-taking-that-again, is interested in methods: how will I remember what people say in such a way that I can be sure it's accurate? For the last thing Medjugorje needs is more *lies* about it. She tries to make me believe that it's the lies of such as myself that bother her, though I choose not to mention the Bishop of Zagreb and his objections to the place.

Feeling under a little bit of pressure, as much a result of my thick boozer's head as anything, I try to offer a more rounded picture of what I'm up to; that I'm thinking about childhood, youth and exile, how I find myself on the outside of the faith in spite of all the lavish blandishments of a good Kafflik education; how it's time, on some level, to take another look. And wondering if I've gone too far, I say how I envy those who are pupils in the Diocese of Liverpool's Kafflik primary schools, where Lourdes Roger does his business, who are not compelled to go to mass because, his version of the official policy says, every individual must find his own way to God. And that seems a remarkably gifted idea for this day and this age (and this person).

Well, this causes a little dissension. Cecilia and Eileen fulminate with old-fashioned, tub-thumping Irishry: 'I don't see what was wrong with the old system,' says Eileen, to which Cecilia adds wise words about acquiring habits early which remain with you until later life; good old-fashioned Kafflik respect for learning by rote, in other words. But Vicky, who, it turns out, is an Anglican, says she can see what I'm talking about, and says so patiently and quietly and courageously. But Eileen has a doggedly Donegal point of view. 'A bedrock,' she says, 'that's what I received, and I think all children should receive the same.' And – something of a non-sequitur it seems now, but since we're in praise of freewheelery we'll let it go – she starts on a long saga about a certain convert in her parish who came over from the Anglicans but who feels that she can pick and choose which parts of the faith she likes and which parts she doesn't. The hardliners, Cecilia prominent, curse their name; Vicky is silenced by the discourtesy; and Nora Batty, her face badly bruised from her fall, falls asleep in her chair.

Well, I say (being of a provocative frame of mind, and this being a pilgrimage where it's time to search, to do some seeking): 'What do you do if you find yourself in difficulties with certain aspects of the faith? Or with one specific aspect of the teaching that you just can't accept? Let's take birth control,' I add, and it's still an attack as far as they are concerned, even though I suggest we take it not necessarily on a personal level but on the basis of what John Paul II has been encouraging the Third World to think and do, viz., not worry too much about bringing starving babies into the world so long as the evils of contraception are strenuously avoided. Eileen looks like she might walk out; Vicky looks faintly embarrassed; Cecilia, trying to find a formula – perhaps she feels the camera's on her and it's her job to be reasonable – says that rather than freewheel our way through that issue we should allow each person in turn to answer.

It's Lawrence that starts. (In fact, Lawrence is the only one from the proposed *ordo* who manages to make a statement; because as soon as he's finished – indeed, rather before – Cecilia is in, intolerantly, her speaking skills more developed than her listening ones.) But Lawrence does say something substantial, and substantially honest; he details the way in which he made his own, individual, conscience-driven choice to use artificial birth control. Up to now I'd assumed it was only the pretend Catholics who reached that point and that situation, but he, the Kerala Kafflik, and sincere as the day is long, has done so. It seems to come down to this: faced with the facts of life and with the facts of his economic situation and the facts of the wishes of himself and his wife, he had, via conscience and prayer, come to a common sense conclusion that there was not much to give between artificial contraception and the riskier, approved version that people used to call Vatican Roulette.

There's a stunned silence when Lawrence is finished; I'm not sure anyone expected this response, certainly not Eileen, and absolutely not me. The hot sun burns on the blind we sit under as Cecilia starts to talk. It's not what you would call a response; it's more of an autobiography, made up by a transposition into the third person, and dressed up to look like a contribution to the debate. 'Let's say there is a woman at home,' she says, and you're supposed to understand it's a hypothesis only, and forget it has very little to do with what has gone before. 'A woman who doesn't work but who is devoting her life to the family. She gets tired, she gets older, she gets fatter. She has the children all around her all day, and soon, she can't find the energy within herself to do . . . all that. You know. The *sexual act*. Especially when he's busy with his work, preoccupied, and men's interest in sex being different, well, more urgent, what is it she can do? She tries to say to the man, well, what I need is slightly different. Why not spend some time with me in bed cuddling and holding, not *doing sex*?' (The italics are hers, somehow.) 'Or when I'm at the kitchen sink, why not just come up to me and hold me from behind and tell me that you love me?

'But meanwhile, the man goes to work' (if she said 'there was this friend of mine', it couldn't be plainer who it was) 'and there's a younger woman there, his secretary, *say*, and that young woman flatters the man, makes him feel special.' Well the story's predictable enough, but it's hers, which adds a horrible fascination; we're safely still in the plane, but she's jumped out, and we're watching her tug unsuccessfully on her ripcord. She's taken a plunge; in the hot afternoon we have a feeling we are coming somewhere in defining where we are and where we go; her thinking is away, leaping between idea and idea, every one from the inside of her own life, even if she doesn't quite want to push on over-explicitly. 'You know, a man goes to a priest and he says, "There's this woman on the train, and I think I'm in love with her: I see her every morning and she's beautiful and I care for her and I think I could settle down with her."

And the priest says, "What train is this?"' Which half the table think is the punch-line, so that when the punch-line comes it's almost lost: 'Well, the man says, "The ten past eight." So the priest says, "I have the answer. Get the ten past nine." But he doesn't – he carries on on the ten past eight until it's too late.'

What this has to do with anything that's been said I don't know, but things go back and forth, and round and round, and pilgrims pass, and come in, and sit down, and eat pizza, and go away; and I hear twenty good things ascribed to the intercession of the Virgin, to her blessing; and I hear ten bad things ascribed to the Devil and his works. Angela chips in, quietly, asking me to have a look at bits of St James, and telling me I should read the holy book more often, and Vicky gets turned on, for a bit, responding to someone's speech on the theme of 'no disrespect to the Anglicans but they shouldn't be taking our communion for we're the one true church'. At which I get troubled, and say that I think there are too many rules and regulations, that they should take anyone who's gentle and lowly at heart. And Cecilia, to be fair, agrees: anyone who is sincere is more or less all right, she says, anyone who's not mocking. 'If they feel a need,' she says, 'it's all right.'

And she tells a tale of a Holy Willie woman in her church, who got stroppy about a late-life conversion; and Cecilia, formidable as she is, got stroppy in turn, making sure the woman remembered the story of the workers in the vineyard who arrived at different times of the day; made sure that she remembered the rejoicing that apparently occurs in heaven when a single sinner repents. Yet strangely, she does not regard herself as a converter, and she doesn't regard her own conversion as an overnight thing. 'A woman may be twenty-seven years away,' she says, once again resorting to her royal third person, 'but when she comes to Medjugorje and suddenly finds she no longer requires the tranquillizers she's been taking because her marriage has ended'

– suddenly all that's gone before, all the wander and confusion, is simple and transparent – 'and no longer has to sit in a room wasting away and looking at the ceiling, because in Medjugorje she's discovered the love of the Lord and His Blessed Mother – that's not a momentary change – that's been building – that moment has been coming. And those of us who come year after year or time after time – all of us have had a moment like that. A conversion.'

> St Giles (Aegidius)
> Feast: September 1
> Patron Saint of Cripples
> (also Beggars and Blacksmiths)
> When visiting Rome, Giles was given two beautiful wooden doors by the Pope. He threw them into the sea off Italy, and they were miraculously washed up near his abbey on the south coast of France.

So, next Lourdes morning, ready for conversion, I go to find what's special: as instructed by Win, I make for the baths. Actually, that's rubbish; rebellious at last, I don't intend to at all. After the Grotto experience I'm taking Win's instructions with a pinch of salt, for all my admiration, and anyway I had been thinking I might go and have a look at the Stations of the Cross – the official round of the Stations, great wooden things planted on a hillside – this afternoon. But as I come out of the hotel I see Roger there, standing behind his mother's chair, with Margaret. They're waiting for Eric and his wife, who've travelled in an independent group from Widnes; a group that goes the easy way, by boat to Bilbao with a short bus-ride up the coast, across the Pyrenees and over into France. And Eric, with an impressive tour-guide manner, says they are going to take Roger's mum to the baths, and so I go along for the walk.

As we go Eric witters amusingly about his sister's farm in

America; she's left her Liverpool home years back and lives in wealth in Maryland. A far cry from this as a vacation experience, he seems to be saying. At the entrance to the baths queues are beginning to form for the afternoon session. Once we've got Roger's mum in the ladies' queue it's the work of a moment for Eric to chivvy Roger and I into joining him in joining the men's, and with a well, why not? shrug both of us end up sitting on the concrete bench outside the low, flat, brutalist bathhouse with the healing waters inside; the place where we'll find what's special.

After five minutes there – or five minutes chat with Eric, who knows everything – it's clear what the main Miracle of Lourdes is: that no one falls sick as a result of passing through these baths. For on an average day hundreds of people pass through each of the tubs that contains the holy water, and the holy water is only changed once a day. Which is unhygienic enough. Add to that the fact that of those hundreds at least a quarter are suffering from a life-threatening disease, and your imagination constructs quite a combo of bacteria and germinology. 'You could say to Saddam, why bother nerve-gas bombing the Kurds,' says Eric, 'when you could just convert them to Catholicism and send them down here.' Some say, Eric reports, that the water neutralizes the germs in some fantastic, other-worldly way; others say that sooner or later someone's going to get typhus.

Roger is uneasy sitting in the queue; at first I think it's because of what Eric has been saying; later I'm not so sure. He keeps looking up to see where his mother is in the queue, on the other side of the wire run that divides the ladies and the men. 'I came down here yesterday,' he says, troubled, 'while my mother was out with Margaret, and I saw this building. I couldn't believe it was the place. Couldn't believe this could be the baths.' He points to the concrete flat roof, the dark, shadowed canopy that sits above us; it looks like a stillborn model for a Sixties tower block. 'I saw people waiting to go in, queuing up tamely just like we are now, and for some reason I thought of concentration camps. And now I can't get that image out of my head.'

I can see what he means. Here we are, all waiting to be herded in, not knowing to what particularly, and a set of officious officials has been given the job of seeing that the queue moves forward in an orderly fashion, which means that whenever there's a space we're to be budged up as far as possible. The *Oberleutnant* nearest us looks like a village-idiot type: stooped, hunched, balding, and speaking in clipped, village-idiot Italian. 'At least Lurch there wasn't here yesterday,' says Roger. 'He was off being fitted up for his gold teeth.' We shuffle along the benches. Hymns are sung, and *morituri te salutant* pronounced, in my heart, anyway. Uncle Fester makes sure we all sit three to a seat, which makes jolly Eric even jollier; he tells some story of a canon in his parish who used to organize jollies at very cheap prices, on the basis – as you only discovered when you got there – that it was three to a seat in the coach. Roger laughs mildly, and I laugh, but Eric laughs loudest of all, earning all of us a scowl from the querulous Quasimodo.

Rog is still thoughtful, scanning the crowd and their faces. 'I wonder what's going through their minds?' he says, looking at the sick. 'I wonder if any of them *really* feel that they're going to come out cured?' There's a restlessness in his tone, which I don't quite pick up until I hear it again, later, for now Eric's on my mind as we notice a couple of obese Italians and record the fact, once again, that miracle cures do not extend to lardy arses. (Eric laughs: 'Miracles are only effective when used as part of a calorie-controlled diet.') Roger is not so sure. He's face-watching, which I initially take for looking out for his mother as he scans the women's queue; but which instinctively I begin to feel is something else.

And only when he sees I feel this does he tell me about his own trip: here for his mother, yes, but really here for his wife, who died four years before of a brain tumour. Eric looks away, stops gagging; he knows the story. 'It was inoperable,' Roger says, matter of factly, 'and we knew that, and we made a conscious decision to be as normal as possible, for the sake of the kids. About halfway through her last year she decided she wanted to go to Lourdes and – normality, you see – I stayed at home, which I was happy to do, for the sake of the plan we'd made.' We move up the queue; Lurch watches admiringly as an Italian harpy sings *Ave Maria* in a frog-croak; she's on the Third Sorrowful Mystery and it's twice as sorrowful than it needs to be. 'When she came back,' Roger goes on, 'when she came back she was changed. She wasn't cured – she knew she wouldn't be cured when she went. But she was sort of firmer. More focused. After that it was me who was the more shaky, the more worried, the more sort of – disturbed. She was – well, kind of fine. So I'm here,' he says, matter of fact again, 'to say thank you, I suppose. To thank somebody for that change. Even if I didn't scoop the jackpot, as it were.'

He begins to face-watch again and now I realize why the eyes are so thorough, so restless; I realize that the worst thing for him is not the obvious sick, as it is for those of us not involved; it's the hidden sick, those whose scars are hidden under clothing, those whose baldness lies under wigs; those who we see as stout but who were thin, those who we see as well but who were weller before the chemicals started coursing round their veins. The queue moves on and we get inside the building only to find that there's another queue within: we're squeezed up on another bench. ('Three to a seat, remember,' says Eric, brightening up again.) In front of us are a series of cubicles shielded from our gaze by blue-and-white striped shower curtains; behind each is a single concrete bath, and we are plucked from our seats in turn as a space appears, taken away from our friends and made to walk alone. 'But if you didn't get a miracle – well at least you got a miracle of the mind,' I risk, before I am led away.

'Indeed,' says Roger. 'Bringing my old mother's nice – she loves it, and as I say she has that old world sort of simple faith. But she hasn't seen what I've seen. It was a hard year until she – I mean my wife – went, at Christmas. We tried to be normal, as I say, but she ballooned, she suffered from the chemotherapy, she lost her hair. My mother doesn't really know this, doesn't really know what it means. Her faith is intact. It's not been – how would you say it – tested in quite the same way as mine has. But that doesn't really matter – because I'm really not here for her. I'm really here for me. And to relive my wife's journey, I suppose. To see what I missed when we decided to be "normal".'

A silence falls between us all for about five minutes of queuing; I see Eric place his hand on Roger's, give him a squeeze. Time passes, and Roger is still pensive, but Eric has a sudden thought that springs from all our nerves at this suddenly odd, scary situation. He laughs, and says: 'Roger: were you going to go in when you came down here?'

'Not till you were,' says Roger.

Eric: 'Well, I didn't come intending to come in at all.'

Suddenly we're with a tour guide who doesn't know the way.

'Well neither did I,' says Roger, who then says to me: 'What about you?'

'Me?' I say. 'Well, no. I was just following you lot.'

'Then let's scarper!' says Eric.

We all laugh, and *Lurch II: This Time It's Personal* scowls at us. We sit in enforced silence for a bit. I watch Roger process each person that passes, categorizing them for sickness, for state of hopelessness or hopefulness, processes each condition he sees, imagining his wife here. But she's not. He seems to anticipate my thought: 'Things were very difficult for a while,' he says. 'They're all right now.' And all the way round to the next stage he makes himself kind of jolly, as if to prove it, and I have a sense that if this is one step backward then it's only to take two forward later; that he is a person whose own mourning is moving towards completion, even if the pain of the present is intense; even if his ordeal is also a solitary one.

In time we're led off separately. Behind the curtain things are even more uncomfortable. In the small cubicle, above a soaking, swimming-pool floor are six bare wooden chairs and six rudimentary hooks. A minute Englishman, a post-war-stunted PE teacher type, asks us if we'll strip down to our kecks. Understanding that it's a rhetorical question, I do, then stand and wait. He tells me to sit down. My feet are cold on the grey marble floor: it's wet, dismal, and I look at my fellow bathers, and observe (as you do) their underwear, judge them by their briefs. There's an Indonesian with impeccable Calvin Klein Ys, who looks like a man who would look elegant in an accident; an Italian in boxers and on crutches; and a fat Venezuelan sexagenarian with a skidmark in his voluminous, off-grey pants. I raise a silent prayer when, thankfully, only the Indonesian is called before me.

I pass through the next available curtain and into the world beyond. '*Italiano?*' asks a branc, one of two who stand around like sentries.

I look down at my lilywhite skin, my undeveloped dugs. No chance. '*Inglese,*' I say, or rather, qualifying: '*Scozzese.*'

'*Inglese?*' he says, ignoring me. '*Perfetto.*'

Why it's *perfetto* he doesn't say: perhaps he just has it in for Anglophones. Whatever – a terrifying event begins. They ask me to face the wall, a grey, damp surface without feature. They tell me to wait until the gown is in place behind me, then to remove my pants. I do, then shiver as the Italian boy wraps my loins in a soaking, freezing piece of blue cloth in which other balls than mine have recently shrivelled. Then he turns me round so that I am standing at the top of a set of rough concrete steps that lead down into the bath. The bath is a deep, frightening grey, a frightening, heavy weight; a few feet deep, bathroom-bath-length long, it has parallel steps on either side so that the brancs can take the weight on either side as they lower disabled pilgrims in.

With a deep breath I'm ready to walk straight in but the Englishman stops me; it's not allowed. He indicates a sign up above asking me in no uncertain terms if, before I go in, I Might Like to Say a Short Prayer. This is no less rhetorical than the order to undress; I have to recite the 'Hail Mary', and, that I have the prayer to (as it were) hand, even under duress, I quietly thank the rote-learning procedures of my youth. At *Amen*, the Italian boy takes my arm and walking down his steps begins to lead me roughly down and into the water. 'Seedon,' he says. Not surprisingly, I don't quite understand what he's up to, what I'm supposed to do, and I keep walking, before half-stumbling into a sort of half-kneeling crouch which I can identify by the feeling that the hem of my garment is riding up over my floating testes.

The arms that are holding both of mine pick me up pretty roughly. (I hadn't noticed another guard flanking me on my left.) 'See*down!*' the boy repeats. This time I get it; but by now the bottom half of my body, completely unprepared for the arctic winter beneath me, is convulsing with the cold and this time I have little choice but to do my crouchy kneel once more. 'SEEDOWN!' the Italian voice screams in a most un-Christian fashion, and I try to shuffle round but end up completely on my knees; he who kneels for no one is kneeling now, and by the time – helped by a few tugs and crunching barges from both sides – I do what I'm told I'm shivering, I'm lost and – irony of ironies – I've put my back out.

I stand up at the far end, up to my knees in the water, on my feet again. The Englishman appears and makes me pray again; he thrusts a little plaster Madonna into my hand, suggests fiercely I say another 'Hail Mary', and when I have tremblingly completed, performs a little litany: 'Our Lady of Lourdes, Pray for Us, St Bernadette, Pray for Us'. Only then do they let me go. There are no towels in the changing room; you are simply untied, passed your soaking kecks and dispatched to change quickly before you return to the world of Quasimodo and the Sorrowful Mysteries. My fear begins to subside after a bit. And while I don't feel uplifted in quite the way Win says, there is, as the dust settles, a very weird feeling in the air. I'm not buzzing, nor do I feel particularly close to her Ladyship, but I do feel like I'm walking strangely tall, like I'm strangely invigorated; a feeling that, once again, must be reinforcing if you start from a position in which you have something to reinforce.

Eric and Rog are waiting outside. 'What did you think to that then?'

'Funny,' I say.

'*Cold* and funny,' says Eric.

Roger, again, is more thoughtful: 'They made me say a prayer,' said Roger. 'Forced me. I have to be honest and say I didn't like it.' But if he is thinking of his wife and what she endured, he has no chance to say so; his mother appears and she coos with remembrance at what it was like, and we all have to shut up; the watchword is 'simple faith', and her simple faith has been reinforced by being similarly, if presumably more gently, doused, perhaps in English, perhaps by Win and Carol and big, beefy Margaret.

I need some time, as he clearly does. They go off to take 'Mum' to one of the services; I decide to go to the banks of the Gave to have a scribble and a think. As I walk past the entrance to the baths the queue is still there. Amongst them is the

Archbishop: presumably to avoid Lurch propelling him to the front, he's taken off all his accoutrements and is sitting like an ordinary pilgrim, a plain priest, sweaty but serene, not at all the portly Chaucerian figure my satirical self had hoped for. He, and other people like him, are still emerging when I pass later. No one is shouting and whooping or taking up their bed and walking, but Win has made it clear that that is not to be expected, even if such miracles are how and why this whole place lives and dies. As far as Roger is concerned, his mother is better off; that's his little miracle, though – because his wife didn't get a big one – maybe he's in need of a little one himself.

'Stephen closed his eyes and held out in the air his trembling hand with the palm held outwards. He felt the prefect of studies touch it for a moment at the fingers to straighten it and then the swish of the sleeve of the soutane as the pandybat was lifted to strike . . .'

Like Joyce's Stephen, Stephen has to move house, is uprooted from a certain certainty in his early teens. Stephen Dedalus, driven to poverty by his father's taste for the drink and for prodigal company, moves from the pretty house in Bray, in the airy suburbs south of Dublin Bay, and winds up in the grim, hell-like darknesses of the inner north city, off the top end of O'Connell Street, where he wanders nightly in a welter of self-regarding disgust and self-demeaning curiosity. The cause of this Stephen's move is not disastrous husbandry, and nor is his motion so emetic, even if it is disappointing. He moves from Edinburgh to Glasgow, from place to displacement, from company to solitude. Like Stephen Dedalus's, it is a move to the rougher edges, where voices are more clipped, where his own voice seems over-refined and garishly cultivated; and where – if one really wants to trudge out the parallel – in the streets around Blythswood Square, he sees the prostitutes working their patches as the other Stephen in Dublin does on his nocturnal rambles. (Stephen

Dedalus, of course, steps forward and samples their wares; this Stephen is much more timid.)

For his father, at least and especially, the move has a great boon to it in addition to his own advancement; from east to west a perfect offering may be made. His older brother has already shown signs of falling victim to the strains of the Sixties, to the secularization of society, to the wishy-wash of the current teaching and its moving away from proper doctrine and reinforcement; and his father, quite reasonably, does not want Stephen, and the other brothers to come, to fall by the same relativist wayside. (His sister is not in the same danger; at her convent school she is − and will remain − devout.) The solution, for his father, lies in a return to the past; he and his brothers, particularly James Ignatius and Francis Xavier, learned to love and serve the Lord under the beady educational eye of the Jesuits; respect was paid in full (and the scholarships offered to the nine-children-in-two-bedrooms family reclaimed) when the two joined the Order, when the brothers became fathers. The Jesuits, unrepresented in the panoply of Edinburgh's great but Protestant-dominated academies, had a solidly green-blazer school in Glasgow. Give me a boy at seven or whatever is past, of course. But this boy, this Stephen, can be given them at eleven, and the object of the exercise remains the great Jesuit educational objective, the production of a Kafflik gentleman.

The vibration at home is good; that here is a development that is full and exciting, and the new green blazer − the golden Holy Cross of his earliest years has been traded in for a golden Gonzaga eagle − is tried on with alacrity, is worn with something like pride. But the school itself, when he gets there, gives off a slower, more fearful rhythm, emits a mustier fragrance. Behind the great, unsentried doors, the place turns out to be in the grip of a clique of old, conservative men, a particular species of men of the cloth whose cloth is dusty, a handful of dead hands whom the Jesuits will shortly pension off, who stand at corridor-ends in their long soutanes, their black wings trailing behind them in the breeze, resisting anyone who seeks to shake the motes off the shroud. Stephen's age is permissive, of course, and they know it; they know the Enemy is at the gates. They respond in the way they know best, these men who have learned by rote: they feign the non-existence of change, to lecture and to hector, insist that what they offer is absolute and that anything else is relativism, keep all minds and windows shut. In the catachetic world of God the Father, God the Son, and God the Holy Ghost, who are three persons in one, all is to remain entombed, encorpsed.

These storm troopers of the Church cannot be blamed, of course, if the horses don't drink; they do enough leading. They provide the mountain, and we Mohammeds must come to it. Written into the routine of the day is mass each morning at ten to nine; the services are dreary, bleary, conducted 'twixt sleep and wake, if organizationally useful (they act as a temporal buffer zone that allows the middle-class boys from Bearsden and Milngavie and Pollokshields to arrive late without being noticed). On Fridays there is another service in mid-morning, and sometimes a mysterious Benediction in the afternoon, with the monstrance gleaming on the altar for a reason never fully explained.

In the classroom, in the great Jesuit tradition, each activity is routinely dedicated to the Maker. On day one the message is given; all schoolwork is to be marked with an AMDG at the top of each page in the exercise-book – Ad Majorem Dei Gloriam, 'For the Greater Glory of God'. Under this heading we study French, and History, and Physics, and Latin, and Mathematics – all the secular subjects which will bring the exam passes which will ensure that the sons of doctors can become doctors, that the sons of Italian ice-cream makers can become accountants. (For Kafflik gentlemanliness, for some of those who attend here and those who brought them up, is a matter of class and money, not a matter of right and wrong; it will take more education than this particular brand of men in black can offer to make any kind of dent in their second-generation immigrant assurance that that is so.)

So all the trappings of the spiritual life are here; all, that is, except spirit and life. The one opportunity for glimmer might be the scheduled lessons for Religious Education that Stephen is offered; time in which, free from the restrictions of syllabus demands, one might enjoy an exploration of the faith, or discussion of the nature of the world, or direction as to how that explored faith might be better used to change the nature of the world. This would seem to be a reasonable expectation of R.E., though there are some amongst the Jesuit corps at the school for whom it is still known as R.I.; Religious Instruction, that is, for education is, after all, a putting-in, not a drawing-out.

For the Greater Glory of God *comes, for instance, old Father R, a creaking ghost of a man, a dry-as-dust fossil; a good old-fashioned English Jesuit. Stephen is eleven, twelve; Fr. R is that plus a hundred or so, living in a world that has gone wrong, but which can be righted if England can regain the Ashes and the important things about the religious life are restored to the curriculum. Since he can do nothing about the former, he concentrates on the latter. Not for him any new-fangled heresy of Personal and Social Education; not even for him any moderately old-fashioned heresy of Moral Issues. There is not a word about doing things for others, or helping your neighbours; there are not even warnings about not coveting their ox; this is the bones of Holy Church saved as a relic, drawn out of a cask to be displayed as perfectly preserved. And who cares if it crumbles at the touch? Horses will have been led to water, so don't spare them.*

Lesson plans, such as they appear in memory:

Week 1: class will learn the names of the different parts of the priest's vestments. Method: *teacher will talk, students will make notes in book, be tested at end of week. Any failure to recall the detail: six strokes of the ferula at bill-cashing time at the end of the day.*

(*And so, Stephen possesses some of it even now:* The inner garments: the amice and the alb, of white linen. The outer garments: the chasuble, the dalmatic, the tunicle. *They're remembered well, these words that pour back through a fearful memory of the possibility of a fearful flaking.* The vestments are put on over the cassock, in this order: amice, alb, cincture, maniple, stole and chasuble. The cassock must be black, except in certain missionary churches, where a white cassock is permitted owing to the effects of the heat of the sun.)

Week 2: *class will learn the names of all the Saints in the Canon with a Jesuit association.* Method: *teacher will talk at some length while students make, in a book, half-hearted notes on which they will be tested at the end of the week, at which time they will feign or engineer a little interest so as to avoid six strokes of the ferula at bill-cashing time at the end of the day.*

(And so Stephen can still, just about, run through the list. The obvious ones, with the usual mnemonic of the initials that are painted round the church he sits in each morning. SFX: St Francis Xavier. SIL: St Ignatius Loyola. SAG: St Aloysius Gonzaga. SRB: St Robert Bellarmine. *(The same Bellarmine, that is, who was a friend of Galileo, and who clothed the poor in tapestries from the wall of the Cardinal's house in Milan, and who lived exclusively on bread, water and garlic.) The less obvious too, the footsoldiers of the Storm troopers of the Church:* SSK: St Stanislaus Kostka. SOP: St Oliver Plunkett. SJB: St John Berchmans.)

Week 3: *class will learn the names of the different utensils found on the altar.* Method: *teacher will drone endlessly, half-conscious pupils will make, in a book, no comprehensible notes on which they will be tested at end of week; most will fail and hardly care about the six strokes of the ferula at bill-cashing time at the end of the day.*

(And so Stephen, an obedient child, still possesses a half-sense of what consists of and what sits on the altar of the Lord: candles, missal and missal stand, the veiled tabernacle, the altar-cloth, the veiled chalice and burse. *And the other bits and pieces that surround:* Chalice: the law of the Church is that the chalice must be made of gold or silver, or that the inside of the cup, at least, be silver-gilt. (In times of persecution this is not always possible.) The thurible or censer: a cup-shaped vessel, with a lid suspended by chains, in which incense is burned during High Mass, Benediction, Processions and Solemn Requiems.)

Is it any wonder Stephen feels, as hairs grow unexpectedly, as hormones queue up to collide, without a tiller in this rough world? For the Faith of his Fathers is taught in the same way maths is: by bullying, by rote, by tricks of fear and memory. If only someone might tell him that he learns trigonometry or algebra so that fundamental aspects of his physical existence can be explained, then perhaps he might learn a little more studiedly, a little more purposefully. Of course it is possible that he is simply not, by nature, a mathematician. So how would he know?

IV
Confirmations

St Augustine of Hippo
Feast: August 28
Patron Saint of Brewers and Publicans
Invoked to Cure Sore Eyes
While living squalidly as a young man in Carthage (the Doctor of
Grace cohabited with an African woman for fifteen years, fathering a
child named Adeodatus) Augustine framed a motto for all who are
saving up their virtue for later. 'Da mihi castitatem et continentiam,
sed noli modo' – 'God give me chastity and temperance – but not yet'.

Saturday, 7.15 a.m. In the queue to get back on the bus as our
ferry draws into Dublin Bay there's a wacky old couple, Mac
and Nancy, and they're holding forth at this godawful segment
of the early morning – or Mac is – about what the word 'special'
means on his newly acquired duty-free Special Filter. (It's an
important aspect of pilgrimage, I think.) 'Maybe they roll it a
bit finer,' he says, 'I don't know. Stronger. To me it tastes like
paper unless your tongue burns when you smoke it. And they
don't give coupons any more, you know.' He goes on in this
pre-breakfast stream of consciousness fashion as we return to
take our seats. He and his wife are marked out by having identical
haircuts – white for age, short for style. His is a little spikier,
hers a little smoother; he has sideburns. Their mouths are un-
identical: his never stops, hers never starts. With what I take to
be an Irish exile's sense of the right thing to say he wishes me
the top of the morning and shakes my hand. 'And a beautiful
morning, isn't it?'

127

No, I'm tempted to say; darkness is on the face of the deep, and I feel pretty bad; without form, and void. Up at the back, with a due sense of spiritual priority, Edmund is squabbling with his neighbours. The black woman in front of him, whose neck is wrapped in one of those wraparound cushions from the World of Innovations catalogue, has put back her recliner, which is interfering with the interface between Edmund's capacious girth and the fat bag of sandwiches and duty-free he has on his knee. 'Sister, sister,' pleads Edmund. 'Come on, now. Move your chair to the upright position. After all, you're in my space.' Sister (we're talking brother-and-) is unmoved. 'The back is too straight,' she says, in mitigation, and the issue hangs between them, heavily undecided.

I'm watching the crates and the cases and the pallets on the dockside; the perpendicular corrugated boxes soar into heaps of brand-names and slogans and ports; tough tough toys for tough tough boys. Then we're through a big iron gate; the run through the dockyard stockyard becomes a nice run along the Liffey, in towards the city. Edmund mutters under his breath at me a little bit, but otherwise all is quiet – that there's no singing now is something to thank God for. I stare out the window. It's a modern world of building sites and Euro-election posters hanging on every newly sparkled lamp-post. Sinn Fein, Fine Gael, Fianna Fáil, the old names. (The candidates are a little map of holy Ireland in the rare old times: Hanrahan, Gogarty, Duffy, Ahern; but also in the rare new ones: Banotti, di Rossa, del Vecchio.) We pass the Halfpenny Bridge and the General Post Office and O'Connell Street and the Customs House and the Winding Stair Bookshop; we pass the places of Stephen Dedalus and the locations of *Dubliners*; and some of the other Stephen's places – Blackrock, where I was conceived in the months before my parents returned to England, and Maynooth, where my father taught Latin to seminarians in the 1950s.

It's a private journey already, and it becomes more so: soon, all around are the sleeping and the dead. Sister Pius comes, of course, to survey the battlefield of corpses, the arms and legs hung out to dry over chair backs and armrests, and she whispers: 'We're only not singing because they're all sleeping, you know.' Thank God for the gift of narcolepsy, then. The landscape around suggests the growth of wealth in holy Ireland; on the outskirts of Dublin there are buildings going up everywhere, and as we move westward on to the road towards Sligo – the rurality is told in the place names as we pass Clonard, Mullingar, Ballynadrummy – I see trim bungalows sprouting by road-gang caterpillars, and jeeps sitting proud at the front of neat white gardens. In the towns, it's more of the usual, though: Guinness bars and graveyards.

Guinness bars and graveyards, yes. And what else, as we reach the fourteenth hour of this, the long day's journey through the night, this pilgrimage through this barren land?

Lakes and hills. Hurley posts and dry-stone dykes.

(The Maltese woman up in front of me wakes and starts saying the rosary.)

Road works and sheep.

(The black women in front of me surface too, and, fearing a falling, rearrange their duty-free up above my head: 'We don't want you drunk without drinking' – a joke that is also above my head.)

Pine trees and scrubland. Food stores and lounge bars.

(Edmund stirs, mutters, but re-closes his eyes.)

Disused sheds and holes in the ground. Kiernan's and Kellehers, Luigi's and Macari's.

(With the microphone unintentionally switched on, a discussion starts up at the front about the best time for morning prayers.)

Pebbledash and tussocky grass. Extensions and septic tanks.

Slippery Road Ahead. DUTCH FURNITURE – a crazy business in the middle of nowhere; somewhere in the central west of Ireland.

(A busload of pilgrims beginning to wake, a people that dwelt in darkness seeing a great light . . .)

So *Sing a new song to the Lord*, it begins, from the front. Yahweh's people, sons of the morning, shout for joy, get their oil in their lamps as we pass Craggy Island. Sing hosannah: if music be the food of love, as Rab C. Nesbitt would say, then this is the colostomy bag. 'We thank the Lord for this bright new day,' opens Fr. Jude from the front, jaunty and cheerful. Watchman, what of the night? The bright new day – give or take another three hours of soporific conversation, of terraced houses and Euro-money-fiddling Christmas tree plantations, of increasingly curving, endlessly narrowing, terrifyingly undulating road – sees us turning into the car park of Knock almost on the far west coast of the Emerald Isle, right on the button for twelve o'clock mass. There is – seventeen hours from the good Sister's flat in Portland Rise, London N16 – an arrival after all.

Saturday, twelve noon. Knock: the end of our pilgrimage. Gold and silver, ivory, and apes and peacocks; or so it should be. But the only sign that there are treasures laid in store for us is the presence of the coaches of the English tour companies, parked on a rough concrete concourse, with their 'itinary'-titles in their windows: IRISH SCENIC SPLENDOUR, says one, and BEST OF ENCHANTING IRELAND the other.

So why is it neither splendid nor enchanting? Where is the ivory? Where are the peacocks? We pass through rough houses, closed toilets, dreich tin shacks set up to look like welcome-places, through to a market zone that makes the commercial centre of Lourdes seem like Taste City, Arizona. The shops themselves are rough-hewn – breeze-block topped with a few ramshackle tiles – and what they sell is appropriately rough-cast. Leprechauns are everywhere, and shamrocks, and other shenanigans of shebeen secularity; while the religious tat – artificial bouquets to lost mums, dads, brothers, sisters, grand-fathers – is not top-drawer. I buy modestly. Only a stick of sticky pink 'Rock From Knock', an 'I PRAYED FOR YOU AT THE SHRINE' 20p holy water receptacle, and (of course) an I ♥ PADRE PIO bumper-sticker prove irresistible.

We drift towards the centre, to the 'domaine', a concourse that's rather better put together than the periphery, and I'm surprised to find that the chapel where Fr. Jude is to say mass for us is actually relatively tasteful, all toned greys and whites, all architect's paint-effects, as if a TV DIY programme had got a hold of it; the tabernacle, for instance, looks like its components might be the standards of such tat-making, a few cut-out pieces of aluminium sheeting, some jigsawed MDF and a hunk of reclaimed granite. In the centre of the altar is a shocking-white tableau sculpture-piece, in which angels swirl around a lamb on an altar as three figures look on from stage right. (The golden crown on the head of one of the figures is the only taste no-no; as if the veil wasn't enough to let us know who it was.) A plaque to my right, above the door of the church, explains the sculpture; and explains the shrine.

On 21st August, 1879, fifteen people of varying ages witnessed, over a period of two hours, the apparition of Our Lady, Saint Joseph and Saint John the Evangelist on the gable of the church.
To the right, in the centre of the gable, was a plain altar on which stood a lamb. Behind the lamb was a large cross which stood upright. Angels hovered around the lamb for the duration of the apparition, which was enveloped in a heavenly light. Two official

Church Commissions of Enquiry, one held in 1878 and the second in 1936, found that the testimony of the witnesses, taken as a whole, was trustworthy and satisfactory.

As I jot, irreverent, Jude preaches nicely. There is none of the Lourdes myth-and-magic bullshit from him; it's refreshing to discover these things, these places in the company of someone who knows no more than we, who is not immured with the frightful, self-defensive rhetoric of a particular place; he has no cosy archdiocesan deal with the travel agencies, and no hostile bishops look over his shoulder. The theme is general, not specific; the notion that you take from God what you can give to others, and you take from others what you can bring back to yourself, so glorifying the effect God had on you in the first place – a kind of love exchange programme, a good-vibe lending library. He reads from the story of Elizabeth meeting the Virgin Mary and feeling the child leaping in her womb, and, cutely, on my left, a couple who've wandered in kiss chastely. They're Irish stereotypes, in a way – a red-haired man in a tweed jacket, a little, slender woman with tough-looking farmer's hands and long hair – but it's nice: the man taps his wife's belly paternally, and it's clear some little bugger – another carrot-top, perhaps, the image of mine – is getting a blessing today.

Outside, Sister Pius gathers us all together, apparently so that she can inform us of the price of a cup of tea in different establishments around the town. Various people look irritated and bored; everyone looks at a loose end, which strikes me as strange, as we stand at the end of our pilgrimage. (When you have walked the dusty pilgrim roads to Compostela and finally stand before the towers that have been your long life-journey's dream, do you stand about on the street-corner having the spiritual equivalent of a desultory fag?) The shaven-headed pair look especially impatient. Mac is smoking his latest B&H,

puffing deeply, searching for the burn on the tongue; while Nancy stands looking all around wearing a wacky purple jacket, big beads, and a pilgrimage holdall from some other trip. She has it hung round her neck, like a train-spotter's picnic, like an evacuee's gas mask.

I join up with them. Mac, the husband, chats away twenty to the dozen as I go with them, forsaking all other company, down for an hour at the Knock Museum, a stone's throw from the Basilica. It's a hotch-potch of horses and carts, of late nineteenth-century folk-photography, of Bishops' Vestments of Other Eras. It hardly catches the eye, but Mac talks as we go, tells of the reinforcing of his wish to come, of the pressing content of this week's prayers: 'Last week. At the end of our road. A young mother, murdered. Just shot. Bang. Bang. Bang. Just like that. Imagine. At the end of our road.' Nancy shakes her head, says something about a terrible world, which he echoes in his strange, combination accent – a little Irish, like hers, a little London, but a little something else, too, which for the moment is invisible underneath the scars and palenesses induced by seventy-five years of living. Only when he talks about coming with the army through Chittagong to Burma does one realize that although he fought for the British Army there, he was also born there, son of an Indian woman and a late-Empire squaddie.

He talks me through the other fragments of a life lived: that half-caste birth (his word, not mine), a spell with the railways when he came to Britain (he produces a beautiful old ID card in which his spiky white hair is jet-black-wavy, and his pale, yellowy skin is dark and deep), his time as a freight manager with KLM out at Heathrow; his decision, fifteen years before, when lying in hospital traumatized by a brain tumour and 'something down below' (he points towards his groin, to his orchids, with a nod-and-a-wink gesture) to leave his marriage and the shape of his life to become Nancy's partner for the rest of it; a serious decision for a middle-aged Catholic man with a wife (to whom, he says, he still pays maintenance from his pension, fifteen pounds a week) and six children, by whom he had played the game according to the rules, conceiving them under the eye of the Church, with himself, herself and Jesus Christ in the bed, bringing them up to know and fear their Lord . . .

He breaks off, abruptly, suspecting himself of being maudlin, complains that he can't stand this way of travelling, this dirty, sleepless wandering, and asks me what I know about the shrine, about the site. I tell him what little I can. 'Oh, yes,' he says, as if remembering, as if it's all familiar, and he talks Indian shrines for a while. A healing Virginal Apparition down around Bombay. The figurehead of the Virgin – a carving from a wrecked seagoing boat, washed up on a river bank in Bengal – which was rescued by some peasants and taken to a church, where it surprised an onlooker or two by suddenly leaping up and taking magical residence on the roof. We look at more of the exhibits, and at first (pictures of Knock at the time of the Great Famine) they're prosaic by comparison. But soon we're in mumbo-jumbo territory, with an advert for a sodality based at the place called the Volunteers of Suffering, who apparently offer up their own sufferings in order to help others, and in the tale of how Archbishop Murphy of Tanzania travelled sixteen and a half thousand miles to return thanks for the restoration of his sight through the application to his eyeballs of cement from Knock Church.

But the most fabulous elements of Knock and its museum are the tales of Monsignor Horan, curate, and then parish priest of Knock, resident there from 1963 onwards. He was the Mad Monsignor who elevated the place to where it stands today in the Marian pantheon, by raising hundreds of thousands of pounds to build the big, circular church that John Paul II blessed as a basilica for the centenary of the shrine in 1979; he was the Kubla Khan who, his passions inflamed by the prestige of a papal visit, went on to raise millions of pounds to build, in the middle of miserable Mayo, the fabulous pleasure-dome known as Knock International Airport. And though 40,000 turned out to see the first flight to Rome in 1985, and though the airport does carry West of Ireland traffic to England and America and Lourdes, there is something deeply ridiculous, and perhaps obscene, about the concrete sheds of the terminal and the vast runway running out to the middle of nowhere. There's a Christy Moore song to make fun of it, with a chorus suggesting that amongst the great miracles of the Christian world – the Lourdes, the Fatimas, even the Bethlehems – should come that marvellous example of word becoming flesh known as 'the airport up at Knock'.

Mac, uninspired by such an unexotic miracle, looks and listens, then gets bored and goes off to find Nancy. 'I can't bear to be dirty like this,' he reiterates. 'It doesn't feel right not to have had a shave, not to have had a meal. I'm never going to come travelling this way again.' We agree to go for a pint, to find a sandwich at any rate. 'Those folk I see at my pub back home were taking the mickey, saying how would I survive a day and a night on a coach? And you know, what I'd love is a big plate of Irish stew, a big plate of cabbage and bacon. I've lived with this long enough to get used to it, you know.' He laughs largely, infectiously, as he always does, and smiles at her; and she, eyebrows raised in a disapproval that is mock only, smiles away serenely as she always does and says nothing. They are *compañeros* of a longer and a harder road than this one is; it shines in everything they do; their life is a pilgrimage.

We're about to go pubwards when Edmund appears, fussing:

'I thought I'd lost you, y'unnustand.' I have obviously failed as a 'travel companion' and Mac wheezes irritatedly when it becomes clear there's a tacit agreement that we'll take Edmund to the bar too, since it involves giving Edmund a few minutes to look at the turn of the century classroom, the potato planter, the photographs of famished peasants leaving the dock at Cork bound for Liverpool and Glasgow and Ellis Island. Even I begin to wheeze irritatedly, though, when we also have to give Edmund time to chat up any woman he meets on his travels – the curator at her desk in the museum, and a handmaid all dressed in white for purity, are soon giving him their telephone numbers – and to take some photographs. He insists on Nancy and Mac holding hands in a flowerbed and then, ludicrously, of placing me in front of the Basilica, which may not sound too silly unless you know that he also makes me take my jacket off and swing it casually over my arm, and – this effect of self-conscious leisure being considered inadequate to give the right visual message – he makes me borrow his big, Starsky and Hutch, fuck-off-reflective sunglasses. *The Writer at Leisure in Knock*, he says; the photograph is to have a title, like a picture of a famished peasant in an exhibition.

Ten minutes later the writer at leisure is at work in Knock's most prominent pub, with pints of porter all round. The scene is familiar: smoky, thick air, unventilated, wreathes the heads of our oddball crew. A wedding, or a pre-wedding party, comes in; it's a *Ballykissangel* scene, with a stunning, pale Assumpta you can't take your eyes off surrounded by thick-looking tyros in ill-fitting blue suits and shiny brown shoes atop gleaming white socks. Needless to say, Mac makes a beeline, beating even Edmund to grab the attention of the young colleen, while Edmund sits and talks about Sister Pius, denying those who say she's no longer up to it, making clear his feeling of responsibility: 'Someone who is strong in the mind, as she is, but weak in the body like that – is someone who needs some help and protection.'

Mac returns to the table and sits down, makes a joke about weakness in the head, starts yapping. The chat is general, not laden – it's a jolly two pints we have, a conversational song and dance. ('You make too many jokes,' Edmund says to Mac at one point, to which Mac replies that Edmund is off his head.) They talk Lourdes for a while: Edmund singing the praises of Gavarnie, the Pyrenean mountain outside the town, and Mac, on the subject of mountains, recalling a time when he thought he'd lost his passport there; and how he walked miles and miles down the hill from the hostel they were visiting, and through and into the Domaine, where he stood in front of the Crowned Virgin's statue and, in desperation, told the Lady that even if he'd never needed her before, then he needed her now. And, lo and behold, the passport turned up, in the duty-free bag, where it had been since being produced to the checkout girl on the boat. 'A little miracle,' says Nancy, quietly.

We decide to go; before we go, he and his wife decide to go. 'I'm going to the building society,' he says, his way of seeing a man about a dog. It starts a run of related jokes: going to the hole in the wall, how his wife is with the Woolwich, and we peg back to the bus just in time to wait an hour while a batty old lady and the woman from Stamford Hill are querulously dragged from the healing service in the Basilica of Our Lady Queen of Ireland, as it's sparingly known. We have reached the destination of our pilgrimage, spent three hours there, and it's time to start making our way home. We realize as we go – and how about this for a snapshot of the Catholic Church in this day and age – that everyone who was sitting at our table, pilgrims all, and all except me regularly attending as well as fortified – is divorced and currently living with a partner in a state of relationship that would not be approved by the Holy Roman authorities. I don't know whether I should – it's paradoxical that it happens

137

on this, the least impressive and most chaotic of these journeys – but I feel kind of at home here at last, in this world of unsanctimonious sufferers, in this circle of real-life-livers, in this Thoroughly Modern Millie-version of the people of the Lord.

St Fiacre
Feast: September 1
Patron Saint of Cab-Drivers
Invoked Against Sterility, Fistula, Syphilis and Haemorrhoids
When Fiacre, a seventh-century herbalist, asked the Bishop of Meaux for land for a garden, he was offered as much land as he could entrench in a day. Wherever Fiacre's spade touched, trees toppled, bushes uprooted themselves and soil turned itself over.

In Medjugorje things are not so clear. I am still feeling repentant for my drunkenness (for wine is a mocker, and strong drink is raging) and inclined to believe that I have some ground to make up, so I accept an invitation to join Nora Batty, Lawrence, Angela and Valerie on a walk up Podbrdo, the Hill of Apparitions, which lies just outside the village. The hill, as can be deduced from the motley crew attempting the climb, is not a problem even for the most paraplegic of pilgrims; it's small, compact, and no chains on the feet are required, even if the odd barefoot is visible from time to time. Even the fact that they want to leave at five in the morning is not really a problem, given the kick up the backside my sense of deadly sinfulness offers me; I am so keen I get down to breakfast before any of them, and sit for a quarter of an hour in the pre-dawn light.

There being no drying paint at hand, I am watching a field of capsica grow when Nora appears and – for my own good, but from behind, and by surprise – sprays me with some foul-smelling mosquito repellent, uttering strange Yankee-Irish anti-insect imprecations. Lawrence, the Kerala Kafflik, and next down the stairs, has the advantage of seeing her coming. 'I am myself a repellent,' he says, in a tone of indulgent wisdom. Nora tells him not to be so obstinate, and sprays him anyway, flirtatiously, like Blanche DuBois does to Stanley Kowalski, and we hit the road running not long after our scheduled set-off time. Lawrence walks ahead in the grey, pre-dawn light with Angela while Nora, Valerie and I follow in their pesticide-cleared wake. 'The thing you've got to understand about Lawrence,' says Nora Batty, 'is that he's so *wise*. He's studied the eastern religions, you know. He is a kind of – what do they call them? A seer.'

Now maybe the sight of me on such an expedition is likely to send the earth into convulsions, but even I'm surprised by the drama that occurs almost as soon as we leave Tomas's Pansion. For there, in the middle of the pavement across from the Church of St James, sits – with its back arched, its head cocked – an ugly brown snake. I say, to no one in particular, 'Oh – what an ugly brown snake', which I imagine is the average person's response. They – perhaps to me in particular – all immediately, and simultaneously, mention the name of Satan, envisaged as a physical entity, just like the thing before us, and not just as a metaphor. In time we walk on, but the incident delays us, however, what with all the Sign-of-the-Cross-making everyone has to do, and Nora Batty, who feels we should get to the bottom of the hill quickly so that we can avoid the midday sun when we are on our descent-return, offers to pay for a taxi to get us there. When we get out of the cab of the only driver on the streets at that time in the morning, he is sitting at the wheel of his Mercedes counting five dollar bills – US, of course. Wearing a leather cowboy hat, he looks like a gambler; I notice the military marque he's branded himself with, a serpent tattooed on his arm.

The morning is lovely out there on the edge of the village,

and I forget that even arms dealers have a patron, and consider instead St Bernard, who cleaned up the Alps on behalf of the righteous. As we start the climb cocks are crowing in the gardens that lie along the rough roads. The smells from the farms and the houses are rich and primitive, part-agricultural, part human; smallholdings sit fair in the thin, clear light. As we begin to move up the hill, the pilgrim path starts, and it's rough and stony, covered in thick clods of mud and jarring, jabbing stone. Soon we're climbing away from the houses and the vineyards that lie in the fields between us and the church, between us and the village, between us and the world; but what I haven't banked on, in my pitifully partial piety, is the fact that this is not just a promenade, not just a walk to the top. Two hundred yards up we come across a slab of bronze with a relief illustration of the Annunciation, and the party of Poles in their dumpy floral dresses and cheap Eastern Bloc suits murmuring to themselves in a devout but certainly early-morning fashion give the hint that the path we're on is the Way of the Rosary, that the party I'm booked in with are planning on doing the whole shish kebab, and that I'm invited.

Stuck, I panic a little; I haven't done this for years, can't remember any of it, and, in any case, whatever praying I've ever done has not been done in this form. At first it seems there may be some room for individual consciences, as Angela, who's in some kind of a strop with Nora Batty and seeking solitudinous solace, is working on trying to go at her own pace, which gives me cover to hang around aimlessly at the back while they get under way. But Lawrence the Kerala Kafflik is having none of that, and soon I'm enjoined to cast aside my recalcitrance and join in. 'The Annunciation' is the First Joyful Mystery, and (as you'll know, especially if you were born in Ireland before 1930, or were educated by Fr. R at my Jesuit school in circa 1973) there are five Joyful, five Sorrowful and five Glorious Mysteries, each mystery being made up of a decade of the rosary, viz. one 'Our Father', ten 'Hail Mary's, one 'Glory Be to the Father' and, at the end, as a closer, a little snatch of 'Sweet Jesus, Save Us From the Fires of Hell'. I can mumble along as well as the next person, but when we have come through the 'Visitation' and the 'Presentation' I have a sudden realization that the leadership in this ritual is circulating; and that it's coming to me next.

Suddenly the world seems hardly far away at all: and I'd like it to come to swallow me up. Not so much because it's a big deal – I'm not being asked to brand my forehead with a crucifix or anything – but while I don't want to follow this form of a form of words, and don't want to announce belief, nor do I want to be insincere; I don't want to spoil it for them, this encounter with the early morning, and I don't want to spoil it for myself, for the day is rising out of sight, over the hill, and down in the valley the village is becoming bathed in light. I really feel I ought to kneel for no one, yet this is a public thing, and I've no wish to spoil anyone else's kneeling. So though I'm self-conscious at first, and tentative, I do it. I join in; and my voice, I'm sure, acquires a little more certainty when I see that, for Angela at least, this is a gesture, when I begin to know that I don't feel insincere within certain limits; soon my turn is over, and we're working our way towards the 'Finding of Jesus in the Temple'.

It seems that now I've done something everyone relaxes a little, which is nice; it feels as if they all come together, sort of, as if the embracing of me becomes their day; and who's to say there isn't a little prayer for my soul going on if not in the cool blue heart of Nora Batty, then in the considerably warmer converted core of Angela, or in the middle-upper-left of one of the other epauletted hussars in Our Lady's Cavalry Regiment? We all stand together and look at the faces on the monument in front of us, and chat about how wise the relief's face of Jesus looks; *that* Jesus, you'll remember, who went AWOL, and was gone three days or whatever before he was found in the Temple arguing with his elders and betters. Angela says she herself has always had a problem with the idea of becoming like a child; but that, on reflecting, it has to be seen not as an instruction to be half-witted, but as something to do with a manner of acquiring trust.

Nora Batty retires a little and takes our picture, all of us standing there, and I jib a little; I have a terrible feeling that what's going on is the recording of a hoped-for moment of conversion. For who's to say that odd-looking white-shirted man in the picture, with his head bowed, isn't rapt in religious thought, and not just looking at his dusty boots in order to avoid over-scrutinizing gazes? The camera never lies, after all. Fortunately, we move on. As we do, the Kerala Kafflik pipes up with a tone-deaf incantation of *Ave Maria*. Nora Batty says, with the rough laugh of a New York cop, 'Youse are all lousy singers, you know.'

'It's not the sound, it's the intention,' says Valerie, in her piped Irish-Toronto, which I reinterpret for the rock 'n' roll audience within me as meaning the singer, not the song; though of course it's actually the other way round. Beyond, the whole valley is now full of light; it's a strange accompaniment to the next stage, the Sorrowful Mysteries, when we are urged to meditate on the suffering and crucifixion of Christ, and one really feels the sky ought to be going black, with thunder, lightning and Temple curtains being rent in twain and so on. Nora Batty, having already demanded a fairly high price for my admission to this holy circle, raises the stakes further by insisting that since I'm 'the teacher' I should be, in this next section, the one to read from the text, the commentary that punctuates the decades. Which, for a while, as I relax into this, I don't actually mind doing. You can be drawn in: the valley is lovely, far below, and there's silence and peace, and perhaps milk and honey, maybe even apes and peacocks, and I've come to accept that the point of the process – perhaps the point of the whole pilgrimage process – is not to reach the top but to endure the stages; the point is to stand and to think and perhaps even to panic, for the pilgrimage is life and life embraces these things. And if – though I am slow of speech and of a slow tongue – I can read well for them to read well, then so be it.

There's another thing, too: the landscape where we are is full of evergreen thorn bushes and red rock, and the cock crowing in the distance promises a biblical conclusion. Heat-oppressed, I start to feel that I might be in Sinai, in Judah, in Galilee. And there is a kind of poetry in the dark passages of pain and grief that make up the Sorrowful Mysteries, which make up the path to crucifixion. *You asked your father to let the bitter cup pass by*, I read, aloud, and, my voice growing with the sun, add *it must have been an all too bitter agony to make you sweat with blood*. I feel moved by the phrases, by their originality in this text, but also by the sway of it: *They go on mocking you, and crowning you with a crown of thorns . . . My God, My God, Why have you forsaken me, far from my prayer, far from the words of my cry? I cry out by day and you answer not; by night there is no relief for me . . . To my friends, they who see me abroad do flee from me – I am forgotten like the unremembered dead, like a dish that is broken* – and even the mumbled platitudes of the repeated prayers, the endless circular-izing around the feveredly clutched beads, even that stupid *Fires of Hell* postscript can't remove a sense of being up there, of being elevated, of being on top of the world; of being in sure command of a stony place full of temptation.

I can't be sure of myself: this experience, this feeling of being poised in air, goes far beyond my comprehension. I am touched by their need for me, I suppose, their need and hope for something to touch me, and able to free myself from their demands; they are relaxed, not vulture-like, here at this distance from the end of our journey; I too am relaxed, with the awkward uselessness of Lourdes behind me as I find warmth here. And here and there are parties of Croatians and Frenchmen and Poles and Italians and Germans and Japanese, and little crosses made of twigs, and messages of thank you in many languages. MAJKO! it says, and HUALA! – Balkan voices have given thanks here. The language of the text, like some terrible sonnet, moves and disturbs. Grasshoppers are waking up and chirping, and a green shiny beetle flits across my vision and shines translucently, nature-callingly, enthrallingly in my eye. For a moment there, up on the edge of a biblical world, called for, I seem to answer at some tiny level.

But the spell breaks as we begin to descend back towards land again. The Mysteries become Glorious, and although I'm still reading, it's suddenly tedious. It's suddenly hot, too: and it's suddenly taking a long time to cross Podbrdo. Suddenly the text is revolting, is gaudy; it's all the ornate divinity of the Virgin, instead of the stark, pure suffering of Christ, and the language loses its majestic resonance as it moves from agony to a trite sort of painted ecstasy; suddenly it's all ritual and no pain, all surface and no depth, and suddenly I can no longer find any heart to agree with it. *I glorify you because you did not leave your apostles in suspense . . . We praise you because you sent the Holy Spirit, the comforter, upon them . . . Be praised O my Lord for having crowned your mother Mary Queen of Heaven . . .* All the old nonsense, of crowns and thrones, in other words. It's a defining moment, a moment that foretells the end and, in déjà vu, touches me from the past; I sense that while I can empathize, while I can feel for the man with the wounds and the cross, I find myself unable to glorify.

I begin to long for the world down below, and the only glory

I find is when the decades end and we appear to have come to a close. But even then it's not the end; for at the last, just as the crowd comes on to the pitch and I for one think it's all over, Lawrence produces a leaflet from his bag with a novena – some form of nine-day prayer I don't understand – to that same Indian deity that Mac later tells me about, Our Lady of Good Health. He's clearly about some intention, though he won't say what it is; a wife, perhaps, or a mother or a child or a grandchild; and we have, of course, to respect him by joining in with him. And though everyone's weary, and the sun's up, and hot on our backs and faces, everyone stops to listen. The prayer, which is pretty, he reads prettily in his Indian singsong, and as he stands there, first one gorgeous green Galilean butterfly, then two, settle on the very cheek of Lawrence's face, as if it's not just the face of a Brahmin, or whatever Nora Batty says he is, but the face of St Francis himself. No one laughs, or anything; there's just a gleam in everyone's eye, a fruition; and as we make it to the bottom of the hill he announces that the day before he had been feeling 'down in the mouth' – hard to believe when he's so pert, so perkily easy to patronize – but now he feels that he has achieved his purpose in coming here.

I talk it all over as we meander back to the Pansion: it's Angela who becomes my conscience. Prompted by my thoughts on the poetry of suffering – which I am offering to anyone who asks as evidence that it was worth bringing me there, in spite of my refusal to brook a wider conversion – she tells me the rest of the tale of her childhood: how at three the TB or whatever it was got into her bones, how she wore callipers until she was seventeen, how the whole package held her back socially and – no doubt, though of course she doesn't say so – sexually. 'But you know,' she says, near-proudly, 'although the thing left me with – with what you'd call a disability, I suppose – to me this limp in my legs is the cross, my cross, the cross that makes me.' The suffering it gave her, she explains, is what gave her life shape, what formed her, what en-faithed her. 'You can't underrate these things, you know. Don't feel bad, if you just happen not to have had that cross to carry, if you can't find it in you to make the leap from there into glorifying.'

I hum and haw a little at that; it seems an odd criterion for membership, but it does seem to link them somehow – Angela with her limp, Cecilia with her divorce and her tranquillizers, all the mob of the bereaved, even Lawrence with his sick child or wife or mother. We talk for a bit about climbing mountains – she's sure it is something utterly fundamental, even if her sister can't quite grasp it as she plants another notch on her bedstead – and she throws me a quote from the Psalms, among her other soothing assurances that I mustn't worry about not doing the right thing:

For who shall climb the mountain of the Lord? The man with clean hands and pure heart, who desires not worthless things.

Back at the hotel from our ascent of Podbrdo, the Mountain of the Lord, I doze for a few minutes before Nora Batty wakes me and physically takes me down the road for Sunday mass. (On the way, she tells me about the beautiful St Rose of Lima, who sought to maximize her chances of remaining a virgin by scarring her features with rubbed applications of pepper and lye.) The preacher is a strange half-American, half-Croatian Franciscan who spends a quarter of an hour first telling, with a pendulous sense of the dramatic, and then explaining, with a pendulous sense of the humanly decent, the story of Sodom and Gomorrah. I have forgotten that it's pretty weird in the original: fifteen shaggy dog variations on a question-and-answer dialogue between God and Abraham (*A. If I find fifty innocent people I will spare them all. Q. But if there are forty . . .?*) before God gets round to telling Abraham whether he's actually going to kill all the poor buggers or not.

I'm bored, but then something happens that I have not been prepared for. Whether it's the walk up the mountain and the beads; whether it's the effect of the sun on my head; whether it's the shaky remains of the slow-waking morning doze; whether it's the congregation, the madding crowd of Yanks and Francs who are filling the church; or whether it really is some sort of intervention, some sort of intrusion by a divine force – I begin to have a curious experience. I start at first to feel odd, and alien; then I seem to become woozy; and then, as the voices intone *Lord, on the day I called for help you answered me*, positively surreal.

It reminds me of that cave in Lourdes, the odd power it had to make an inward stirring, to make a kind of trouble in my heart. I have at this moment, or feel growing, this odd sense that on some level I want to belong, even though it seems entirely clear what happened this morning, even though it is utterly apparent that something was defined. But at the same time it's as if twice today something has taken hold of me, and the feel of that call is difficult to resist. So much so that for a heady, unsteady minute or two I am seriously considering shouting out some sort of declaration; some sort of affiliation, even as the priest continues with his anti-sodomite theme; for a second it sounds like the message they've all been telling me I'll get; and later, in hindsight, it seems a remarkable testimony to the place that something in the air of the morning and the music can so shake my manly faculties.

But the mass ends, and out on the street outside, on the steps of the church, an old Croat beggar approaches a party of wealthy-looking Americans who are coming out of mass. (Coming out of Sunday mass, for that matter.) And the Croat man is as beggarly as a beggar can be: he's not an artful gypsy with a cute kid, or a meths-smelling wino with a surreptitious bag of booze. No: he is eighty if he is a day, and he's thin as a rake, and he is emaciated, and he has the demented features of someone struggling with slowness in the head, and his right hand – well, his right hand is not there, having been removed by a bomb or a mine – more than likely in the place where we are standing – or a piece of agricultural machinery. And the old American folks, schooled on the religious-tourist doctrine that says you don't give to beggars hanging out in Holy Places, and schooled by an American priest, who unlike them seems to have some Croat in his vocabulary, turn away and say they have no *kuna*. And just as a minute or two before I had longed, in some small way, to shout out that I belonged, now I long to shout out the opposite – some sort of act of disownment including a description of the number of dollars in their pockets. And such is the giddy state of me after the morning and the mass and the music, I feel, as I walk down the stairs towards the statue of the Virgin, that in some way I've been saved. However paradoxical, I feel the heat on the base of the brain must have been talking: *Lord, on the day I called for help, you answered me.*

At our pilgrims' lunch, needless to say, the beggar becomes my text (I'm coming to rely on this lunch-hour as a peregrinative high-point) as I talk to Lawrence and Cecilia and Nora Batty and (unhappily, for him, stationed at the same table) some Croat-American from Ohio on a package tour. I give an impassioned description of the incident to those who haven't heard it. Perhaps under the influence of the rosary, I'm beginning to acquire a considerable gift of repetition, as I wander the streets and meet pilgrim after pilgrim, become part of the crowd.

Needless to say, those who love Medjugorje are appalled at the idea that the spurning of the beggar might become the point of representation in anything I have to say about the place. Nora Batty and Cecilia recite a righteous litany of all the false beggars of all the tourist traps of the religious world, and Cecilia crows that, after the event in question, she had seen the man in question pass by with a carrier bag full of money. Cock-a-hoop, she also tells the tale of a beggar in Assisi or somewhere else who was discovered to have a Mercedes at home in the garage; though this proves to be a mistake, as the day before, it seems, she'd railed against James for judging by appearances when he, in turn, and differently motivated, had railed against the Mercedes-owning habit of the religious-tat, souvenir shop owners. But in any case I have a clincher too: I know that when we were down by the statue, all on our own, and the beggar could have come and claimed a tithe from us all, he didn't; I saw him come and kiss the railing round the effigy, and sincerely thank his providence, before he wandered off to wherever he was going.

We have Croat chit-chat for a while as the Ohioan holds forth. He's an American cliché: eighty-five if he's a day, in fedora, open-necked shirt with string vest showing, uttering clipped, amusing gags without substance in the manner of George Burns, whom he somewhat resembles. He's one of ten million Croats who live outside Croatia, he says. There are only four million inside, it seems, and he too offers statistics we've already heard from Branimir, about how many Croats were on the westerly bound boats in those pre-war days. (The only thing he spares us is Branimir's little golden nugget – that the Croats, the 'Hravats', invented the necktie.) He's been travelling with a party, not for the first time, and he talks of the other cities of the place – of Split, which he likes, and of Dubrovnik. 'Not a bad place,' he says, 'if you like swimming and girls with no clothes on.' Lawrence is the only one naughty enough to laugh aloud. The Ohioan goes to rejoin his party as they move off to Zagreb, where he hopes to meet his long-lost relatives.

When he goes we turn to the Franciscan's sermon, and the talk once again gets feisty and spirited in the cool of the canopied shade of Columbus's restaurant. Cecilia is on hot form, and Nora is spiky too. The preacher's theme becomes ours for a bit: he had spent some time kicking around the old chestnut that forgiveness is only worth its salt if the thing that's being forgiven you actually find unforgivable: that if you find something easy to forgive then there's no point in making the pretence of forgiving it in the first place. But when we get into the small print of this (that things disliked have to be embraced) Cecilia and Nora Batty get edgy. They want a line, they say: certain things have to meet their punishment, there's no two ways about it; there are virtues and there are vices, and no two ways about that; there are sins and there are penalties for committing them, and no two ways about that either; the only way back for many people is the journey through repentance, and in that sense it doesn't matter whether the person they've done whatever they've done whatever they've done to decides whether to forgive them or not.

Well, it's hot outside, and even the walk back to the hotel is likely to be an ordeal, and the beer is cold, and consequently I'm not going anywhere this afternoon, and so (in the interests of religious debate, you understand) I drop in that thing my uncle, one of those fearful Jesuits, used to say to me when I was little, to the effect that although he was a priest, and to some degree a traditionalist one, and certainly brought up in a trad-itional way, he couldn't bring himself to any kind of belief in hell; or rather, that he was prepared to believe in it, but, given that his God was an all-forgiving one, he found it impossible to believe that there was anyone in it; and 'anyone' included the devil, who, he argued, would always find forgiveness no matter how many times he turned to crime. Now of course I am aware that this is an attitude that will not find universal approbation; but it does seem to me to be an idea that demands a certain kind of serious consideration, and I'm surprised at the vehemence of disapproval when it arrives.

Needless to say, Cecilia, for one, is not buying any of my family's wares, and she blows a holy fuse with me. It's heresy, she says, to say that there's no hell; that people who do wrong, who sin, have to find some kind of reckoning; that all-forgiveness is not a thing that's simply randomly given, but something that has to be earned, through repentance: that the choice is there to be saved if you want to but that you have to choose to be so, through repentance, but if you don't want salvation and are happy to be chucked out into the abyss for ever, then that's your choice, the fruit of your free will, your freedom to choose wrong. 'I mean, what does the Bible say? It says there will be more rejoicing in heaven over the repentance of one lost sinner, over the finding of one sheep that was lost . . . so that means you'll be welcomed in if you repent. But that doesn't mean that you'll be treated the same way if you don't.' She doesn't manage to come up with a passage to justify the black damnation of those, including me, who seem bent on another path, and, I imagine, her ex-husband, for whom no fire can burn hot enough; but that's of no matter.

I disagree: for me – and on a certain level, although my lack of belief disallows me an opinion, some might say, I'm sincere in this – it's a matter of fatherhood. An all-powerful, all-forgiving God, I say, surely takes a different line from this: no matter how often the transgression takes place, for me there's still a bringing-back. (It's a strange part of a Kafflik upbringing: people tend to think of it in terms of hardness, in terms of black-and-whiteness, but I've met more Kaffliks who feel an urge to forgive than feel an urge to expel when something in their lives needs sorting.) So we discuss fathers and children, shepherds and sheep; lost sheep, prodigal sons, the faithful shepherds; as a father, I say, I'll always let my children back in, whatever they do, because I'm their father, and they're my children, and in my conception of things, however un-spiritual I may be, however ungodly, I can't let this God, that god, any god be less of a good father than I am.

Well it turns out another vein of Cecilia's life story is being unintentionally tapped into: this woman, who the previous day was hard-heartedly breaking her heart over unfaithful husbands and their running off with their secretaries, now embarks on the theme of ungrateful sons. James gets away pretty lightly in her description of things, although he didn't do well on her last birthday, she says, and in general doesn't do well compared to his sister, and it upsets her that he can spend so much on designer clothes and cachet gizmos (he's carrying a digital camcorder to make a video diary of the trip, and the fifteen hundred quid price tag comes in for some flak in this respect); but Andrew, her eighteen-year-old, is the real problem. Eight when his parents separated, and not a bad guy according to James, he became problematic in his teens; surly, uncooperative, unhelpful; marked by the tranquillized ceiling-stare of his mother; and equally marked, perhaps, by the charismatic energy of the newly converted model.

'He must have kept bad company,' says Nora Batty, asserting in a sort of kind way that Cecilia would not have been the one to raise hell in that way. But it was worse than her un-wildest dreams, as it turns out; he had begun taking illicit steroids he had got hold of from a gym, and had become ape-like and stressed out, and one night had come home from exercising, and when an adrenalin-pumped argument had broken out about this or that aspect of his domestic behaviour things had turned nasty; there's a suggestion from Cecilia that she was hit on the back, where she had already been suffering badly, no doubt since stress and absent fathers and the burden of bringing up her sons alone and all the other elements of a life that had turned off the rails began to weigh so heavily on it.

The table is quiet at the end of all this, apart from Nora Batty's vague, pat messages of support; it's a terrible tale, and it brings me up short; partly because my provocation led to the discussion, but partly because however much I believe in the generosity of this God they're speaking of (although how it's my right to comment I don't know) and however much I believe in and hope for the unanimous forgiveness of the unforgivable, I also have a certain feeling of zero tolerance, and I can't quite find a way to bring this all together.

'But James,' I say, 'is a good son.' And he does strike me as that, even if his blindness to her faith is not to her liking, and even if, on the eve of a Mother's Day lunch (as she now tells) he took Andrew out pubbing and clubbing until five in the morning so that neither of them was capable of even a modicum of filial chat when the day itself, and the bouquet-strewn luncheon, duly arrived. My opinion of him is a mere sop, and she lets me know that it is, and she returns to the main theme. 'Well, I kicked that boy out, and that's what God does to sinners. Yes he'll save you if you want to be saved. But if you don't want his salvation then you won't get to have it.'

She clearly feels that she's been talking too much; and Nora Batty feels it too: she doesn't like these intense sessions, I sense she has begun to lose faith in my conversion, which should have been inevitable but is proving elusive; she twitches in her seat whenever things get deep. But the Kerala Kafflik she knows she can rely on, what with him being a font of eastern wisdom and all that, and so she turns to him and says, 'Lawrence, what about you? What are your thoughts on forgiveness?' and she sits back and waits for the conversational flood that will wash sinners like me and my detestable ideas away and leave only herself as the worthy person sitting atop the mountain of the

Lord, perhaps with Lawrence himself for flirtatiously pious company.

But Lawrence doesn't play ball; he's been silent all this time, but for an occasional pat on the arm, an occasional concealed gesture of solidarity. But now he comes out in the open. 'I actually agree with him on this,' he says, pointing to me. (He shocks me, in fact, but they – well, they are on the floor.) 'My God, too,' he says, 'is a forgiving one. I think to be honest I too sympathize with the idea that there is no hell, or no inhabitants of hell if there is or has to be a physical place as such.' I look around the table at a line of dropped jaws. Nora Batty's face is drained of colour: all that stuff about the all-wise guru is disappearing as I watch. It's a slap across the spiritual face, and across the spiritual back, too, and Cecilia needs reassuring words from him, and from me, and another beer, to get her round, resilient face back into resilient roundness.

But there's no returning to the cosy pilgrimage discussion; it's victory at all costs, it seems now, not an open exploration of the possibilities. It's a Faith is a Gift of God, a Take It or Leave It scenario. Nora Batty, living under the New World protection of Rose of Lima, and Cecilia, whose own saintly namesake's head kept singing after it had been removed from her body, go off to pray and to shop. Both, incidentally, and part-forgivingly, for me; in their rich, generous hearts they've promised me some rosary beads, which, presumably, they feel I need now more than ever.

St Patrick
Feast: March 17
Patron Saint of Ireland
(also Excluded People and Engineers)
Invoked Against Snakes
St Patrick was actually a Scot who was enslaved and taken to Ireland.

In just thirty-three years, he expelled all the snakes and converted all the inhabitants.

Saturday, 4.30 p.m. We have drunk at the crystal fountain. Less than twenty-four hours have passed since London, and we have seen the towers of the Holy City of Knock, and yet Sister Pius's 'itinary' is not meeting with the grateful satisfaction so comforting and completing an experience deserves. There are grunts and grumbles about leaving Knock so soon, once we're back on the bus, especially from those who have had to be dragged out of a moving healing service in the Basilica of Our Lady, Queen of Ireland. An Indian bloke called Brian – a sort of Young Turk in the operation, a busy hymn-book-counter-cum-furrowed-brow-soother – and I are sent to round up the stragglers, running back and forth between bus and church, eventually picking up old Mario, a dithering widower, a couple of the African women, and the woman from Stamford Hill. ('What's the point?' she asks, as we remove her from her well-ensconcedness. 'What's the point of arriving in a place on a pilgrimage and then not even being able to stay for mass?')

Although there are a few voices telling her not to be selfish – after all, we did hear mass there earlier, and more crucially the saga of her trip back home to collect her suitcase has not of course made her the most welcome face in the party – there is a mild problem, which is that Sister Pius seems to be making up the route as we go along, heavily influenced by our new driver, Paul, who came in the night while we were sleeping like whoever it was that stuck the spear in the other one's tent. Paul, it seems, is an experienced fellow-traveller of our esteemed party leader, and she shares Edmund's view that the weak in the body require some physical support; which means, in short, whatever Sister Pius says from now on will get short shrift, and we'll do what he says.

At his insistence, we suddenly pull off the road on the way to Westport, our overnight stop, and drop in at a place called Balintubber Abbey, even though according to our programme we're due to visit there next day to hear mass. (The note on the Abbey in what passes for a brochure says that 'mass has been said there continuously since the twelfth century' – I have a mental image of three and a half people in a nave for years at a time setting up an endless mumbling.) We park up at 4.40, and look in disbelief as Paul announces we're to be away from here at five o'clock; no easy task, since the various geriatrics aboard make loading and unloading the human cargo a matter of ten minutes minimum. The Abbey's nice, as it happens: a nice stillness, unusual brown stained glass, an unusual history on the old pilgrim road from Cruachan to Croagh Patrick. But as for the continuously said mass: well, what they really mean is that when the Reformation brought its walls tumbling down, the locals continued to huddle under a bit of tarpaulin of a Sunday morning, or whatever, that Henry VIII didn't manage to knock the place out altogether; it's not the continuous showing of the oldest movie of them all I'd imagined.

As I climb aboard I suggest to Sister Pius that given that people are beginning to grumble a bit about changes to her 'itinary', she might like to let her passengers know if there are any other changes forthcoming. So La Duce, with all the certainty of someone who believes she can make the trains run on time, and with Paul the driver up above with strings attached to her limbs, announces forcefully that we are not coming to mass here at the Abbey on the morrow, but are going instead to Achill Island, to The House of Prayer. This adds further confusion; beforehand she'd told me and several others, with equally forceful authority, that although they usually went to Achill on a trip to Knock, they weren't this year as there'd been some sort of controversy about the place, some sort of Padre

Pio-style holy banning order. But now she is reassuring, or magnificently improvisational, or simply demented: 'Of course; we always, *always* go there. We'll spend the morning there, and then we can have mass at our hotel at night.' (Our hotel, the programme says, is back over at Bray, near Dublin; all the way back across this sodden island.) Then she has the driver put on some sort of soppy hymn tape – it sounds like Dana singing 'Christ Be Beside Me' – and our mad, megalomaniac Ahab leads our maddened meandering party on to Westport.

We stand in the hotel lobby as our keys are distributed; there's a minor kerfuffle with Mac and Nancy, who are glad when I step in to say they are a married couple, not a pair of single-roomers. (Sister Pius has put them apart, responding to their different surnames, even though I suspect she has a shrewdly chill knowledge of what the situation is – Mac and Nancy certainly think so.) I am to share a hotel room with Edmund, which is fine; he has a nice number in maroon string vests, I see. Dinner is fine – I chat affably with Fr. Jude, who, it emerges, is doing a masters in media at London and is not really a regular on this kind of thing. We talk movies – *The Last Temptation of Christ* and *Dead Man Walking* – and he tells me he's due to set up a media unit for the Indian Bishops' Conference when he returns home in a year or three.

His interest is in a kind of media outreach – 'Catholics have traditionally worked to spread the message not directly, but through things,' he says. 'Through education, through social work, through medicine. Why not through the media?' The aim, he says, is to influence, to be generally moral, not specifically evangelistic – he is no Jimmy Swaggart in waiting. He has worked with the Vatican-established mob in Brussels who give out an annual gong for film that has made a contribution to Kafflik life, and this year it has been given to *The Garden*, which, he says, is a Jarman piece with a vision that is deeply moral but

157

very challenging. 'If Rome had seen the film,' he says, 'they would shut us down', for Vatican finance is given to this body on the basis of how it started, which was to reward *The Robe* and *The Greatest Story Ever Told* and the other great works of the Hollywood Studios, not to recognize films in which the central scene features, by the sound of it, a Calvary-parodic crucifixion of three lesbians.

For now he is writing a project on different types of archetypal character in a number of movies; he's looking at the differences between Jesus-figures (such as Scorsese's, or such as the protagonist in *Jesus of Montreal*) and Christ-figures – any character who seeks redemption through death and self-sacrifice, even the retired gunslingers in westerns who come back to save the town even though they know it means their death. We talk a little about the Sorrowful Mysteries, and about the power the speeches had, even for me on the mountain of Medjugorje. These characters are of interest, he says, and he's interesting on the Muslims, and how they can't compete in media terms, since 'representations' of God – pictures, images, metaphor – are not allowed by order of the Koran; although Hindus, for whom camera-readiness is just as possible as for Kaffliks, are in hot competition with him and his lot for the hearts and minds of the peoples of India.

We're joined by a nun from Knock, a friend of Sister Pius, who's been invited to have supper; she's a wide-eyed gaggle-toothed woman who butts in relentlessly with inane pieties. She wants to know how the inane pieties relate to Kafflik Southern India, and so Jude (even though he has carefully explained that he is from Bombay) runs through the connections; how St Thomas the Apostle went there, and how St Francis Xavier pitched up there as part of his global conversion scheme. 'Imagine!' says the nun. Yes, said Jude; he arrived there before moving on to Indonesia, to Japan, to – he hoped – China.

'Imagine!' says the nun. Yes, says Jude, and he lectures a little on the Jesuit technique of inculturing, the historical *modus operandi* by which the language and culture of local religions were studied, learned, then used as a weapon in the war of missionary conversion. 'Imagine!' says the nun before adding, wide-eyed, 'my sister used to say that Francis Xavier could convert one hundred thousand souls in a single day . . .'

Yes: just like Saint Ursula (the victim of a typo, since some medieval monk read M for martyr as M the number, and created a potent myth) sailed the world with eleven thousand martyrs. Jude looks at her like she just stepped off a banana boat, and when she goes, he is moved by her to ask what sort of people come on these pilgrimages; it's clear he feels critical of those around him; not censorious, but troubled by their veniality, their (I suppose he wouldn't use the word, though he's sharp enough to know it's appropriate) stupidity. I give him a garbled sense of who goes, from the little I know, mention apologetically the fact that there are in the world pilgrimages with more hardship than this or the others I have made; it's clear that in taking up the invitation to come he had expected those present to have the sense that he identifies as being characteristic of Indian religions, the sense that a hard-road pilgrimage is a centrality, not an oddness. This twenty-four hours on a soft coach seat, he seems to be suggesting, is a bit of a joke, perhaps even a farce, though he is humble, too, about what he knows and does not know.

The farcical aspect continues after supper. Luisa, a tense, good-looking, half-bright woman with flat estuary vowels, objects, on a grand scale, to the woman she is obliged to share with. (We singletons are merely told where to go at the desk; there is no capacity to review arrangements, no possibility of doubling up voluntarily.) The room-mate is the woman from Stamford Hill, in fact. If Luisa is to be believed, during the first hour they room together the woman sticks her hand down her knickers and starts talking about her estranged husband; which Luisa, for reasons which might be obvious, or might be best known to herself, finds disturbing. Luisa complains, and, although the hotel is full, is given a camp bed in a staffroom at the end of the corridor. A retired gunslinger myself, I end up giving Luisa some kind of moral support – it seems only reasonable, since the rest of the party has turned against her on the somewhat spurious grounds that there was to be free tea and coffee in her camp-site room which they now can't have; and since I'm an ex-coach courier (a student job, long ago) I'm able to suggest various strategies for getting what she wants.

I get away from that, have a walk around the town, find it's almost midnight, and make my way back to the room, where Edmund, in crimson vest and underpants, is lying on his bed watching *Doctor in the House* and quoting verbatim, and with perfect timing, every lounge-lizard line uttered by Leslie Phillips as he ogles bathing beauties – even the cleavage jokes. As I drift off to sleep in my own bed (and my nightwear is altogether less spectacular) I consider the fact that the journey from home to this, the first bed of the journey, has lasted for getting on thirty-three hours; that we have touched base at our destination for little more than three; and, pondering Jude the Obscure's baffled sniffiness about the Western failure to embrace the hardship of pilgrimage, I wonder what he was talking about.

'They would meet quietly as if they had known each other and made their tryst, perhaps at one of the gates or in some more secret place. They would be alone, surrounded by darkness and silence: and in that moment of supreme tenderness he would be transfigured . . .'

'THOUGHTS? *Are you having THOUGHTS?*'

Normally Confession is a simple matter, a routine. Recite a few transgressions; receive a small penance; the job done. But Fr. F, Stephen's Hammer House of Horror Headmaster – he has white hair but thick black eyebrows, a Christopher Lee mouth (innocent, until it opens) and of course looks the Drac-part in the long, black soutane in which he is always seen – becomes frustrated with the routine banalities that come so routinely to him in the confessional, and he occasionally bursts out in this reckless, olde worlde manner, like some voice from the another time and another place, his voice echoing round the hushed, apparently reverent church outside the box.

'THOUGHTS? Have you been having IMPURE THOUGHTS?'

Stephen, as penitent, would have to leave the box, watch the faces smirking as he re-entered the main body of the congregation; as he would smirk were someone else the victim. Of course, at twelve or thirteen, Stephen is beginning to have such thoughts, but, not having been brought up to consider them, he does not know what to call them, and he lets most of them pass quietly, ships in the night, in his sleep; the sort of thoughts that pass during those dark hours, he knows at some unconscious level, are better kept there in the dark where they make their presences felt in fashions unusual enough to warrant no comment. His world is smut-free: sexual desire is not an acknowledged entity. There are no posters of Pan's People on his walls, no Top of the Pops album covers (naked women decked only in a Christmas hat and a long fluffy scarf and suchlike) on his shelf. In his house the television goes off during clinches, ITV is not watched, it being conspicuously more vulgar than the BBC (it is known simply and condemnatorily, as 'the other side') and he himself suffers unspeakable embarrassment if one or other parent comes into his room while a fruity passage of a song emits from his Bush mono-player with its automatic hand. There is an air of shame hanging round such things, heavy and preponderant as night-smoke round a dingy lampshade.

So he comes to think of women not in possession-driven ways, but

161

as figures utterly – and absolutely – steeped in romance. The girl-heroine of Moonfleet, *for instance, which he reads at school, fills his mind for a month or two. She has a plainly beautiful face, virtuously tied-back hair (she lives only in a plain black-and-white line illustration) and she waits faithfully for an eternity as the hero endures a press-ganged seaborne adventure, from his cursed diamond finding in the company of old Ebenezer to his imprisonment by and escape from the dirty Jew of Antwerp; her candle, a good deed in a naughty world, John sees burning in the window as he sails back to shore, and she makes with him a little John in the bright sea-salt-driven house they share when he returns. Nothing in the tale jars with what he knows he should know of the world; there is no stain of sin about so virginal, so pure a woman. If she inspires thoughts, they are entirely laudable.*

He romanticizes hopelessly, in other words. (Joyce's Stephen Dedalus does so, too: he dreams of scenes involving gallantry to Mercedes, a heroine of The Count of Monte Cristo: *'Madam – I eat only muscatel grapes'.) Meanwhile the real life his fantasies run parallel to offers few opportunities for grandiosity of gesture. At twelve and thirteen his mother and other virtuous women conspire to arrange parties which will bring together Kafflik children of his age. There are plenty, drawn from the Jesuit school and from the convents and, for the parents, brought up in an earlier world in which Kaffliks worked and played together without the threat from the alternative systems of morality Protestant children might bring (and Fr. F has warned already that Protestant girls are in the habit of carrying contraceptives in their handbags) the idea that their children will meet and be matey (but not mate) with those of the same persuasion is most desirable. Since True Love Waits, Kafflik hang-outery is a non-consummation devoutly to be wished.*

So the firstlings of his admiration grow at parties whose hosts' names ring with Irishness or Italianism or association with any of the other cradles of the Church: Kilbrides and Gilbrides, Reillys and Flanagans, Gregoris and Ferraris, even Churches; for the children of these Kafflik families are his more developed admirations bound – even expected –

to grow. He, in classic leisurewear of the period – the purple Wrangler flares, the pink floppy-collar shirts, the loud wide-lapel sports jackets – gasps with admiration at girls called Colette and Patricia and Margaret and Bernadette. (No Philomenas unfortunately – he is ten years too late.) And he is strangely at ease under the spell of innocence that sits over these parties – the dancing, the gallantry, the courtesy that exists before drink changes the sense of how things go, before tongues and breasts and thighs become the objects of silent, soul-deadly trysts on the periphery of events. There are best moments now when closeness occurs without touching; when intimacy comes from the mind, not the body; when romance appears without the staining shadow of sex.

And so he becomes (as the rest of the world grows into the taking of what is theirs) a pained, romantic boy. He spends, he remembers, blushing, a whole summer cycling miles just to look at the house of one of these Colettes. He spends, he remembers, blushing, all his worldly goods on ineptly thoughtful presents for one of these little Patricias; he spends, he remembers, blushing, the best of his intellect forming elaborate (and unappreciated) comments. But he does not consider how today turns into tomorrow. He has no capacity to connect properly. He is utterly naive, utterly without the firstlings of understanding of his rights and responsibilities within the world of sex and relationships, somehow robbed of the important connections that make plug fit socket.

And at this time when perhaps some knowledge of how plug fits socket might be desirable, or at least useful, who might step forward to offer an apprenticeship in the art of electrical connection? His Kafflik world has no mechanism of information, none of that trickle-down reality that the rest of the world gets; it holds the line, does not inform overmuch. The world is morally cleansed, which is fine and dandy, and will leave its traces in a concern for his fellow human. But there is no hard edge, no Joy of Sex, no sense that one is on the path towards the inevitable for which one ought to be prepared; no French father taking him to the brothel-door and paying the Madame for a sentimental education on behalf of the son; no expectation that such things have *anything to do with normality. There is no sex education in his world. Where does one look for such things?*

Once a year, in each year of his school life, Stephen has three academic days set aside for a retreat. At some level, these days are where the boys' Personal, Social and Moral awareness is to be developed. A large group of teenage boys, dropped out of class for a day or three . . . so hire some up-front holy hotshot to wow them for a day or two? No, no, no: the job falls to some retired on-the-premises buffer who can be had for nothing. Fr. M, the rector, gives the three-day session in about the third year at school, eighteen hours in all, on the theme of relationships, of which Stephen can remember only one godly thing: a story about two people who got married because they both liked Elvis Presley. Not the soundest base for a lifelong commitment, Fr. M concludes sagely; a memorable snippet but not of much practical use.

In other years the retreat-givers, the advisers on relationships, are similarly limited. Fr. S, whom his grandfather despises for some affair with his housekeeper he's had as a curate in Lancashire. Fr. d'A, who has been sent to die there some twenty years before and is widely believed, at the age of ninety-four, to have forgotten what he has come for. Fr. M, an oversize narcoleptic who falls asleep in the middle of Greek lessons and wakes believing he is saying mass. And, of course, top of the pile, with oversized incisors, Fr F, Drac himself, who wants urgently to know whether we are having thoughts.

V
Marriages

St Isidore of Seville
Feast: April 4
Patron Saint of Internet Users
(also Computer Technicians and Farmers)
Beaten by his brothers for being slow, Isidore ran away from home. A
drop of water forming a niche in a rock in his cave gave him understanding
of the gradual nature of learning. Back home, he compiled a Dictionary
and an Encyclopaedia and wrote a History of the World.

At Pansion Tomas, Sally-Ann and Paul Simpson are sitting on
the verandah smoking; there is no new thing under the sun,
and God works in mysterious ways. Whether it's the boredom,
or whether it's the heat of the morning, or whether it's being
away from her Steve, who is the normal keeper of the tattoo
and who is at home back in Plymouth, Sally-Ann is getting
impatient, tetchy. The hot weather's getting to her, she says,
though – contradictory, somehow – she gives a hedonistic, sun-
worshipping account of what she would be doing if she were
back at home. It's clear that's not the problem. Finally she yields
up her secret; there's another group of post-breakfast pilgrimage
women, sitting at the table inside, in the dining room. I peek
in; it's Valerie, Angela, Mary-Ann and Sheila; I can see no evil.
What's the problem? Grit-toothed, in a stage whisper, Sally-
Ann lets on: 'They're talking about the end of the world . . .'

'You're educated,' Sally-Ann says in her rich Plymouth.
'What's the difference between devout and fanatical?' I do a
decent job on the difference, which satisfies her, but it sounds

like what's going on inside is definitely verging on the fanatical. They're on to messages, apparently, or so Sally-Ann says; the sort of messages that came via the Virgin at Fatima, and at Guadalupe; the sort of messages that say that our time is coming and our number is up and our dice are cast and our end is nigh. We talk seriously for a bit. Sally-Ann says she doesn't mind, but it does upset her, that talk. She's had to listen to a lot of it; for her mother is a fully paid-up apocalypsist, and it makes her miserable. 'It's like,' she says, 'say I had a real interest in porn-movies and I sat and talked about all that right in front of them. It would upset them. So I wouldn't. What they're talking about actually *upsets* me.' And, of course, in the way of Kafflik parent-and-childhood, and the awkwardnesses that come when the former remains true and the latter drifts away, to be upset in the open would upset her mum, so she doesn't want to object.

To cheer her up, I (hardened, in a way, by where life has taken me, but also aware that I am unhampered by the presence of my own mother and the baggage that I once carried) make the jokes that she doesn't dare make even *sotto voce*. We start to speculate about what the last messages from the Virgin might be. Suggestion number 1: the last vision will be the music from *Countdown*. *Be-bum, bee-bum, bee-bum-bum-boooo* – with the last *boooo* fading into a great apocalyptic blast. Or suggestion number 2: the Virgin hands the visionaries a note or makes some big sod-off message in the sky. It says: *How do you keep an idiot in suspense? I'll tell you later.*

Buoyed by her appreciation, I foolishly accept the Ginger Ninja's invitation to stroll downtown and sit in a tobacco fug watching the people pass; cradling, needless to say, a beer, at whatever hour in the morning it is now. Ten minutes later I am glazing over. He is explaining to me the intricacies of the Japanese system of honour. It's probably – he'll understand when he knows himself, and life, better – his way of fulfilling a Kafflik need to be good; like James, as I've yet to discover, his inner self won't allow him to have no belief system, so, in the absence of a faith in Kafflik orthodoxy, he constructs his own. You know the stuff. Samurai. Seppuku. The Satsuma Rebellion. The Feudal System. *How can he get wisdom, whose talk is of bullocks?* My mind drifts, constructs an alternative iconography. Sega. Nintendo. Hai Karate. Kendo Nagasaki. (This last, a Seventies tag-team wrestler.)

I say a little prayer for him: that the years of his studies, which lie ahead when he returns home, will give him the strength and the distance to know that no faith is (not necessarily, if you're nice to people and don't do anything your Kafflik mother would be ashamed of) no absence. Because – by and large – people brought up the Kafflik way have, to go with their guilt, an extra layer of conscience and decency; and it's enough.

I have a long talk with Valerie, the other Canadian woman, at Tomas's lunch: she seems to be profiting from the week. Her head is up; she's better now, too; there are no more complaints, though she's covered with mosquito bites. She's interesting, too; has been working with the deaf, first as a court interpreter back in Toronto then, when living with criminals became too much, she moved into working with deaf college students as a registered note-taker. So she's not here specifically; she just has some decisions to make, and (of course) heard Our Lady calling (whether the call came in Sign she doesn't say). She seems an intelligent, rounded person.

When coffee comes I'm at a loose end, so I wander down to the Catholic bookshop halfway down the road on the way to the church. The Phoenix shop seems liberal enough; there's a nice cool atmosphere, a bit of New Age-y music playing, a general air of calm and unbothersomeness. But scan the shelves, and it's

169

a nice introduction to those who come here. *Hell and its Torments. An Overview of the New Age Movement. The Reign of Antichrist. Miracles, and How to Work Them. A Guide to Catholic Home Schooling. An Introduction to the Devout Life. Rome Sweet Home. UnGodly Rage: the Hidden Face of Catholic Feminism. Facts on Acts* (bathetically subtitled *Of the Apostles*). *Memoirs of an Anti-Apostle. Do You Believe Jesus Can Heal You? Liberalism is a Sin. Freemasonry is a Sin. The End of the World. The Magnificent Prayers of St Bridget of Sweden. The Last Crusade.*

When I go back, Valerie's on the porch, reading. Feeling a companionship, I pallily flick the cover over to see what she's got her nose in; I expect a novel, a travel guide. What I see are two titles from my walk: *The End of the World* and *Liberalism is a Sin*. I go and lie down.

Tomas makes us an early supper, as the entire Medjugorje party – from oldest to youngest, from fattest to bulimiest – is due to climb Krizevac afterwards, in the cool of the early evening. Krizevac is the second mountain of Medjugorje: while Podbrdo, where the apparitions took place, is just a hop, a skip and a jump, Krizevac is a longer haul up to a huge crucifix which the pious villagers of the region put there as long ago as 1933 and which the contemporary pious, especially those from outside, take as one of the signs and wonders of the place. Nora Batty is typical: all week she chants a mantra about how the church was built when there was no real congregation, and how the cross was built when there were no pilgrims – and isn't it a wonder then that years later the Virgin chose for her latest appearance on earth a place with suitable facilities already intact?

At tea I'm opposite Mary-Ann, the Yukon yakker, and I ask her a little delicately about her husband. I needn't have worried; as her grief was on her sleeve from the start, so is her relief from grief, the clear and visible sign that Medjugorje has been just what she wanted and needed. I tell her so: that she looks to me like she's well on the way to recovery, well on the way to completing the circle. She happily tells me about Dick – this is Electric Dick, of course; how he was half-gypsy with a wild streak in him, how he loved a game of rugby but also a four-egg omelette, how he would never see a doctor even in what turned out to be his last years, how he would never change his diet, even when she pleaded with him; how, before he died, she had a premonition, a sort of anxiety attack, at some distance from the event. But, as I say to her, she seems already to be at the point where she's glad for what she's had, and less anxious about what she hasn't. She says that's true: that suddenly, since coming here, she's begun to sleep again. 'Because I've had a message, and I've seen him, and I know he's all right. And I've got so many people praying for me . . .'

She sounds sane as can be, almost there; and whatever they sell in the bookshops, she has plainly been picked up by this place, these people. We talk about the sea, and about being far from it. She reminisces about summers in Mexico with Dick and about winters with him in Filey, near Scarborough. She talks about living in Zambia, about going to Canada, about moving to the Yukon; tells me about all the nuts and bolts of their lives together. 'Look,' she says, 'I know I cry every day; I cry when I pray. But look, too – we had twenty-five years together, and we had two lovely kids, and that's not something that everyone gets. And I look at my friend, whose husband looked after himself in every way and died at forty-seven, and I think I wouldn't have changed my Dick for anyone.' Inspired by a Native American practice which she learned from some hippy-froody Californian Franciscan, she takes prayer-stones to the top of the mountain, and leaves them there, where Dick can, if he chooses, collect them; messages on his eternal answerphone.

After this, the exercise of climbing Krizevac seems something devoutly to be wished; the mountain of the Lord, and all that. The main group, it's clear, will be saying the Stations of the Cross, which involves fourteen stops on Christ's journey through passion, death and resurrection; I have in mind a swifter, more solitary journey, so when Danjela the Courier calls some taxis for the rest (I expect, like any other holidaymaker-taker, she has her ten per cent from the cowboy-hatted sharks of the town for arranging such things) James and I strike boldly ahead, walking the half-hour route through the town to the bottom, and overtaking the party on the first Station.

Striking out alone, yes, but the talk is properly pilgrim, albeit in our own fashion: James is preoccupied by Cecilia's inability to understand his mental processes, and is seeking some closeness, some repair. Even though he wasn't brought up as a Catholic – his mother had drifted away during his youth, in the time before her husband took another train – he still feels the pressure of her wanting a conversion from him; it's not the same pattern as I or the Simpsons have gone through, but it's similar, in that he maintains a feeling that nothing will satisfy except that one result. Like the Ginger Ninja, he has been on a little search himself, and what he's come up with is a mix of embracing, pseudo-Eastern faith and a bit of New Age gizmo-belief. On the way up we talk about Zen, about the search for a suitably adapted Buddhism, about whatever type of cyber-power it is that New Englanders use to conquer their fear and their ambitions. Another non-believing Kafflik child, another strategy for making sense of the world. Another attempt to do some good in a naughty one . . .

We work the mountain together, driving hard – this is a steep one, a hard one – sweat dribbles down our faces as he talks about his work with video. He works experimentally as well as mainstreamily, and has been developing a process of condensed storytelling that in one form involves taking old B-movies and other tedious pieces, removing the establishing shots and other dross, and coming up with an intense, punchy narrative. (The other form involves multi-screen showing, *Man Who Fell to Earth*-style.) The path is rocky and hard, and the sweat flows, and becomes cool in the cool of the evening; but it feels liberating up there, to climb away from the town and to not be tied up in the ritual of the Stations and the rosary; this is life cut to the chase, religion without ritual.

What lies at the top is truly special – the Yugoslav sunset, which tonight is the most beautiful thing in the world; and it's impossible of course for anyone – and the sun plunges its way down behind five, six layers of mountains, wavy, gorgeous – to not feel a gush of something visceral, a deep enmeshing with the living things of this universe, when all is quiet and still, when the world plays its hand. Rumour has it that the sun at Medjugorje, like the sun at Fatima, dances and spins in the sky as a sign that the Virgin is near, but what we see is something far more inspiring; not a miracle, just a process. We watch it slide slowly down then slip, like a blip, down the last few notches of its splendidly un-greasy pole. 'Here it is,' says James, back in Zen-like mode, 'no hierarchies, no order, just nature. Miraculous.'

The perfect evening has a perfect end. We pass the others on the last stage of their upward journey as we begin to walk down the hill with two lovely eighteen-year-old Croats, both university students on an annual one-day visit they have done together since they were ten. Their belief is as simple as anyone on earth's. Sheila, the Simpson *mère*, is halfway down, puffing and wheezing, but determined to make it, whatever the tarred-up state of her lungs. ('Did you know,' she says slightly mysteriously, 'that religious doesn't mean "devout", it means "repetitive"?') At the bottom we meet up with and have a drink with Annie, Errin's tall, strong, upright daughter, and Linda, a young and feisty black Londoner, who are happy to mark what was seen at the top as an experience of sorts; who, as young, are happy without a proven, dogmatic, doctrinal development.

When we get back, at eleven, Cecilia and Nora Batty, non-climbers both, have Laurie and Errin's son, the Little Prince, having a hymn-singing contest in the lobby. And Laurie and the Little Prince know Kafflik life well enough to know that there's no harm and the prospect of dosh in pleasing the oldsters with a religious ditty or two, so they're giving it the full works and being promised the earth in terms of ice-creams on the morrow. I feel a warmth, even a tinge of envy in all this: the former for the adults, and the benevolence the place brings out in them; the latter for the children, and the innocence and belonging of their lives.

St Vitus
Feast: June 15
Patron Saint of Czechoslovakia, Dancers, Actors and Comedians
Invoked Against Nervous Disorders
(also Against Dog-Bites and Rabies, Snake-Bites, Epilepsy and Syden-ham's Chorea)
Vitus, son of a Sicilian senator, was converted by his nurse and tutor; all three were arrested for sorcery. Tortures did not trouble them, and they were freed amidst a violent storm through which an angel guided them home.

Sunday, 9.24 a.m. *It's hard to dance with the devil on your back.* It's a bleary Irish morning in some ways, heavily overhung with the long day's journey into night of the day before. We are enjoined to rise for a seven-thirty breakfast, but Edmund, zealous, rises at five and wakes me at ten to six; no joke on no sleep. As we go into the coach he straight away resumes an earlier argument with the cushioned woman in front. Maliciously, I loudly take the woman's side, mock-jolly, mouthing platitudes about Christian charity; and Edmund gets a bit stern with me: 'It's a matter of principle,' he says frowning. 'This is my space. It's important not to let people take what is not theirs. Space is one such thing. Y'unnustand?'

Sister Pius gets a hold of the microphone, and on the hour or so's run out to Achill Island she tells us where we're going. (This is obviously her customer-care-led response to the moans and groans of the previous day.) The House of Prayer was once, it would seem, the home of a housewife called Christina Gallagher, who, in 1988, began to see apparitions of Christ and the Virgin Mary at a small grotto in County Sligo, and later (much more conveniently) began to experience the same within the comfort of her own home; and who, like Padre Pio, is reported to have endured the appearance and discomfort of stigmata. 'Yes – that's where we're going. She will usually see us without any problem,' she says, 'and we used to have mass there, but priests aren't allowed to say mass there now.' 'Why not?' someone calls from the back. The answer is the same as that to the same question set, the same restriction placed, on Padre Pio, but rather than commenting sagely and judiciously, Sister Pius says: 'God only knows. Some people didn't believe in her, but then again some people thought that Jesus Christ was only a carpenter.'

We are fifty kilometres from Achill; we pass a pub miles from the nearest building, surrounded by empty fields with nothing but sheep in them; there's not even a hovel for migrant tinker or mad king, let alone a house or a shop enticing residents or visitors, yet there's a sign saying CAR PARKING FOR PATRONS ONLY. We pass a little town; on a winding road there's KELLY'S FILLING-STATION, KELLY'S KITCHEN, KELLY'S QUALITY MEATS and KELLY'S THE CHEMIST. In honour of the ubiquitous

Mr Kelly, the singing and preaching starts: 'Thank God for a good night's rest,' Fr. Jude says, but of course the priests get single rooms and are not haunted either by night-walkers in crimson underwear or by lonely women prodding their own pudenda. 'We're asking the Lord to be with us every step of the way today . . . we have one more day to live, one more day to love.' Edmund, suddenly and for no concrete reason re-irritated by the seat controversy, and sensing that the issue has gone to sleep, gives the seat in front a *sub judice* shove. But the woman in front is resolute: 'Edmund. Understand. I am Mrs Thatcher with her handbag. You shall not pass.'

Jude, unaware of the cold wind blowing through the back seat section, leads the singing from the front:

'Bind us together, Lord, bind us together
With cords that cannot be broken . . .'

and it's an enjoyable ride. A bit of ritual can get you going; I find myself in the warm here – free of the stress of Lourdes, more comfortable with my own position than in Medjugorje, singing along, relatively unselfconscious, happy to be on an island in the sun, enjoying the way that each of the cottages, however tussocky and grotty the land around, has still carved for itself a little patch of walled and fenced perfect lawn, as if boundaries have to be kept and the amoral wilderness out there kept at bay in holy Ireland. Ditto on board; the prayers finish, and Paul the new driver puts on a muzak-style soft-rock album of songs you know without the words: that one about feeling it in my fingers, 'Raindrops Keep Falling on my Head' and '(They Long to Be) Close to You', which I ruthlessly use, making a joke at Edmund's expense about his enforced proximity to Mrs Thatcher up in front. We're out on the edge here: another town passes, once more marked by family ties: SWEENEY'S

176

SUPERMARKET. SWEENEY'S RESTAURANT. SWEENEY'S FASHION STORE. SWEENEY'S BUILDING PROVIDERS. Sweeney's rich, too, I suppose, in a town in which the only viable opposition is a hairdresser called Deirdre's Clip Joint.

Sister Pius makes her usual important spiritual contribution as we roll up to Christina Gallagher's front door by showing us how the path round to the right, which leads to the chapel, can be ignored in favour of that to the left, which leads to the shop. 'You'll want,' she says, presumptuous, 'to buy one of the matrix medals they have here. They're in a design that Our Blessed Mother passed on to Christina. But make sure that you pay the extra twenty pence for the stainless steel one. Some people have had problems with rust with the cheaper ones.' Pat the Baker's van passes (SO FRESH IT'S FAMOUS, it says, which sadly can't be said of the good Sister) and we file out of the bus to enter a big, slick, white, double-glazed building with strip blinds; not at all the country cottage of the imagination. A smart woman in sharp-cut clothes greets us as we enter the chapel through the back: 'Welcome to Our Lady's house,' she says.

I pick up a leaflet by the door, seeking clarification on the ownership of the said property. It says that during a direct communication between Christina Gallagher, our resident mystic, and the BVM herself, in 1991, the question of building a House of Prayer was brought up. 'I will be there in this house, with many angels, praying with all my children,' the Virgin is supposed to have said. 'I will disperse darkness and surround you with light.' It's certainly bright, certainly white; it's a securely rendered place in a big tarmac car park; not the ordinary housewife's gaff I'd expected, although to judge from what we've passed, the ordinary housewife's place is like this. The location is cottagey: the top of a hill on which sit four or five other houses, which slope their way down past rough wire fences to the Achill Sound, at the end of which the Atlantic winds its way towards Americay. A sign pointing right shows the way to the shop, where I pick up a postcard or two and accumulate a couple of matrix medals, in stainless steel of course, for only the best materials will do for this pilgrim whose faith is so ersatz. To the right a sign points us to a chapel – an extension that Christina's husband might have put up, had he been so inclined – a stained-glass, be-statued silent zone with St Philomena statues and Laura Ashley curtains.

Most in the party take Sister Pius's advice and head left first, then right afterwards; I do the same. In the chapel most are quickly on their knees. I wander outside, and find Luisa still harping on about her last night's experiences with her roommate, still seeking support and justification. She doesn't understand why we have so long here, and it is difficult to tell – the local equivalent of Deirdre's Clip Joint is closed, so it's not as if we can have our hair done or anything – so we wander down to the village together to have a look around. As we go, her bright estuary vowels clip out a sort of life story, if veiled in vagueness and suppression. She's studying counselling, from which start it's easy enough to know what the next gambit will be: 'Of course I've really been on two courses; learning to counsel, just like the others, but learning to understand, to counsel myself . . .'

Cloud lies low over the hills on the other side of the water, and the road winds off along the coast; we walk some of the way, climb across a long rough bridge, cover some distance. 'Yes, I had to learn all about myself, learn about my own needs. To be perfectly honest.' But she never gets perfectly honest; something about a husband and a divorce, of course, but no more; just hints of another life, and a skilful manner in turning the conversation away from herself whenever there's a risk she might give something away. She moans about the ritual aspects of this journey, about the lack of feeling that seems to persist in the party, and tells me that her own penchant is for healing services, as practised by those celebrated for the Kafflik versions of such things – she mentions a Monsignor Buckley, a Sister McKenna – and what she witnesses weekly at some kind of priory in Cockfosters, where prayer is free range, charismatic, not bound by the old rituals of Pius's pious pieties.

It all seems fair enough, in a distant sort of way, and there's no way she's going to be anything but distant; something's lying too deep for exposure, yet crying out for it. 'Stuff has happened that means I need hands-on healing,' she admits, but it's hands off if you want to get closer than that. It's not physical, though physical healings are achieved where she goes; it's 'mental, inward, warming, refreshing' when the Holy Spirit comes out to play. We come to the edge of a field: rough, dungy, half-defined. 'If you're interested you really ought to come along, really ought to encounter the Holy Spirit,' she says, talking of her regular weekly services; 'it's remarkable.' But the descriptions she provides of the feeling of the thing coming down upon her are a little obvious, and sort of unhelpful. The Holy Spirit is a 'white light', she says at one time, at another a 'warming hand on the head'.

We wander back towards where we came from, passing the local Sunday mass coming out. She tells me something I knew, that Christina Gallagher is supposed to practise healing in that little chapel with the Laura Ashley curtains; I tell her something that she didn't, that Christina Gallagher was expected to arrive just a few minutes after we left; and seeing a chance to have some hands laid upon her she insists that we make haste back there. She tells me I ought to come and see, but when we get in, Paul the bolshie bus-driver explains that (just for a change) time is not on our side, so Christina is going to see the first ten and do a bit of group work with them, but that individual consultations are not possible. It seems a bit unfair for me to

179

take one of those ten places, and anyway, when Sister Pius grabs my hand at the back of the church and asks me if I need healing, my instinct is clear: call me pompous, but I kneel for no one; call me repressed, but I heal for no one.

I leave them to it, then, slightly regretful of my generosity, slightly irked that it all has to happen behind closed doors. Out on the road I meet Edmund walking around, and together we walk down the other side of the hill, towards the hamlet, until we can't go any further. He chats up a local woman – it's de rigueur, of course, and de rigueur for Mac and Nancy to arrive to make fun of him about it – and takes a photo or two, equally de rigueurly. He stands by a roughcast wall until he has a look at the backdrop and says, 'I can't have this; my friends will think I took my holiday in H-block.' He has an amusing little dig at me when I get my notebook out. 'Make sure you have all the names,' he says, pointing to a field of sheep, then insists that I copy down his interpretation of the natural world that we can see across the airy waters of the sound: 'The hills – level and plain,' he says. 'The water, drawn to a certain depth. The seas, calm. No sound, not even a bird. Create an atmosphere. Y'unnustand? The hills, with mist and low cloud, like rainfall in the distance . . .'

While we stand there a man drives up in a red van – ear-ringed, tattooed. He asks what's going on in there, in the House of Prayer. Edmund tries to tell him, and they chat, and two minutes later the man's moll, a fat, sly-looking woman appears, asking for money to feed her two babies. I provide my usual ungenerous, no-questions-asked pound. 'Can I have a fiver?' says the woman, asking for more without acknowledging the first; 'I've three babies at home, y'know, and nothing to eat.' Edmund searches diligently, but he only has English pounds, not punts, and he tries to offer a couple of them, but the girl isn't having any of it. 'They're no use to me. No use at all,' she says, extraordinarily brusquely. She wants quids in Irish if it's quids, though what she really wants, she repeats, with a sort of ugly directness, is 'an English fiver. That would be all right.'

My inclination would be to tell her where to stick her two (or is it three) babies, but instead Edmund, the space-preserver, the defender of territory, begins to look around all over the place, asking all and sundry (the healed are now emerging from their healing, ready to catch the bus) if they can change the English coins he dredges from the bottom of his wallet into punts. One of the Nigerian women aboard gets stroppy in the extreme when, her hand deep in her handbag, she realizes who it's for, and she turns on and sherricks the beggar's woman: 'I don't work hard all week to feed people like you.' But Edmund is undeterred, impressively determinedly helpful, and goes on until he finds two or three pounds, and he gives it even though the bloke in the van has backed up to where Edmund is, saying that they need the money for gas, not babies, and entirely blowing the mother-of-two (or is it three)'s cover.

I leave him to it; my attitude to these things is simple, and it's up to him. When he comes on the bus, he makes a little speech about it, about Christian charity. He decries the Nigerian woman as ignorant, under his breath – he says it's an 'African way of thinking', as opposed to his own Jamaican way – and says he feels a duty to help even if the person helped is either ungrateful or patently dishonest; that you take a chance, as part of the equation you encounter when you 'see how the people of the world live'; when you travel. I nod; it's a generous perspective, a thorough one. 'And anyway,' he says, grinning, 'that man I asked for change – he *gave* me a pound, the pound that I gave on to the girl. Y'unnustand? So you can see that life – that God – is good.' He mimes, with his hands, the giving and receiving. 'You see I gave, but I didn't lose anything.'

If only everything was so simple in this game of celestial

Family fortunes, this *Jeopardy.* He hands me a newspaper he's picked up in the lobby of the chapel. *Michael* is the title, and it is 'published by the Louis Even Institute for Social Justice'. The headline – this is front-page news – runs YES TO CASH, NO TO THE BIOCHIP UNDER THE SKIN. It's clearly a matter of common Kafflik concern:

> No to the replacement of cash by electronic money! Smart cards will lead directly to global control over each individual! They are only the forerunners of the microchip being implanted under the skin, the mark of the beast, which **no one** can buy or sell!

After which, the first actions aboard the coach – an old Chinese man handing out songsheets for 'The Dear Little Shamrock', and singing away through the microphone in a *Kung-Fu* accent – seem perfectly normal. As he does so, Sister Pius segues in perfectly with a lecture on the way in which the three-in-one in the shamrock, the trefoil, is what Saint Patrick found to offer the Irish people as a symbol of the Trinity. 'The dear little scchamrock, the scchweet little scchamrock', the man sings, incomprehensible as a takeaway phone-line. I'm almost sad when Paul, the driver, cuts right across the singing and puts on a video by some ever-smiling Irish harpy-crooner called Bonnie Stewart. *Che Sera Sera* never seemed like such an anticlimax.

I hide away by reading my Christina Gallagher leaflet, and drift off to sleep on the section about the Virgin's direct orders that a medal in honour of herself should be struck, with specific instructions for the design, as follows: 'My son's cross, me on my knees praying for my children. On the other side two hearts weeping tears of blood. Simply call it the matrix: my son wishes to mould it.' Three notes follow. a) *The medal claims cures, healings, conversions and protection from air disasters. b) Medals are 30p, but 50p for stainless steel.* (How wise our leader is.) c) *Please note: Christina Gallagher does not have any representative in the US.*

St Leonard of Noblac
Feast: November 6
Patron Saint of Coal-Miners and Greengrocers
Invoked for Protection Against Robbers
A Frankish noble at the court of the pagan Clovis II, Leonard turned an invading army on its heels by the power of prayer. Clovis was converted; Leonard went to the Forest of Limousin to live on herbs, wild fruits and spring water.

What to do now, here in Lourdes? I feel the need of some redefining, some spiritual guidance; but everyone is out doing good works. The grand events of the place I have seen and witnessed; and I am stiff from my encounter with the sacred baths. So I decide to see what the secular ones can do; for backs and necks, a few lengths of the pool. I fear to go in the outdoor municipal pool looking so white, so I instead head indoors. But there's a hitch; you're now allowed into the Domaine without long trousers on (my pious father was asked to leave some years back, when the rules were tighter) but up at the pool you require 'le slip'; a note on the wall, with all due solemnity, informs bathers that *le Bermuda est interdit*, because *ce n'est pas pique-nique*. I decide to look for a pair of trunks: but foolishly head downtown instead of up, and discover that it's impossible to find a shop selling anything normal in Lourdes.

The chief trade in Lourdes is, of course, statues. It's the most familiar image of the place, the pictures you've seen of the emporia of the pile-'em-high/sell-'em-expensive traders dealing in religious *objets*. I walk from the Place Jeanne d'Arc to the end of the Rue de la Grotte, and literally every shop is a religious one; you can't buy a paper, let alone a pair of Speedos.

But the shop names are pious and proper and each claims a patron. Padre Pio's. À L'Avé Marie de Chartres. St Genevieve. St Pascal. St Firmin. St Julien. St Etienne. St Sebastian. St Charles. St Joseph. St Vincent de Paul. St Michel. La Providence. All these lie within two hundred yards of the Domaine, like the Magasin Paul VI, which is typical, stuffed to the gunwales with religious knick-knackery and low-class tackery: grot all the way to the Grotto. A brief break for the Domaine and the Grotto, and on the other side, it starts again – another Circle of Hell, another shopping street. St Anne dal Romagna. Saint Honoré. Alleluia. Little Flower. St Madeleine. Ste Cecilia. Croix de Jérusalem. St Andre. La Vierge Sainte. St (a new one for me and sounding like an Irish conman) Laurence O'Toole. Did I say all shops? I was wrong. There are hotels as well. And what are they? St François d'Assise. Le Vatican. L'Angelus . . .

Now commerce has always been a feature of pilgrimage sites – the Spaniards of Galicia were selling scallop shells to visitors to Compostela from the twelfth century; in the nineteenth enterprising Lourdais sold herbal cures to sick travellers. But the place is ridiculous now; nothing useful, nothing even pretty. I walk the On-High Street shops. Crucifixes. Rosaries. Holy water bottles. The odd pilgrim's staff, in something like wood. But mainly statues; statues and pictures. Christ dies his death here in a multiplicity of forms – stripped, robed, clothed, hologrammatic. But even more centrally, Notre Dame de Lourdes appears before Bernadette with miraculous multiplicity. There are Dames plastic and wooden; un-fragile and breakable; plain and illuminable; Virgins crowned, starred, beaded and flowered; and Blessed Ladies whose robes act as barometers. They cascade from huge to teeny-weeny, from five-inch to five feet. She appears, miraculously, on key-rings, medals, plaques, and saucers; in bronze, in plaster, in plastic, even in plasticraft;

painted and unpainted; on plates, cups, spoons and mugs; on hats, scarves, jerseys, sweatshirts, pants and coats; on candles, in candlesticks, in tubes; standing, kneeling (never sitting – for the Blessed Virgin, a good housewife, never sits down); sometimes on her own, sometimes with a baby, sometimes with Michael the Archangel, of whom you don't see much these days; in colour, in black and white, in frames, in bas-relief; in Nativities, Assumptions, Annunciations and Flights from Egypt; veiled (threatening) and in music boxes that play 'Ave Maria'.

It's a hot day in sultry August, and watching this stuff – this place – I feel my temperature begin to rise on the inside. The notion of pilgrimage – the eager searching for a place where heaven has been – and the reality of it – a heap of tat mementos pursued with fervency by dried-up Spanish matrons – have never seemed so far apart. *You cannot serve God and Mammon. In Carthage then I came; burning, burning.* The heat is stifling, worsened by the passing of the pilgrim band – a heaving, seething, sweaty mass of pilgrims, each picking up their cards, their statues, their prayer-sheets. *Lay not up for yourselves treasures upon earth.* Some take ice cream or beer in cafés. But most just wander from A to B, stopping off in the gunk emporia and browsing for bargains of which – in August – there are of course none. *For this is a den of thieves . . .*

It seems, suddenly, to be a place from which one needs to escape; this public city, this place of shopkeepers and hoteliers, this place without peace. Above me, I see a bridge: the way to the outdoor pool, where Bermudas are allowed. I climb there and catch a breath as I reach the safety of the high un-pious air above; I dive in the pool with the fat, brown boys with their shaven-crop haircuts and the thin, airy girls of the town, who age me with their assurance and their poise and the dusky skimp of their swimwear. There is a world outside. The blue water is a little dusty, so it won't matter if I too am carrying a little dust; it washes off me, round me, over me. I get relief – an awful parody of a miracle of Lourdes.

I lie awake that night, my body restored, but my mind still striving for some direction. Somewhere in the night I realize that if the problem is external – the people, the shops – the solution must be internal; somewhere along the line what's said about the place in the places that matter, the churches, must hold whatever hope of redemption there is.

So, making my early morning way down to the Domaine, I join a very long queue on the way to the 'Outdoor Mass at the Grotto' – an included excursion on the programme of our popular peregrination, admittedly, but a sort of chance to find a way that's more inward than the others the place has so far offered. The grey skies are changeable, and the old ladies up ahead are singing *Nothing Compares 2 U*, although it might be *None with Thee Compares*. The Liverpools have gathered under the banners of their travel companies (Tangney Tours, Leisure Time Travel, Pax) and behind them are the hardy souls who organize their own trip and refuse to put money into the pockets of the religious travel agents. By the statue of the Crowned Virgin a little boy in a red shirt with FOWLER 9 on the back is quietly snivelling on the ground.

We all watch the sick pass; they're to lead the way. Some, like before, are casual; some are stretchered on the ancient cripple-wheelers, complete with standard-issue crocheted blanket. We follow on with the old cock linnet to the Grotto, where the priests are already assembled, their backs to the wall of the cave by the Gave. By now the assembled faces down here are becoming as familiar as those up there; the Ghanaian, and Fr. Des-how-you-doin', and Father Gerry; Roger and Eric; the many Margarets. *Whoever has God lacks nothing*, says a voice from the massed surpliced ranks, and the guitars and flutes segue into a folk-mass intro. Looks like I'm on my own, then; the imagination of man's heart is evil from his youth.

But the preacher is the Archbishop, and he strikes one as the best hope for some sense in this time and place. He is a small man, quiet, humble and precise, and his preaching has a kind of muted glory. Unfortunately a woman next to us in the crowd faints and the brancardiers hop in, officious as football stewards, space-clearing, and the pearls of his wisdom are ironically punctuated.

We need to be still to be silent, he says, *to discover how to open the door of our heart.*

The brancs bustle around the prone one, fighting off photographers passing with their ladders, anxiously eyeing up the best spot.

Sin is noise and din drowning out the word of God.

A set of Japanese pilgri-tourists pass, clucking contentedly, cackling traditionally, one eye on the altar, one on the kerfuffle.

In stillness we ask to be renewed.

The fainter is moved ostentatiously to a ringside seat and Tony the Treasurer, his job well and efficiently done, stands with his back to the altar like a bouncer at a rock concert.

For Bernadette, at this spot, was still and silent and prayed. Bernadette, at this spot, opened her heart. Just a few feet away, she dug in the earth and a fountain of healing opened up.

Now there is a moment's peace: a pause.

We should, in the next thousand years, seek a world in which doors are opening for such as Mary of Nazareth, or for Bernadette Soubirous – people who say, 'I am gentle and lowly at heart.'

Amen, I think, and watch the others around me kneel. Soon it's communion, and underneath that washing-line of discarded crutches that hangs over the Grotto the priests begin to file out, ready to distribute: each, like some cartoon potentate of the

187

East, has an acolyte carrying a big blue umbrella, as if the poor dears can't be expected to feel the heat of the sun for five minutes. The brancs, meanwhile, physically point priests in the right direction, as if they're blind or incapable; an Italian branc waves the communicants forward with two fingers raised in a universal, if unintentional, symbol of what he feels.

The communicants communicate, and the umbrellas return towards the Grotto, Babar's caravan returning from far-off lands. The *Ave* starts and we dutifully make our way away, on to the next stop. Maybe tomorrow . . .

At the 'Bernadette Mass', next day, the Archbishop continues with thoughts of humility; another chance for something here to strike home into the arrogant sickness of my soul.

Who were the Soubirous? he begins. *A humble family despised and looked down upon by the other Lourdais . . . If we want to join and enjoy her story then we must dispense with anything arrogant, boastful, proud* He segues into a reading of that line again: *those that the world thinks common and contemptible are the ones that God has chosen.*

The youth appear en masse to do a big demo-mass designed to reinforce the theme. A bundle of them arrive on stage, each carrying a big placard. It looks like a fourth-form assembly; but I suppose that's excusable, since most of them are fourth-formers. Each board has, in big capitals, some youthful problem. WORRIES. JEALOUSY. SELFISHNESS. LONELINESS. PARANOIA. ANGER. And twelve others, each identifying a contemporary deadly sin. Once all the boards have been read everyone in the party turns themselves around so that their sides are to us, and they put their hands on each other's hips to make a big train. A narrator explains, in case it isn't obvious: an admission of vulnerability fuels the train, and the train can make progress if we have faith that we all belong to one another.

Along from me, Roger takes notes: he will use this again.

The Archbishop – he who has sat quietly waiting his turn at the bathtubs – watches this with a suitably indulgent expression, and then preaches again in a still, quiet, impressive, telling way, in what comes to me as the true voice of a pilgrim, a quiet insistence that something valuable exists beyond the tat in the shops and the trumped-uppery of the officials.

If you want to know what it is to trust in God, you must be willing to pray not according to what you deserve but as deeply as you are allowed by the Holy Spirit.

His gaze takes in the massed ranks of the sick, who again are lined up to the side of him; he feels for them and with them, creates a goodness. Then he looks round towards the rest of us.

Never say to the sick, How are you? They have to lie if you do. Don't make them hide their feelings; there's no point. Christ and prayer, he says, are like two yoked oxen. Don't worry about the plough, He says. Talk as we go. Tell me the story as it really is. I'll tell you my story, Christ says. A story about my home.

My home is the place where it is necessary to be gentle and lowly at heart. This is the truth of Lourdes: not that we're gentle and lowly of heart so that we can rule the roost in heaven: but that heaven is to be gentle and lowly at heart. If in the sick you have a glimpse of what is it to be gentle and lowly of heart, then in the sick you have had a glimpse of heaven.

It's rather lovely; rather pure; the sort of voice that was sometimes present but often missing from childhood; the sort of voice that might not convert, but that might have kept one attached. I'm with Roger and Margaret, and Margaret smiles as, as the Archbishop finishes, some branc walks past, head up, on a very important mission to nowhere in particular, taking communion on the hoof as he allots priests to people. It's another place in which Christ is blocked out by something only too human – a total eclipse of the Son.

Outside, irritated, Roger's Margaret rants about how the brancs in general were striding the aisles as she tried to contemplate the things she wanted to ponder. 'It's just not necessary,' she says. 'You don't have to do everything in public.' (She is a primary head, too, and knows that offices can be carried out discreetly, indirectly.) But as we talk I discover the real source of the fume, the real fire: it emerges that at a mass for the sick Roger's mother was not anointed; as she was not Official Sick, the brancs had simply pushed the priests by.

We go for a Coca-Cola in the Little Flower tea room. She is thoughtful today: she has clearly reached a point in her pilgrimage, an edgy moment, though she remains positive. She tells me about the day before's trip to Bartres, to Bernadette's wet-nurse's village where Bernadette, in the myth, tended the sheep in the months before her visions. And she's interested in what she's learned, in extrapolating the psychology: that while she tended the sheep Bernadette was left in the fields, all alone, away from the house; she slept out, it seems, saw no one for days on end, had nothing but her rosary beads. And her face says that she reserves the right, as a teacher and a person with some knowledge of the workings of the minds of young people, to draw her own conclusions about what would emerge from an adolescent mind in such circumstances.

We get personal. She's a clear-faced woman, charming in her way, with a ringing voice, an honest tone. She wants to know about me, and we talk about the difficulties of nowadays; she allows me to be honest, to acknowledge that I can't really belong to this lot in any full sense because of the way I live. 'It's not so bad as it once was,' she says, and she tells me how in the 1950s Catholics marrying Protestants would be made to marry on the side altar rather than the main one, even in their own local parishes. 'Many friends of mine feel bitter about that now,' she says, and, lowly and humble at heart, she lists some other things that distract her. But she has an answer. 'If you want to continue to believe,' she says, 'you have to look up rather than straight ahead every now and again.'

Roger's mother has no such problem. Even if Roger is beginning to sag under the strain of offering therapy to her while needing it for himself, his mum is being uplifted by her experience, and her wappy, off-the-wall monologues are moving into full swing as she sits in her chair, lovely-spindly in her T-shirt and shorts. Her conversational medium is sparrow-leaping, topic-hopping, but returns always to the nest, to the praise of the nest, to the fact that her son is a good boy and never drinks and has a good job and should have had that other job and comes in to see her whenever he can and always looks after her. When the dust of her loquacity settles, I ask him how *he* is. 'I'm glad I brought her, but I have to admit there's a burden in that too.' He lowers his voice. 'I was looking through my wife's photo-journal last night, after we'd been to the baths', and for a second it's obvious how painful this is; this isn't just laying a flower at the grave, this is walking in the footsteps on the way to the cemetery. And as if to illustrate the difficulties he has in concentrating, his mother starts to chirp again: 'He's a good boy. Such a good boy. He always looks after me. He's got a good job, you know. I've got three telephones. He should have had that other job, but they didn't give it to him. He's an angel. And I have three telephones . . .'

Margaret catches me by the hand and tells me a story, something that's been disturbing her, something she can't tell them. She'd been standing by the procession the night before ('Do you mind if I tell you this? Do tell me if you mind . . .') and a man in a wheelchair had come up beside her in the procession; a sick man, an Italian or a Spaniard. She'd smiled at him, and he'd taken her hand. It had been gentle, at first, but, after a minute or so, when she'd tried to remove it, the hold had turned into a grab, a seize.

'You don't mind if I tell you this, do you? Stop me any time, if you need to,' says Margaret. She had felt his need for comfort, and so had submitted cheerfully enough; but after a few moments she had looked in his eyes, and what she could see were not the eyes of someone taking succour, but the intense eyes of someone transfixed by desire. And, she says, with a glance at Roger's mum, she realized then what's it's like to be in that chair; not just unable to move, but unable to express the deepest part of yourself. And since then she'd been shaken by all the cosy bits and pieces that she saw as she walked around. And found it necessary, she says, to be lowly and humble of heart.

I know that that is what I need to be too. Another day in Paradise, another mass in Lourdes; this time the Mass of the Anointing of the Sick. It takes place in the Pius X Basilica – a vast oval underground car park of a church, a place of concrete and echo rather than incense and hush. The Liverpool mob are dwarfed in it even though there's a good turn-out; it's two or three hundred yards long, I guess, built, practically, to accommodate 25,000 people sitting and standing, the same 25,000 who at the height of the season make up the torchlight procession; constructed expressly so that those great outdoor events, like some celestial sports day, can be indoors if wet.

A Liverpool priest is pontificating through the microphone when I get in there: something about how the sick are the chosen ones. *How Great Thou Art*, they all sing, and the Gospel features, reassuringly, the casting out of demons, before the Archbishop takes to the pulpit to preach. He is again quiet and calm. His is a beautiful preaching voice: eloquence without false rhetoric, articulacy without sophistry. Every time he opens his mouth, it feels, I have some hope; things begin to make a little sense; if you had been brought up with this every day, you think, things might have been different. He looks over the massed ranks of the Official Sick, who are ranged before him, and talks to them directly with his eyes, though to us with his mouth.

What about the sick? Are they useless? Can they be saved? Do they really belong to the family of the Lord? Yes, they do belong, they are with us, and the Holy Spirit is hoping that they will open their hearts. So shall our sick brothers and sisters be raised up today. So shall our Lord make them one of us. Through suffering, as well as death, Christ came to us . . .

A Down's sufferer – prominent only because a certain thoughtful stillness has come over the room – gets all happy-clappy. Oils are collected and candles lit.

These symbols are a sign of the overshadowing of the Holy Spirit – a sign that the sick are with us.

All round the room the priests – Gerry, Des-how-you-doin', the Ghanaian – raise their hands and bless the oil and the youth, Cranberry-like, sing 'The Lord's My Shepherd' into the heavy, significant, un-pasteurized air. The priests circulate, and a candle is held above the head of each sick person. Hands are laid and heads blessed, including that of an old lady who has dropped off and needs to be woken; whose candle is barely lit. And, most noticeably, John the Aviator sits still throughout, physically transformed by what goes on; not so much beautified as beatified, he contrives to look like a chosen one, seems to be raised up; calm, he sits, receives and lets the priest go without a hint of 'again', and though a bunch of camera-clicking Japs pass along the barriers to his right his serene, purified gaze never falters.

Communion, with further urges to humility from the Arch-bishop, finds me half-perched over the front of my seat; for though I kneel for no one I long ago perfected, for moments such as these, a kneeling-like half-sitting position. I am moved by John's peace. Tony the Treasurer, strutting as the Lord of the Aisles, cannot touch him, cannot touch me now. In the face of a real miracle, he doesn't seem to matter; there's sense in it, a sense that even the finale (as Win jigs down the aisle I wish I was a Quaker, wish I was entitled to a long patch of stolid, thoughtful silence) can't take away. *Look up instead of straight ahead now and again* – Margaret's motto comes back to me; and it may be dishonest, but on some level it looks like it works.

'He closed his eyes, surrendering himself to her, body and mind, conscious of nothing in the world but the dark pressure of her softly parting lips . . .'

Just as word must become flesh, so flesh becomes flesh, becomes seen as flesh, becomes something sought and longed for: there are hormones and there is biology, however much it is denied, and these do not discriminate between Kafflik and Protestant, between righteous and wrong-eous. In days like these, when mortification of the flesh is not in fashion, the priests at the green-blazer school find difficulty in keeping the green-blazer boys apart from the girls, especially the blue-blazer girls from the other side of the religious divide. And, if he has said it once, Fr. F will say it a thousand times, to the boys, to their parents, to anyone who will listen: the contents of that type of girl's handbag can bring great danger to the mortal soul of a good Kafflik boy.

On warm Saturday nights at the school disco Fr. F patrols disapprovingly, watching for spirits hidden in the Coca-Cola bottles, invigilating the dancing (the statutory two feet apart rule, at least until the smoochers come on, applies). Fr. M, too, is often seen prowling the corridors, muttering imprecations in his thick Oxford accent, until he comes a cropper one sweaty evening when he tries to separate a couple who, it turns out, have managed to get their dental braces entangled; a visit to the dental equivalent of casualty is necessitated, where the specialist can hardly operate for laughing, though Fr. M, standing by, wondering about the Kafflik youth of today, finds it no laughing matter.

Back at school on Monday, traumatized by the event, Fr. M tries to convince the boys that their behaviour has not sufficiently befitted Kafflik gentlemen who have been subjected to Jesuit discipline. The life-lesson runs something like this: kissing is, or can be, a sin, since a kiss such as those he has witnessed speaks of a certain intention, a certain desire, a certain thought that lies behind the action. In learned detail, he sets out a treatise on the nature of kissing, from the acceptable peck on the cheek of a mother through the chaste kiss on the lips of a 'good friend' to the abomination he has seen, 'kissing with the tongue'. Each is analysed for its virtue or otherwise; the third, he suggests, might rightly be thought of as sinful outside of marriage, where it might be understood as a stage in the making of another young Kafflik soul. (French kissing, it seems, is fine – so long as Christ is in the mouth too.)

And more, too: when someone, satirically feigning religious doubt in order that the disquisition be extended, asks whether the sin of French kissing is mortal (one that is potentially damning the bearer to eternal torment) or venial (a small but significant black mark), Fr. M foolishly puts a time frame on this matter. To judge from what he has seen on his weekend on duty, in his prowling of the corridors with his Transylvanian associate, he defines thirty seconds as the duration at which such speaking in tongues becomes a peril to one's mortal soul. Which strikes Stephen as funny, until he comes to consider that this is all the preparation he, and presumably many of his own associates, has for a sexual life in the late twentieth century. And, as chance would have it, in terms of the order of the universe, the time when he will require such preparation is only thirty seconds away.

Ironically, given the determination it has shown to not provide him with any background for his sentimental education, it is the school that inadvertently provides the opportunity, that sets up the possibility of his word becoming his flesh. Sometime in his fourteenth or fifteenth year *he travels with his school friends to Wales, to a big Jesuit house where there is to be a drama summer school. It is not approved of by Fr. F, incidentally, who is on the last legs of his authority, but the content of the week is innocent; the house is staffed by an eccentric Jesuit, aided by his squad of young Jesuit novices; there is mass every day, and of course all dramatic performances come with the AMDG imprimatur; each is offered For the Greater Glory of God.*

There is another aspect, of course: down in the cellar, in the third circle of hell, a disco starts. There Stephen is given the usual crude message that someone is earnest about him, and, notwithstanding a gap between the stirrup and the ground necessitated by whatever it is in his make-up that twists each relationship into a search for virtue, he reaches out and takes; for the first time he enjoys the full scope of that thirty-second sin. The desire – the intention, the thought that lies behind, snare-like – quickly falls upon him, as sure as the softest touch of a nether lip. He romanticizes it, of course: walking on the beach, jumping in the water in his clothes; he is in love, he will marry this person, he will have children by her. And when he falls in love, it must be for ever: when he returns home the romance continues, and maintains its rose-tint-view of the ways of the world.

Meanwhile, there is a change at home: his family start to attend a hip chapel around the corner. The atmosphere is apparently unstuffy: the priest, an Italian, wishes everyone good morning in the middle of mass, which is nothing short of revolutionary, while a set of novices, young bearded Lanarkshire men called Gerry or Des or Hughie lead the folk-mass services with jokes and resonant strums on big twelve-string guitars. For a while all is energized; but the vibrancy withers when the family of Italian girls around the corner begins to take the boys for walks, and introduce them to other vocations. Stephen, in the novice-free new world, is handed the poisoned chalice of a deal sewn up over his head: a commitment to play his puny six-string, Sunday in and Sunday out, at the folk-mass at ten-thirty on a Sunday.

And, of course, this commitment, this demand that he bear witness, arrives just as all surety that this religion is really his is crumbling; just as he needs a little space to reflect, he is deprived of it. Compared with the rush of love he feels for the girl, the love he feels for his God is a slow and sluggish walk, a perfect reflection of adolescent ennui. Sad to say – and it is a matter of sadness – he begins to grasp that there is no resonance for him when that host is raised above the priest's head, and he moves straight into the sort of guilt that is the real burden of this thing, the sense that he is letting down his people. The Catch-22 for the departing Kafflik is this: they teach you to tell the truth, then don't want to hear it. So he continues to go through the motions of observance; keeping the peace, he calls it. What else can a coward do? In this city, in his world, where he has never met a homosexual, where he has never met a person who is divorced, where people still express surprise if a Kafflik is marrying a Protestant, it's best to stay mum.

Time passes – many thirty seconds – in this state, this wretched stalemate. He does what he is told, and leads the awful songs. 'Colours of Day'. 'Lord of the Dance'. 'Give Me Oil In My Lamp'. Those terrible versions of 'Holy Holy Holy' in mock African or mock Caribbean. If he can avoid it he can, but usually he can't. And meanwhile his feelings the other way deepen and intensify: she dumps him, he suffers, he gets her back; as his spirit weakens, his flesh becomes more willing, and it seems obvious, though not to him, that he is in the final round of a classic grapple between the two. Needless to say, the stronger – the flesh – wins hands down.

Look at it this way, as a choice of destinies.

Scenario 1: he spends his Sundays strumming his way through chord changes of Status Quo-like catatonia, drinks coffee in the novice-free parlour, chats with the virtuous, then returns home to spend the afternoon at his books. He studies and eventually discovers his own vocation, be it secular or divine.

Scenario 2: he spends his Sundays following where his perfectly normal blue-blazered girl leads. She takes him to many places; her main route takes him up that same garden path where the novices have boldly gone before. Somewhere along that garden path is a big tree with apples on it; she gives it a good shake, bringing down (if not an apple) then at least his cherry. His fig-leaf is on, and he is lost to innocence for ever. Now there are thoughts, that's for sure. And lips, and breasts, and hands and hair and all manner of sweet nectar in all sorts of unlikely locations will follow.

But then things are not so clear. At the time it's bizarre; barely dreamed of, hardly considered, never contemplated – a sudden and mysterious arrival of knowledge; Stephen is as innocent as Adam. Only years later does he realize the most startling fact about the end of his childhood. The most surprising thing about this startling and stunningly un-dramatic end of innocence is that, in another sense, he has absolutely no notion of what is going to happen; he has never actually never touched himself in a knowing way, so when he piles in, machetes his way along the strange overgrowth at the top of that garden path, he hardly knows how it begins, let alone how it all ends. It's an utter, utter mystery. The surprise – he has to say, however he prides himself on his physical austerity, his demand for romance – is pleasant, is gratifying.

VI
Confessions

St Germaine
Feast: June 15
Patron Saint of Peasant Girls
(also of the Physically Challenged and People with Unsightly Illnesses)
The deformed Germaine, had an abusive stepmother who made her sleep in a cupboard and feed from the dog's bowl. Accused, in midwinter, of stealing bread from the table to feed a beggar, she opened her apron; a profusion of summer flowers tumbled out.

For some reason some old song of Harry Nilsson's (You can climb a mountain or swim the sea, it goes, yet never be free) is in my mind when our Croatian courier announces, to gasps of approval from the others, that we have this morning (as her odd, strangled syntax has it) an appointment to see Vicka. I clap and cheer with the rest, just so I don't feel left out, and it's Lawrence who has to let me know – or *remind* me, as he says archly (the seer seeing, the all-knowing knowing all) that Vicka is herself a seer, is (though thirty now) one of the children who saw the Virgin on Podbrdo and kicked the whole Medjugorje thing off. Danjela is fulsome in her description when one or two of the matrons in the party ask for more bumph. Yes, Vicka still speaks to the Virgin every day, although the Virgin only graces her with a reply on one particular day of the week – I think she says Thursday – at twenty minutes to seven exactly.

In spite of the nonsense this does seem to hold possibilities; all the miracles on earth can't hold a candle to a personal appearance from on high. So bright and early – it's a half-seven breakfast at Tomas's, and a half-eight set-off – we walk across the fields to the remote part of the town that was, before 1982, the village itself. It's a bizarre scene when we get there. In the garden, under a sort of grapevine bower that all the houses in town seem to have, and on the road surrounding Vicka's small, half-pretty house, a couple of hundred Yanks, Poles, Italians and now English are gathered. They look like they're just hanging round on the street queuing for something, until you see that their faces are alert and not desultory. You also see their multi-nationality – the Poles gaudy in their poverty, the Italians svelte in their wealth-y. (The temptation to make a rhyme for the Americans is almost too great; try bum-bags for size.) I end up pushed into a corner next to Cecilia, who's next to James, whose good intentions in getting up to see the seer are being undermined by a steady flow of demands and strong requests from his mother.

As I get there she's asking him if he would like to take a petition to Vicka. (Vicka, like some celestial DJ, will receive requests, although she doesn't choose her own Top 10, but leaves them in a pile for the Virgin to read.) James, with a barely maintained sense of diplomacy, says he thinks it's more important that others have the chance to put their wishes. It's a quaint notion, that feudal idea that you petition the queen to do your bidding, but there's no shortage of takers, even in these egalitarian times. In fact shortage is the opposite of the problem; the other nationalities are supposed to cede the garden to us Anglophones between 8.30 and 9.30 a.m., but such is the intensity of their devotion that no amount of pleading from the couriers and the guides has any effect and the Poles and the French, here first, appear ready and willing to listen to Vicka speaking in Hindustani if it means they can spend another half-hour in her presence.

Soon duress becomes the order of the day as bulldog-like, the

Brits make a bid for glory; the garden becomes a scrum of would-be hem-touchers grasping their pieces of paper – Great Depression shareholders outside a collapsing bank. But possession proves to be nine-tenths of divine law; bulldog becomes hangdog, and we Brits retire to the street outside, clutching our wilting paper flowers and our limp handwritten requests for intercessionary miracles. This has certain disadvantages, particularly in respect of the traffic situation. For this is a comparatively congested village thoroughfare, and every now and then a diesel Merc taxi, cowboy at the wheel, passes, or, worse, doesn't pass, but hoots warningly instead. Vicka's message – the Message of Medjugorje – is, for me and most of my fellows, the message of Mercedes, is largely the chug of an impatient diesel and the *parp* of an air-powered horn. As the Italians hug the wall, kiss their statues, and absorb the timbre of words they do not understand, I only catch the end of the interpreter's bit: 'Vicka greets you from the bottom of her heart, and she gives you this message from Our Blessed Mother: that message is prayer, fasting, penance, peace . . .' before another taxi passes, taking with it the rest of the words.

It's disappointing: part of me has not been able to resist the idea that I may be in the presence of greatness in coming before this woman; I confess that part of me is feeling pretty feudal too, and I want to know what she has to say. But I have to be content with a visual impression for quite a while. She's a nice looking woman, Vicka, with a big smile and a big forehead and her hair swept back in an Alice band. She doesn't look particularly divine, if truth be told; she wears a beige T-shirt and check pants, not just nothing special but something quite horrible. *Our Blessed Mother is full of love, and we in turn love her so much,* she says. *Her message is the same as it has always been. Just as a flower cannot live without water, so we cannot live without the grace of God. With prayers every day, your faith will blossom in the same way as his love.* Then – just as a sentence or two offers a semblance of coherence – two cars arrive simultaneously, humming low, and we're back in dumb-show-land again: I watch her gestures, her smiles, her hands touching her beating-heart chest; I hear next to nothing, and recall that sin is din and noise drowning out the word of God.

But what I do hear, it strikes me in the pauses, is not all that prepossessing. This is Our Lady the Queen of Peace, Star of the Sea, Mother of Mir, talking, and yet she seems to have nothing to say about the things of the world; peace seems to be narrowly interpreted, confusingly so in a country in which so recently the bombs were flying, were taking people's heads off, even if Cecilia's tour bus was granted miraculous Red Sea-like passage through the shells and the shrapnel the respective militias were launching. *Our Lady invites us to a complete conversion. You have to open your hearts. Our Lady would like us to renew the prayer of the rosary in our families. The best weapon against Satan is the rosary.* It seems almost a mockery to be quite so banal, while there isn't even peace in the street outside; a taxi driver and the driver of a German jeep practically come to blows when one won't back up through the crowd to let the other pass.

Vicka, half-heard and therefore probably unfairly edited, carries on in the same traditional, square-aimed vein. *Young people are in a very difficult situation, Our Blessed Mother knows. Our Lady says that what today's world offers you is just temporary: Satan is working on our young people, trying to destroy our families. What you must do is pray, pray, pray. But remember, if you pray for peace in the world, remember: without peace in your heart, then prayer is senseless.* Fair enough; but it's not that easy for me and my ilk, who have never been able to take prayer without action. And Vicka doesn't mention the poor, doesn't mention the hungry. *Pray for the Pope, for the Bishops, for the Priests, for the Church.* Nor does she mention genocide or ethnic cleansing. *Pray above all to*

Mary the Mother of God. And not a word of Mostar, of Sarajevo, of Srebrenica. It reminds me of something from childhood – that vain search, amongst the doctrinists and the orthodoxers, for someone that would join the faith of the fathers to the belief in the brothers.

I stick it out to the end, but I confess I'm jaundiced by the close, as the trudge back to town arrives. Cecilia, James and I walk together across the fields, through the vineyards, on the way home. Irritated, and having no Angela to angel-like rescue me into sense, I take it out on Cecilia in a most unchristian fashion; I pick a fight about the Virgin Mary. At the time I feel it is something I feel, even if the logic of it is a bit specious, a bit extemporaneous, even if the motivation is sinfully personal. Surely, I say, worshipping Mary is wrong, (a) on the basis that anti-Marians have always had it, which is that it comes near to cultism and graven imagery; and (b) because Mary and the rosary are so ultra-Kafflik in style, orientation and doctrine, then if the Virgin is encouraging a message of pray-on-the-rosary-and-everything-will-be-all-right, then she's actually encouraging anti-ecumenism, is actually fomenting universal un-peace, since no one apart from a Kafflik even so much as dreams of clutching rosary beads.

Cecilia, as one would expect, and as to be perfectly honest I perfectly deserve, gives me well-rehearsed short shrift: on (a) she says she honours Mary, not worships her; while on (b) she says that I'm Satan's mouthpiece (I've come a long way from being one of the Virgin's storm troopers, I suppose) and that it's arguments like mine that result in priests taking down Mary's statue in churches. With some dignity she turns her back on me to go to ten o'clock mass. I wish I had the same dignity; when James and I go to have a ten o'clock Coca-Cola, I rant conspiracy theories about the right wing in the Vatican wanting to encourage such manifestations as Medjugorje for the very reason that they're anti-ecumenical; in a world that's ever-relativist, in which dangerous forces are suggesting we might actually be friends with some of the opposite sides that surround us, it's important to have a few branches of supra-natural protection that vibrantly support the old on-your-knees ways. James, camera in hand, nods and smiles, feigns interest, and goes off to lie in a field.

In the Medjugorje evening, Sheila, the Simpson *mère*, wants James and me to take Sally-Ann and Laurie and her up the mountain. (The Simpson children and grandchild, alone of the whole party, missed the walk the other night.) We're agreeable – up there it's the nicest place on earth. (It does strike me as ironic that climbing the mountain, the definitive pilgrimage experience, should become as much about getting away from the place of pilgrimage as anything else. *For who shall climb the mountain of the Lord? Those who want to get away from the tat of the souvenir shops.*)

They're all game for the walk, the whole walk and nothing but the walk – no taxis here. We make our way through the town as the day begins to cool and the light is starting to fade a little. Sally-Ann, fags or not, is quite quick up the side of the mountain, quite keen and agile; fit in that other sense. Laurie needs a bit of help and encouragement, of course, but James makes himself available to do elaborate mimes of rubber shoes and the behaviour of mountain goats, and she shins up happily enough. I, meanwhile, walk most of the nursery slopes with Sheila, who huffs and puffs a good B&H bit, but it makes a change to see her walking instead of sitting on the patio contributing to the dust/ash ratio of the Croatian highveld.

We breathlessly talk Vicka for a while, and, knowing her to be fairly devoted to all things Virginal, and probably not averse to contemplating the four last things, her response surprises me with its frankness. More than that – I'm taken aback when 'obnoxious' is what she calls the whole scene by the seer's house. It's partly because she was disturbed at not getting nearer the centre of things, but it's not just that, it's clear, and, encouraged, and still on my high horse, I say what's on my mind. How can an Our Lady of Peace not have anything to say about peace, especially in this land of uncivilly civil war, where Ethnic Cleansing Washes Whiter?

Of course and of course she puts me right: if everyone has peace in their own hearts then of course by definition peace will follow because each person, warmed by the daily saying of the rosary, will acquire peace, transfer it into peace with neighbours, transfer that into ceasing all wars and strife altogether. My faith, or what is left of it, will – just as of course – not chime with that sort of expression. Warmed by the encounter with Cecilia, I again speak rashly, saying it seems a hard message to be passing on to the Muslims of Srebrenica, if there are any left: *yes, I know we've spent most of the last five hundred years skinning you alive and boiling your pagan entrails, but just hang on a bit until we say a few more decades, and we'll acquire peace in our hearts presently.*

She's quiet for a minute, and I feel mean; repenting, I collude with her in a pause halfway up the mountain, where strictly contrary to the rules and regulations (there are actually signs along the pathway, pictures of puffers transfigured by a thick red line) she lights a B&H and puffs on it deeply and satisfiedly. Pensive, she instructs me that I should go ahead, not wait for her. Before I go she finds the reply she's been carefully considering; she digs out from her bag a book she's been reading, with pictures of some Virgin apparitionists operating out of Rwanda, and pictures of others in that country that – precisely echoing the state of affairs in the land in which we're now standing – have been slaughtered in the name of ethnicity. Yes, she says, slaughter was a sort of end of the world for the people she has been talking about, for the people she's showing me in her book. 'But it didn't come from above,' she says. 'Oh no. They were slaughtered by another tribe. They shouldn't have been watching the skies,' she says, 'they should have been watching the person next door.'

So saying, and lighting up another, she waves me off, and I catch up with the mountain goats and the rubber shoes. I'm glad that Sheila takes her time: she's not there to see Sally-Ann, in one of the world's least ancient but most sacred places, climb a radio mast and mock-up a crucifixion scene. Sheila takes her time, stops for a few fags, but makes it in the end to the top, makes it in the end for the end of the sunset. It's that that compels once we reach the top, and compels even in a way that Laurie's shrieking about the wasps and Sally-Ann's shriekings about Laurie's shriekings can't deter. I manage to climb a little hill within the hill, manage to find my own mountain of the Lord, where I gaze out over the setting sun. I think about Simeon Stylites, who built columns and lived at the top of them in order to escape the hubbub of his fame. (By the time of his death, hastened by his habit of tying his flesh tightly with knotted palm leaves, he was sixty feet aloft.) More importantly I consider those I've hurt today, and whether it was avoidable, when push comes to shove, when irresistible force meets immovable object, when one truth must face down another.

St Clare of Assisi
Feast: August 11
Patron Saint of Television
A friend of St Francis, Clare established and for forty years ran her own brown-robed order, the Poor Clares. When, on her deathbed, she became too ill to attend mass, an image of the service would be miraculously transmitted on to the wall of her cell.

Sunday, 1.23 p.m. Bonnie Stewart, Sister Pius's video chanteuse, is still singing away as we begin to make the homeward road towards Dublin. 'Daisy Daisy'. 'Goodnight Irene'. 'Goodnight Paddy Reilly'. 'I Belong to Glasgow'. 'The Northern Lights of Old Aberdeen'. 'Blanket on the Ground'. 'The Old Rugged Cross'. 'How Great Thou Art'. Plus, of course, the usual sops to the oppressed: men might be able to build houses, but 'it still takes a woman to build you a home'. I have an idea for a men-strike-back song in this crossover country/popular favourites/devotional genre, something about 'Who Cut the Grass in the Garden of Eden?' with a little sting in the second verse along the lines of the fact that we all know who harvested the apples. The chat is idle, desultory, till we roll up in a little wide spot in the road called Charlestown, where at Walsh's bar Mac persuades Mrs Walsh ('your cousin,' Edmund says to me), in mock-heroic vein ('Madam – we are pilgrim travellers, thirsty from our long road's journey') to give us a couple of after-hours pints. When she does, she is blessed in the name of St Amand, patron of publicans.

As we sup our Guinness, Mac thanks me for sorting out the hotel room situation, delightedly quoting my bolshie line ('They're husband and wife, for God's sake!') to Sister Pius, and hopes I'll do it again tonight if it comes up again. (Nancy, who has said little throughout, suddenly speaks up, aside: 'You know, I'm sick of being treated like this. I've done nothing wrong and neither has he so the rest of them know where to go.') The moral discretion of Mac's righteous riff fades rather when he tries to inveigle Mrs W into giving us another one, at severe risk to her person and her licence. Edmund objects ('Leave a person space,' he says, 'don't say the wrong thing') but Mac insists that his time as a KLM manager gives him judgement ('I know how to deal with foreigners'). We drift out, along the road filled with cars flying Mayo and Roscommon flags; for it's the football or the hurley quarter-finals somewhere up along the road to the next town, and the men are out of mass, have drunk their pints, and are going to the game.

Back on board, Luisa offers her newly-bought Christina Gallagher video to Paul as our homeward-bound viewing, and she comes up to me and tells me especially that I must watch it attentively as the price of not having been to see the woman herself; my generosity becomes my reproach, though I am glad to have the chance. *The Christina Gallagher Story*, after all, tells all, or all I need to know. The woman, it emerges, is Vicka reincarnated; a plain-looking, dowdy old style Irish housewife. (According to the myth, when the Virgin first appeared Christina told her that she was too busy to have an apparition as she was washing the dishes.) As the film proceeds she recites the times and the places: seeing Christ crucified in 1985, starting to see the Virgin in 1988.

By this stage in the journey I'm a bit blah-blah-blah about all this stuff: the mockery she endured from her neighbours, who called her a lunatic, who said she was hallucinating; the marks she's had left on her from the devil's attacks. But one also feels obliged to listen to this kind of testimony; no taxi drivers can run across the screen, tooting and parping, but more – somewhere, there's a push, an edge. 'Sometimes,' she says, 'I've found the cross easy. Sometimes I feel Jesus has abandoned me.' It reminds me of the swell of the words up the Medjugorje mountain, and her description of seeing Christ is painful: 'On seeing the crown of thorns, I wanted to scream with the horror I felt. The *sorrow* I felt that day will live with me until the day I die. When I see him on the cross I want to take my own heart out,' she says, rich with contemplation of the agonies of things. Her descriptions of the Virgin, too, have an edge missing elsewhere; when she says the Lady was 'radiantly' beautiful, she has the grace to point out that she means it literally. 'Her hands were joined, and they contained a glass globe, with smoke in it, whirling around. She swayed her mantle at me three times, then left. I felt that I was completely, I was utterly in love with this woman. I felt something beyond the peace of this world, something you cannot explain in words.' She is doing a fair old job, though.

Her visions, too, are sort of compelling, although perhaps it's the way she tells them. She was taken on a journey to purgatory at one time: a 'dark dismal muddy smelly place –' (she speaks without commas) '– a place of corridors and hallways and doorways where I saw people with brown habits with their hoods up on one side of the corridors with evil spirits on the other. These evil spirits were playing with fire.' (Literally, we assume.) All the people she saw, she says, were suffering, and, as she passed and saw each one she felt the suffering of each one; sensed a yelling and suffering that was 'beyond words'. She says she saw a bright light, saw Jesus and pleaded with Jesus to let the people out, after which, inconclusively, the souls disappeared as she herself was subsumed in a ball of light, a magic trick that had gone wrong. She describes her marks, too: the suffering of pain in hands, feet and chest, the forerunners of a life of Pio-like endurance; marks on the forehead, little spots. ('I asked Jesus not to send the marks; I didn't want the attention they would bring me. But when I told him he could stop, that he could please himself, he stopped – you see he simply wanted my surrender.') As an almost continuous sufferer of the pain of the passion, she seems to enshrine the idea that suffering, like Guinness, is good for you. 'These are just the sufferings of the journey home,' she says, which is fair enough, especially if on the way you get to see the odd dancing Eucharist, the odd bright ascendant ceiling-less host.

St Barbara
Feast: December 4
Invoked Against Death By Artillery
The beautiful Barbara was locked up by her father for disobedience.
Condemned to death, she escaped; her father dragged her back by her
hair, then killed her with his bare hands. He was immediately struck by
lightning and died.

Outside the 'Marian Pilgrimages (Ireland)' shop on the main
Medjugorje drag, a notice says that pilgrims are counselled not
to travel to other places of interest – Dubrovnik and Sarajevo
are within reach, and each carries an interest either touristy or,
just a couple of years down the road from civil war, sort of
ghoulish – since 'peace is only to be found by concentrating on
Medjugorje alone'. *Pray for peace within your own heart*, as the
endless story goes.

And maybe peace is findable there, if you like that kind of
solitudinem faciunt pacem appellant experience, if you like living
in a bubble. I am itchy: the same long strip of street, the same
cold coolness in the white buildings, the same cowboy-hatted
taxi drivers smoking cigars and coursing the main drag in their
Mercedeses. For however many times (and it's plenty of times,
let me tell you, and with fairy-tale grammar) people tell me
how miraculous it is that a bomb never fell on Medjugorje
during all the years of the Yugoslavian war, it does seem to me
to be quite remarkable that beyond that fact no one (save
Lawrence, of course, who knows everything) seems to know
what's going on in the rest of the country. So when I hear that
the rest of the group are taking an excursion (not included, as
they say in the brochures) to a parish which features the statue of
Our Lady that, the visionaries say, most resembles the apparitions
they saw on Podbrdo, followed by an hour at the waterfalls, a

local swimming spot, I want out, and, with James, I wander up to the bus stop, resolved to catch a bus to see Mostar.

Mostar is familiar – a name, a bridge, endless shelling from the hills – from newsreel, and it doesn't take long to acquire some of the post-war paranoia of the place. The taxi driver from Medjugorje doesn't help. He's a narrow, anorexic-looking man, thin as a rake, shorn on top, who tells us he lives in his car – why buy a house during recent times, when there's the possibility that any ticket you take might be a one-way one? – and happy to be in Medjugorje, because there are personal antipathies he'd rather not face. We get him on to football for a bit, but that too is political – how Dinamo Zagreb has become Croatia Zagreb, and how neither Zeleznicar of Sarajevo nor Velez of Mostar are what they once were, for that was in another country, and besides, that league (and probably half of the playing-staff) is dead. So instead of chit-chat he shows us, all bravado, photos of himself in his Croat militia uniform; but once we reach our destination, he won't take us all the way into town, but – arguing that there are too many Muslims there – shows us the bus stop where we'll find our way home, then drops us off on the outskirts.

Suspecting that we're being done in some kind of way – for he does make a small-change second-language quibble with the sign-language-negotiated fare we'd agreed back in Catholic-land, back in Medjugorje – we try to make him take us to the *centrum*. He begins to do so, but after a street it's obvious that he isn't fooling; his driving goes to pieces, as if his nerves are suddenly shot. And given that this appears to be a peaceful city in everything except its shot-to-bits architecture, we can only speculate that it's not the general situation that he fears, but the vindictive instincts of specific individuals. And it suddenly occurs that this is the terrible thing about a civil war; in a normal war your enemy, or the man whose brother you shot, returns to his own country and – your borders being your buffers – you never see him again; in a civil war your enemy returns to the street corners of the next town; the boy next door returns to the house next door.

So we find ourselves a little lost and confused: knowing nothing, seeing nothing, unable to speak, walking down a road unaware what kind of a zone we might be in, in what direction we're heading. IFOR vehicles race the streets in some areas we walk through, and Spanish troops strut around with peace-keeping machismo, but in other parts the place seems entirely normal, entirely peaceful. We stop and have coffee, not knowing if we are in a Muslim part of town or a Croat one, looking at faces. Spooked, we begin to swap tales of lonely places – James has been on the back foot in India, and Zimbabwean troops have pulled guns on me at remote times in the past – but this is different, difficult. As Yugos and Polski Fiats pass amongst the armoured cars, along with the odd tank-like Mercedes, we look around, seeking a bank and advice.

We get both in the Hrvatska Bank, from a teller who speaks English, a Croat who'd rather be out, but whose city this is. As she offers guidance and tells the tale of the place, a thousand newsreels begin to return to mind, so that what she's saying is her story, yes, but is memory, too. A city built on two banks of the River Neretva: an old town, first occupied by Muslims, when they were Ottomans, treating the whole region as their chaise longue, on the far side; a new town, first occupied by johnny-come-lately Croats and Serbs, but later, partly because of forced integration by the Yugoslav authorities, on the near; the Muslim population had come across, traversed the Boulevard Marshal Tito, had taken apartments in the Yugoslav blocks, had settled alongside their neighbours, just as Bosnia, and Serbia, and Croatia as a whole had done under Tito's umbrella. Population of the city before the war: 120,000. Population now: 30,000. Proportions then: 38 per cent Muslim, 37 per cent Croat, 20 per cent Serb. (A reasonably cosmopolitan town it had been under the Yugoslav communists, she says; however forcibly they had been put together, people had rubbed along.) Proportions now: impossible to judge, she says, but she is able to say how many Croat families live on what was once, and then hadn't been, but was now again, the Muslim side: four.

It seems remarkable, until the newsreels start to revolve again in one's brain. 1992 and 1993. The Serbs take the hills around the town and begin to rain down bombs. Where do they aim for? The Turkish quarter, of course, the Old Town, for Ethnic Cleansing Washes Whiter. And when eventually the machine stops, when Milosevic draws his horns, the Croats pick up the marigold gauntlet and begin to do a bit of dirty work themselves; they bomb the Muslims too. And they go on for two or three years, and in the process take out all the bridges that cross the river, make some kind of ceremonial-vandalistic division of Muslim Bosnia and Christian Croatia and Herzegovina; most significantly, the Ponte Vecchio, a sixteenth-century piece of Italianate stone, dropped into the sea by massive shelling for reasons entirely non-strategic but immensely symbolic, particularly to those good Catholic Croats, those people with more churchgoers than Rome, with more baptisms than Paris, with more Pope-peekers than Austria.

Well, the bank-teller says: there's peace now. Yes; business is pretty much as usual; of course we can come and go across the river, now that life goes on, so we begin to walk down the way she's told us. We feel less paranoid about faces now, and the odd Croat football top passes on a kid's back. We cross a new bridge which is nasty and concrete, but which nonetheless has vaguely Muslim-style balustrades. And from the bridge, looking back and looking forward, you have a sense of how this town divided as the Muslims began to head back or be herded back into the Old Town where their Ottoman ancestors had once set up shop, and how the Croats held on to the other side. And a sense, too, of how things turned out when push came to shove. For across the river, on the other, Muslim, side, the top half of any building visible is strafed and pock-marked; on the other side, if anything, worse; looking back there are great swathes of waste land, demolition blocks, safety fences surrounding building sites where you mustn't walk for fear of uncleared mines.

We cross the bridge. Across the river the first port of call is the University, and then there's the Bus Station, where, we're told again, the bus to Medjugorje and all points Croat does not stop. Faces begin to change on the far side of the river: you feel further east, and the faces look not so much more Muslim as more Russian; in Croatia you could be in Italy, here you could be in Georgia, although there's a feeling of no fixed nationality as the town wanders along. There's odd, Muslimesque architecture built from Eastern Bloc breeze-block (an old communist tower block has been built to look vaguely like it could be Casablanca); there's also, as some kind of gesture among the rubble that begins to accumulate, on a street corner behind a ruined palazzo, just down from the wreckage of grand riverside hotels and public buildings, a bright new green Benetton shop.

Here, at the heart of the Turkish side of things, the violence to the architecture begins to take on a wantonness: so much artillery has been fired that it could not have been strategic, and must have been random, for every wall is Gorgonzola. We pass what was once the Islamic Club of Mostar, with traces of what were once minaret windows and are now rough-shod clere-stories. On the ground a gypsy girl begs by holding a baby and keeping up a relentless clicking by hammering an old pair of shoes on the cobbles; I give her something, then retreat, in haste. On the next corner there's a graveyard, which looks almost accidental in its higgledy-piggledyness; you read the gravestones, as you do, and with a sharp tender shock it becomes clear that every one of the two hundred crescent-marked plaques and stones and wooden memorials dates from either 1992 or 1993, that all are men, and all are in their twenties or thirties, except for the odd innocent. *Macsumic Nersada, 1993–1993*; it looks like an engraver's typo, until the horribleness of his one year's span dawns. The temperature rises and the gypsies start to follow us; gallantly, if unnecessarily, one or two locals ruthlessly scare them away. There is no *Ave Maria* here, though.

Another street corner graveyard passes by and we take a wrong turning, and end up walking down a lane, past a third graveyard, again where a building has been cleared. I'm inclined to turn round, but there's a sign at the end, and we wander into what is clearly a tourist trap from the old days, which, unlike the others, still runs. It's the Turkish House, and – pardon the mixing of Arab metaphors – it's a delight and an oasis. Inside there are woven sofas, star screens, pictures of copper-beaters and basket-makers and be-fezzed people making pots and pans; there are hats, prayer-mats, pipes, hookahs, cloths and stunning bedspreads; there are Islamic drawings and photos of river-bank minarets on the wall and poignant shots of the Ponte Vecchio on the wall; the air is still and cool and gorgeous, here in this perfect preservation of a battered culture-in-exile; above all, inside, there's a sweetness in the air, a richness the dry and dusty, flat streets of bomb-preserved Medjugorje can't get near.

On the way out we pause in a shady courtyard and the old woman who watches the place wants to sell us a postcard in exchange for having held the place open a little past closing time. We reach into pockets and produce some Croat *kuna*; and while she doesn't quite spit on it, she makes it clear that Deutschmark or dinar is the only order of the day. We have none. She curses us, I think, as we go, promising to find a bank and come back. It strikes me as ironic that I now have Allah as well as the Virgin to contend with, both of them raining disfavours on my head; it's no more than we deserve, since we don't go back, but move deeper into the heart of dark, central Europe.

The smell of Turkish coffee begins to fill the air, thick and black. Men are sitting on the corners. There's a Turkish consulate, a Turkish flag. The roads get narrower; there's a market of watermelon and bananas; a band of young boys play Kasbah music on the street corner and the tack shops start to appear, selling prayer-mats and hookahs and jugs and pots in beaten brass. Minarets appear, and mosques, along with an American-run office of Restauracija, Rekonstrucija, & Revitalizacija, where they tell me in stern PC terms that there is no such thing as the Turkish community here, and invite us to lunch; but we have no dinar, no dollar, so we wander on to the end, where, just across the bridge, if they could be fagged to make the journey, or if they weren't so full of hatred for the Croats and their dirty deeds, any of them could go and cash in our coins . . .

But, of course, where there was once a bridge there's just a big hole. Yes, say the Americans' documents, up on display, the Old Town and the settlements on both sides together made the stone necklace of the Neretva, and the Old Bridge symbolized the integration of Bosnia and Herzegovina. Yes, they say, the breaking of the bridge, the destroyers hoped, would symbolize the break-up of a relatively successful ethnic collaboration. And, yes, the fact is that the city can be called the European Hiroshima, done over once by the Serbs and the Chetniks, done over again by the Croats and the HVO. As we linger by the replacement IFOR bridge – a rough construction of timber, solid enough, but utilitarian, the mosques start their one o'clock song; and none of the traders even though the Croat bank is just across the river, will take our kuna. Compare Medjugorje, where the Croat traders make sure that every Winking Jesus has a price in sterling, in dollars, in Deutschmarks, in kuna; where every fiscal language is spoken.

We decide to head back, to spread the word, and we stop only to take pictures of the destruction on the other side, where the Stalinist Boulevard had become the dividing line between the two sides. An eloquent testimony to human division: the apartment blocks are in tatters, with some people living above burned out apartments. At 44 Lunescukova the Bosnia symbol is on the wall of a blacked-out building and the building still smells of burned-out wood; we pick the shell of a bullet out of the wall. We look into a huge wheelie bin, turned on its side, riddled with bullets; placed, no doubt, in front of a sniper. On the Boulevard, the trees are cut down and every building smashed to pulp. A big graveyard runs up the hill towards where we're bound. Every stone – or hunk of wood – is, again, a 1992 grave. But this time – on the near side of the river – some are crosses, some are crescents and stars. Made from bricks, from stones, from pieces of picket fence; some have people to look after them, some not.

It seems to me like the saddest place in the world. We head back to the happy Catholic bubble, to Medjugorje, where the Virgin still recommends the inner peace to be found in the rosary. It's another of those moments when we return to the Pansion at another time from the rest, and, again and accordingly, we're given a little clap, are the objects of much clucking and communality. But this time we are prophets not really welcome in this our country. We show our testimony – James's digital video machine can play back in miniature. But what we meet is a group armed with Danjela's tour-guide tales. The rest have cruised the country while she's told them stories of massacres of Franciscans by Muslims. 'Isn't it wonderful,' says Errin, 'how

the Croats kept their faith, in spite of all that happened to them?'
Lawrence and the Essex girls slightly demur, but from Nora
Batty and Angela and the Yukon Yakker there's more forcible
agreement when Valerie says, with an attempt at troubledness,
'It's because of all that out there that the peace you find here is
so special.'

The longing for someone to confess becomes almost
unbearable.

'His flesh shrank together as it felt the approach of the ravenous
tongues of flames, dried up as it felt about it the swirl of stifling
air. He had died . . .'

*How does a young man react to his sexual initiation, when the rose-
pink flush to the face − and the rose-pink flush to other places, too −
finally fades and dies? In the secular world, the world of non-Kaffliks,
Stephen supposes male youth responds predictably: by being smug, or
embarrassed; by boasting, or by being discreet; by becoming determined,
or resolved; by getting to work on it − working to bring about more of
the same, to develop new knowledge, to become a comfortable expert,
as one would with any life skill; naturally, in other words. Even a quasi-
egghead such as he is might be able, by reading and study, to become a
normal member of the normally sexually driven human race by − in
calm periods − gradually acquiring the skills to attain new and greater
heights, to be more and more pleasing, ever more thorough, ever more
knowledgeable, ever more fulfilling. But Stephen does none of these
things; what Stephen does is to go to confession.*

*This act of repentance, this apology for an apology of an act of love,
does not happen immediately; he is not immediately thrown into
repentance by a hell-fire sermon, as Joyce's Stephen is; he does not feel
the flames of hell licking round his feet, nor feel the sharp edge of
conscience emasculating him; he does not seek to amend his life, as
Stephen Dedalus does with misguided intensity, before the sight of the*

girl on the beach at Howth prompts him to reverse his well-intentioned decision. In the case of our Stephen, various other encounters occur; other scenarios are played out between the girl's curiosity and thirst for knowledge and experience and his hapless capacity to go where her music takes him, his ill-defined ill-driven determination to pursue that heady and mysterious final moment. (For, as Marlon Brando likes to say, the penis has its own agenda; as the months go by Stephen places several items in the minutes of the last meeting.) There remains something like love there, too, though the romanticism gradually gives way to opportunism, and it's buried too deep in all the other stuff to be spoken of too evangelistically.

No: Stephen's act of repentance happens when, in another echo of the story of the other Stephen, he finds himself being eyed up by the Jesuit vocation-spotters. This happens less for his piety than for the sake of family tradition, he supposes, but nonetheless it happens; he is invited to a retreat-house in Liverpool, where certain people make it clear they are working out whether he might be suitable to follow his uncles into the Jesuits. There is talk of a free sixth-form place at Stonyhurst, the Jesuit academy, by way of a familial quid pro quo; talk of a different order of things altogether from the dark stony teenage path he seems to be blundering along, with his trysts, with his finger-fuck meetings in cinemas and bus-shelters. Along with three other boys he is taken away for a week or a long weekend to a house where something ends up being salvaged; where, bizarrely, what seems sure to be dead and buried has a sudden and startling renaissance.

In later life he will have some respect for confession, for the Sacrament now known officially as Repentance, especially when the outsiders have a go at it, when the mockers mock what they see a very convenient Kafflik habit: sin all you like, in the manner of Saint Augustine, then get it off your chest by requesting forgiveness in a dark box with a grille. He knows from some corner of his teaching that there is more to it than this, that in order to be absolved one must reach a state of perfect repentance, a state in which the confessee, faced with the confessor behind *that grille, genuinely and intensely feels so sorry that he is convinced he will not offend again; for otherwise, whatever the penance done, whatever the form taken, the sin will still be there, a great stain on the soul. Even when he has stopped observance, confession, properly understood, seems to Stephen to be a way of facing one's conduct, of being responsible to someone or something other than oneself, and he knows plenty of people who could do with being made to feel that from time to time.*

But at the time when he confesses his sexual sins, confession has not been in the habit of being as significant as this. So what has it been, as he has dragged himself through this time of ritual and romance? Like so many other elements, it has been a routine learned back at the earliest age in this journey, along with prayers and graces and the answers to questions; a rhythm, something scarcely felt, though observed, something under the eye of the priest. The age of seven or eight or nine, he recalls, finds him (having of course been properly prepared) making his way to that wooden box in the side-aisle of the church, hearing the swish of the curtain, using, for the first time, the words that will become familiar, that he will spout four-weekly until he drifts away into indifference towards whatever sins he has committed. Bless me, father, for I have sinned. It has been two *(or three or four – not sagacious to admit to more than this)* weeks since my last confession. I have – *And the list follows: at nine, those harmless, venial offences – disobedience, lies, not honouring thy father and thy mother.*

Later it becomes a routine in a different sense, a sort of intellectual game: the trick, as a twelve- or thirteen-year-old, being to encourage the priest to believe he is in the presence of someone mature and genuine. I've told lies, and I've been disobedient, and although that is all I could think of, but of course – *the voice dribbling with sincerity* – I'm sorry for what I couldn't think of as well. *The priest, seemingly impressed by this young yet all-encompassing voice, offers forgiveness in the words of his own routine, the other part of the equation:* I absolve you in the name of the Father, and of the Son, and of the Holy Spirit *and offers an appropriate penance, according to the* old routine: a few prayers, perhaps, which Stephen says, or half-says. Say three 'Our Father's, three 'Hail Mary's and one 'Glory Be'. And say a prayer for me. Thank you, my son. *And thank you, father.*

A comfortable habit, then – not for everyone, of course (Fr. M tells a story at a retreat once of Blessed Matt Talbot, who wears chains on his knees when he is penitential) – but for the bourgeois boys in green blazers. But suddenly, in this retreat-house in Liverpool, for a half-hour or so, for a minute or two, for a true moment of perfection, maybe – everything changes. The change is unexpected: Stephen and his friends have packed a couple of bottles to get them through the days, since the word 'retreat' is not a positive to them; but the arrival is different from the journey, as all good pilgrimages must be; whatever happens there, in the house, the alcohol is never touched. The place is staffed with three unstuffy Jesuits a mile away from everything he has so far experienced, three new-schoolers who do some talking and a little bit of thought-provoking in the early part of the day, who (it is a revelation to discover) make it clear that some things are discussable without resort to the small print of rules and regulations, without discussion of the significance of alb and chasuble, without mention of any interest in Elvis Presley.

The priests have little else on; it would usually be busier, but this is a free week for the place, and Stephen and his friends, this little group of potential priests, are the only guests. So they play snooker with the boys in the evenings (cue-racks are the outstretched hands of statues of St Francis of Assisi, St Martin de Porres, St Joseph and St Theresa of Avila, stripped modernizingly from the chapel up above); and in the daytimes they talk to them a little about this and about that, about moral questions and about behavioural ones. Mainly they act by leaving the boys to themselves; there's a deal that they mustn't leave the premises, but otherwise they are free to think about their lives and the places where they've been, and to decide what is going to happen next in them.

And something does happen next. Sure, he already knows that he has not the patience, the other-worldliness, the meditative wish that will see him join this or any other Order. But something else: at the end of the week Stephen seeks out the company of one of them, a bear of a man in a dog-collar, and asks for a few moments to discuss certain events that have been occupying his mind. And face to face – not hidden behind a swishing curtain, as it is usually done in the Bless me, Father mode, but in an open office, sitting on interview chairs, he confesses, in a detailed way, to everything he has done in the weeks and months before. The Jesuit laughs – chortles kindly, at any rate – at his opening, when he starts talking about 'sins of impurity' (he has no other phrase, no other language to describe these matters); but he does go on and listen carefully as Stephen describes how push came to shove.

Of course it is embarrassing, is blushworthy, to lay certain cards on the table, for Stephen to, metaphorically speaking, place his flaccid organ in front of the priest for inspection for vile disease, as if the priest were a venereal disease surgeon. But, significantly, the priest is not interested in when, my son, or where, my son, or how many times, my son. He cuts straight to the chase, to the more important part, to the human part; with a deadly, unchortling seriousness, he comes to examine the reasons why, or why not we might have done these things, and whether, or whether not to carry on doing them. He says that the important thing about sin is not to count it, but to understand it, to probe the nature of it, to feel its relation to the world in which you live and the people that you meet and against whom you may have offended; a silly phrase, he says, but what is meant is true: he asks him to examine whether, and to whom, what he has done is harmful.

Stephen does examine, and still does; to this day he is not sure of the answer. But there is a shorter immediacy of efficacy: he leaves the room feeling better, lighter than he has at any time in these months of deceit and darkness; feeling that the slate is clean, experiencing, for the first time – and probably too late – the sense of the possibility of things that religious people, people of faith, must feel every day. He knows later that there are other possibilities, that all he has done is find an ear to listen and a voice to speak. But what was clear, and is clear, is that *for a moment there, in the idealistic sense one is supposed to be, in the purest possible way, Stephen is a Kafflik, in tune with the world in which he has been raised, but also in tune with what he has turned out to be.*

And what if, the first night he is back home, he is led up the garden path again for a quick sin of impurity behind the bike sheds? He has felt something which – whether he believes a word or not now – means that he is different; means that he has had a vision of something endlessly possible.

VII
Last Rites

St Lydwina of Schiedam
Feast: April 14
Patron Saint of Roller-Skaters
(also Figure Skaters and Sufferers of Bodily Ills)
Injured, aged sixteen, in a skating accident, Lydwina suffered a plethora
of pains. Abscess, gangrene, migraine, vomiting, fever, chronic dehydra-
tion, bedsores, toothache, muscle-spasm, neuritis – all were cheerfully
ascribed to God's plan for her, and Christ himself is said to have come
to administer her Last Rites.

It's the last evening in Lourdes, though there's near enough a full day left to endure before we actually leave. When I moan about too many nights spent on my own Roger tells me that there's going to be a party at another hotel, the Solitude maybe, and why don't I come? It's a group who travel together, his mate Eric's group, in fact, from Warrington or wherever it is, who come every year; and on the last night it seems they always have a sing-song in the hotel bar, apparently, for there's a piano and beer on tap, not out of bottles; it's a home from home, it seems. So we make our way in caravan along there about eight: Roger, Margaret his mother in the chair, Margaret the friend on her own two pegs, and me.

When we get there, the room is divided. The men are sitting along one wall and in the near-alcove booth-like things, while the women are wrapped in a semi-circle against the far wall. Eric buys a round, then disappears into the mob; he's already well-ensconced, well on his way. Roger then buys me a pint of lager and I buy him one back; he drinks all three quickly, as if relieved, for his mother has been carried off into the warm embrace of the women's side where, he tells me, a shift-system of friends and relatives and anyone from Warrington with a large enough dollop of charity has been arranged to take care of her. I can see her throughout the evening, and hear her sweet wayward maternal banalities filling the air like birdsong whenever the human singing stops. ('He's a good boy to me. An angel. Never forgets to come and see me. He should have had that other job. I've three telephones . . .')

The scene is nostalgic to me; it comes straight from my childhood. On my father's side of my big Kafflik family, every wedding and every funeral (before the late Sixties and early Seventies brought more in the way of brass in pocket and jumped-up social aspiration) was held in the Sacred Heart Social Club in my grandfather's town, which was not a million miles from where these come from. Over here, where the men are, would be plates of buffet food – stale white-bread sandwiches and offal-full pork pies; over there, where the women sit, tables packed with obscure cousins, with aunties, with uncles, with nephews. Over there, by the fruit machine, a permanent fixture, a man called Shoeshop Freddie, who'd once taken out my Aunt Monica. And over *there* – a microphone, and stand, a place where (wedding or funeral, it didn't matter, though the dead were usually given a few minutes more grace than the recently married) members of the family would get up and do a turn. Aunties would lilt ballads, uncles recite Stanley Holloway mono-logues, music-teacher second-cousins would sing 'And I Love You So' with the PA system creaking under the un-Perry-Comoesque high tone-rush of the chorus. For, yes, he knew how lonely life could be . . .

And here it's the same. No sandwiches, of course – the Lourdais system means that these people are all exceedingly well-fed, have all been stuffed to their jowly gills at the time laid down by the authorities – but the pints are on the table and have a tendency to multiply miraculously, and the broad faces of the old men, and the slim faces of the old ladies seem nothing if not entirely, and rather wonderfully, familiar. I'm introduced to the men only, as they're, in both senses, on my side. Jimmy. Tommy. Bernie. Paddy. Liam. Fr. Dan. Fr. Fahey, from Canada, just along for the ride, y'know, but as good an Irishman as ever you'll meet and a smashing tenor. And Fr. Brendan, the competition judge, in slacks, sandals and checked shirt, who has, as every year, strict instructions to make sure the 'ladies' win.

The pints – and they're something with a bit of body, something with some bite – slop back, and the banter flies back and forth: where are you, Shoeshop Freddie? He could be here, if he wasn't dead twenty years; but other faces look familiar as through the male repertoire we go, individual Jimmys or Tommys climbing up to give it laldie. Young Billy gives it 'The Wild Rover'. Old Tommy sings 'My Old Donegal Home'. We all chime in when Dennis chants 'Molly Malone', and stays up for 'You'll Never Walk Alone'. Jimmy or Tommy does 'Danny Boy', and Tommy or Jimmy does 'The Rose of Tralee'. And, alternately, one of the Marys or the Junes or the Roses or, of course, the Margarets, putting down her dry Martini or her vodka and orange or – for there is some flash here – her Campari and soda, climbs up and offers a song, sometimes wheezed anciently, sometimes brassed out with wim and wigour and certainly with a brio equal to anything offered by the men. 'Roll Out the Barrel' sings one. 'Auld Lang Syne' sings another. 'Land of Hope and Glory' sing a duo, solo-shy. 'Loch Lomond' follows. And 'Armagh'. Everything except 'These Are My Mountains', which is a shame, since I do feel some sense of leadership.

231

Fr. Brendan makes a good fist of an adjudicatory spoof-speech, and after a humming and hawing of positively Eurovision proportions, announces the result that never varies from year to year; that the women are victorious by the slenderest of margins; and all the men make noises as if they care, faces red and animated and pretend-pugnacious. Roger and I sit and laugh and our intake, fuelled by contributions from many Tommys, happy to have added a stranger to the party, goes up to perhaps six or seven pints, which, pilgrim or not, is far too much for me, and when I get up I'm very unsteady on my pegs. One of the Jimmys – it's the price for the distaff victory, it seems – gets up and does a little encore, a little closer – *There's one little place that I'll never forget*, it goes, *That's Lourdes, the village of St Bernadette* – and those of us not resident in the hotel spill out into the Lourdais night. For some unfathomable reason I end up pushing Rog's mother's chair back to the Roissy, taking a somewhat controversial line as far as my sense of direction is concerned; when they leave me, I go to bed and manage to sleep in spite of the spins.

In the black, shuttered night, I dream of travelling with a friend and a man whose one-armedness is disguised by a long, woollen sleeve. For some reason, in our dialogue, I use the word 'flid', a horrible, disability disparaging word that came into use at school in the wake of a fertility drug disaster, the 'spas' of thenadays. The man produces from his woolly his thalidomide-short arm and it all descends into accusation, and I wake much earlier than I intend. But however early it is, when I wake I do not know that in the black, shuttered night Roger, desperate to talk, has gone down to the Grotto now, at two, two-thirty, pissed out of his brain, but desperately needing to finish off his conversation: a last mother-free chance to talk properly with the love of his life before he goes home.

I have a pulsing headache first thing in the morning – the Virgin

232

of Lourdes unfortunately having roused me betimes, no doubt for her own special purposes and at Big Margaret's special pleading – and one of those hangovers that's vertiginous and that makes me feel the shapelessness of my Lourdes week more than ever, whatever the visible signs of achievement that others show. I am back buying endless cans of overpriced Coca-Cola at the stalls around the Grotto, on the basis that the filling fizz will do more for me than any substance arising out of the spring within, but it has little effect; I'm doomed to suffer badly for my blasphemously boozy behaviour.

When I come by the Basilica I see, by the steps of the church, the Liverpool pilgrims having their end-of-pilgrimage photo taken. It's a big group photo, like a public school shot, and it's a matter of mass participation and enthusiasm; they make the photo-op a hooly, with the youth (especially) singing and clapping along to 'Rise and Shine', 'Pick Up His Glory', 'Children of the Lord', and 'He's Got the Liverpool Yeuth in His Hands'. At first it's a holy-hooly, but soon the religious theme vanishes and instead we're on to local favourites: 'In My Liverpool Home', 'Saturday Night at the Movies' (they make a song and dance of it), 'Help!', and, de rigueur, 'You'll Never Walk Alone'. During this great surge towards the future I sit on my backside on the benches and watch the children play, my head aching in my hands; I do walk alone.

The photographer finishes, and runs off to his next engagement. Everywhere you go in Lourdes you're liable to be knocked down by the pilgrim-paparazzi who, manically scheduled, run everywhere with ladders taking photographs of pilgrims – at mass, in procession, in the street. The photographers display them in boutiques where pilgrims can buy pictures of themselves. I have, over the week, wondered whether, like some demented schoolboy in a long unwinding shot, I can run around the town, my face appearing on the boards of many nations

– on pictures of pilgrims from Roma, from Galway, from Kaiserslautern, from Kuala Lumpur. On a whim I make my way into one of the booth-like shops and – to my shock – find myself depicted.

First I'm big, walking in a crowd of Liverpudlians entering the Basilica on the first day. I imagine a long-lost friend seeing me there and imagining me zealous; or a long-lost enemy finding in my face a reason to track me down, a sinister sub-plot in a detective story. And then I see myself as I suspect I really am, as I was in the beginning and now and ever shall be; at the opening service, the Mass of Welcome, there I am loitering at the back under the ugly, brutalist, fretwork roof, a single white-shirted, faceless figure in a row of empty seats.

Only connect, I think to myself. I wander back into the Domaine in the hope that something will do it. I find myself next to a little room underneath the arches of the walkway that wanders up to the Esplanade above the Domaine, tucked into the wall near the Accueil, I find a little Museum of Miracles, a teeny archive-cum-shrine to those cured while on pilgrimage to Lourdes in the hundred years or so that folk have been wending their way here. Two thousand five hundred names are listed. (Only sixty-five have passed successfully through the committees and the sub-committees, the councils and the sub-councils of the Vatican corridors, but what of that?) These are those that would prove it, if proof can be had; those whose bodies have mysteriously lost whatever ailed them after a visit to the healing waters.

I scan the displays, eager to give the place one last chance. Whoever does the curing in this place seems to have a particular efficacy with tuberculosis; there are a zillion daguerreotypes of skinny, rickety-looking *malades tuberculaires* of many nations. But it seems that it's not just the lungs that are cured when that spoonful of celestial sugar makes the medicine go down in the most delightful way. No, not at all: there's a remarkable collection of diseases, of maladies, of mortifications, and one can't help but be struck as the numbers and the pictures build around the room. I pick out a few as I drift around. Francis Pascal, *merveille numéro 45, cécité et paraplégie flasque post-méningitique.* Vittorio Micheli (Miracle 63), cured of a *tumeur maligne du type sarcome.* Madame Edeltraud Fulda (55), meanwhile, *Maladie d'Addison.* And then, with a sharp tender shock, I discover that one of those for whom a cure is claimed is called John Traynor, and that he travelled with the Liverpool Pilgrimage party – as official diocesan sick – in the early part of this century.

His problems are best described in English. 1914: Traynor goes off to the front and contracts that well-known trench disease known as shrapnel, to which he adds a severe case of bullets the following year. They paralyse his left arm, it seems, and leave him subject to epileptic fits, which gradually worsen to include helplessness of the double-incontinence sort. Pretty much your standard terminal, incurable invalid then – a trepanned skull, drooling, pissing himself, unsaintly in all ways – and when he embarks on the Liverpool Diocesan Pilgrimage of 1923 it is thought he might be one of those for whom the journey itself, let alone the excitement of arrival, will be too much, one of those for whom the best that can be hoped is that they see Lourdes and die.

And there's not much to the contrary to tell except that, on that 1923 trip, not only does he reach the Grotto but begins, as soon as he gets there, to feel something in his leg; that he is soon up and about; and that he is later that year found to be completely cured; and that, when he returns to Lourdes in 1928 he is fit as a butcher's dog and runs barefoot from the hospital to the Grotto. After 1923 it seems he goes home and becomes a haulier, and for twenty years lifts two-hundred-pound sacks of coal every day; he lives until 1945, and dies in doubly appropriate fashion for the ways of his life. His choice of death-day – the Feast of the Immaculate Conception – suits his Marian devotion; his choice of method – appropriate homage to a life of heavy lifting – was a strangulated hernia.

If only all searches ended with such clarity. I am lost and lonely in Lourdes – I haven't done well here, I know – and I take my hangover outside, and climb the esplanade walkway round the side of the Basilica until I'm high, high above the crowds. I see again the ordinariness of this town – its chateau and shops, its piscine and pubs, its higgledy-piggledy houses beginning the climb up to the Pyrenees. I see again the extraor-dinariness – that the roof of the Rosary Basilica is in fact a golden crown, that the Grotto is attended by thousands upon thousands of people on this ordinary morning. I see new things, too: how the concourse around the Grotto-taps is soaked with spilled holy water. (The queuing faithful, from above, look like they're standing in a great big puddle.) How the latest group gathering to get their photograph taken has a comic detail that no one at home will see, for in the back row the dark hand of an Italian branc rests neatly on the pretty, lithe backside of a handmaid.

I walk back down again, and seeking refuge from the sun, drift into the Basilica itself. On the walls people of many nations have left the mark of moments of revelation that I have only momently shared. A graveyard in reverse, it has marble slabs everywhere, but the tablets speak of coming back to life rather than passing over to the other side; in many languages, they make a Babel of miracles. RECONNAISSANCE, O MARIE, POUR TANT DE GRACES OBTENUES. IN ATTESTADO DI RICONOSCENZA PER GRACIA RICEVUTA. DANK DER LB. GOTTESMUTTER. WDZIEZNOSE MITASE UNIELBIENIE METTLIE. CHUNG CON DOI ON DUC ME CHE CHO CHONC

CON LUON GIA-DINH PHERO TRAN-NGOC-LIE. Something
in Cyrillic, too. And names, which bring the miracles closer –
the Comtesse de Canclaux, John B. Flachs of Hamilton, Ontario,
Pham Thuy Tien, Patrick and Nora Duggan, Konstancya San-
guszko and – a man from a limerick – G. Falla of Guatemala.
They list their blessings. One is saved from a shipwreck, another
has a longed-for son, another passes an exam, another has a son
safe home from Algeria; an old woman finds her son suddenly
uplifted; a husband, for all I know, says thank you for the happy
passing of his wife.

Something is achieved, some connection made. Outside again
I come across a mass in the little bandstand on the concourse.
It's the Liverpool one, the closing one – I seem to have lost
touch with the official itinerary – and in the middle of it the
loyalty of those who have helped is being rewarded. Win, for
instance, and Forearm-Smash Margaret pick up their medals
for one or three or five or twenty pilgrimages successfully
completed; some brancs come forward, too, to be rewarded
with a gong and a clap. Works and days have been completed,
corporal mercies delivered, even if no John Traynor has walked
barefoot this year.

Afterwards, there's another line-up on the steps; another
photo. This one's for official sick people only. By now the faces
are familiar – people I've met, or talked to, in one case pushed
around the park by the river. As I stand there, big Margaret
comes up and – kind, forgiving – tells me tales; of those who
are on their last legs when they leave Liverpool; of those who die
en route; of those for whom, at Lourdes station, there's an
ambulance waiting so that they can be brought straight to the
Grotto where, more often than not, she says, they pass away
with the stress or perhaps the relief of the thing, as their relatives
intone the comforting, if platitudinous sentiment that to die

there was just what they would have wanted. Right at the centre of the group, perched on the steps, I see John the Aviator. And his eyes still burn bright and serene, just as they did a day or two ago. He looks raised up. He looks like he has found a belonging. He is not looking for his mother.

So there are successes: miracles, and miracles of the mind, too. It's only me who has failed, who is sick and tired, but mainly sick, since the walk back to the hotel has me going again. So it's more Coca-Cola at the Little Flower with Roger and Margaret. Then it's lunch: a queasy, greasy experience which finally makes me realize that I can't hope to get where I want to get. Only once we begin the sit-on-suitcase resting in the lobby of the hotel do I find relief. And who gives it? Win, of course, even to someone she knows does not believe. Once I've finally decided that I cannot fly like this she takes me down to the storeroom of the hotel, where she has her Alka-Seltzers, and she digs them out, and I take one, sitting in the lobby of the Roissy. It has the effect I want, and I only just make it to the lav, dashing across the Roissy lobby with a mouthful of the stuff, resisting the lure to find it all symbolic of *my* time in this place at the foot of the Pyrenees, this Palma of Pilgrimages.

All the Lourdes pilgrims are brought together in the Roissy bar, waiting for a bus that's late. Win and Carol sit together. Win has just completed her final aromatherapy sessions; on patients at the Accueil, getting them ready for the journey home, but also on Carol, to relax her, on Cheryl, to chill her out. (I too have had her therapy.) The rest look pale with fatigue; she looks irrepressible. Since knocking off at the baths she has taken Albert, some old guy who has lost his mother, for his tea at the Little Flower; and she's taken Edith, another official, shopping. Oh, and she'll be back to do her own devotions, come October-time.

Roger is there, too, telling me he is closer to understanding the mysterious ways of things. He seems in tune, practical, remembers a forgotten present and leaves me to deal with his mother. 'My son – he's an angel,' she witters. 'He should have had that other job. Always comes and sees me whenever I want; and looks after me. Never a thought for himself. And they said that Russia would be converted, and now it's happening! He's an angel – never swears, never puts a foot wrong. Yes – I've a good son, and three telephones.' Roger returns, smiling, with a little package, and he sits cuddled up in the corner with the photo-journal he never let me see.

The Archbishop is in the bar, too, and I buy him a Fanta by way of thanks for reminding me of the good things that people in this religion say. He's relieved, he says: a humble man is relieved. He has five weeks off; he is going away: to his sister's, in Dayton Ohio. What's there, I ask. 'Precisely nothing. A river runs through it,' he says, 'but otherwise it's a place without features. No museums. Nothing at all about which anyone would say do this now, do that now.' A place that has no draw for anyone; a place without din; that's what he wants after a week amongst the miracle shrines of southern France.

In the coach back to Tarbes I manage to keep my stomach intact, though it's a challenge, and I sit and spend my last few francs on some mineral water, praying for the end. At the airport, a cheesy rep tells us the plane has broken down and has been replaced by two, one leaving earlier than the other. It seems a party of priests has already stitched up a flight on the early one. Roger muses cynically about how the party was chosen: 'Like the choosing of the apostles, I suppose,' he says, 'or maybe not . . .'

Fr. Gerry, the programme seller, is not among them. He circulates. When he sees me, he comes over to warn me that the last writer who covered Liverpool at Lourdes had to retract half the things he said. On the plane he leads the prayers for guidance, protection and a safe arrival home. We fly through the clouds over Jersey on radar only. It seems to me to require a small act of faith. 'On a Wing and a Prayer,' says Roger, looking outside at the thick black cloud. 'There's a title for you –' And when we touch down, another Miracle of the Mind is complete, to my mind anyway: I haven't barfed in a bag.

St Drogo
Feast: April 16
Patron Saint of Coffee Bar Owners
(also of Unsightly People)
Invoked Against Broken Bones and Ruptures
Drogo was traumatized to learn that his mother had died giving birth
to him. He became a penitential pilgrim, embracing mortifications and
bodily disfigurement, living only on barley, water and the Eucharist.

Our movement out of Medjugorje is coming soon, too; and I get up on the last day to hear a full-scale family argument going on among the Simpsons, because Paul refuses to venture out and climb even the smaller of the hills. I say climb the hill: what this means, in fact, is that he will have spent the whole week without leaving the hotel, except for journeys at lunchtime to cafés and in the evening to bars. I make a little mental note to try to remember, as the day proceeds, anything he's done apart from sit on the patio and smoke cigarettes. But walking up the town for a drink is all I can come up with by the time I'm walking up the town for a drink with them. Sally-Ann – she has recovered her spirits, knowing it's the last day; she's ready to roll, in tight white jeans and a shirt that shows off her belly-button – says to him, at the table: 'You know what? If you made a video diary of *your* holiday, it'd only last two minutes . . .'

I suggest a more charitable theory which includes his interest in all things oriental and the fact that every night the poor girls who wash and cook for us have to come out and sweep the gravel of the driveway to cover his Superking butts: he is involved in religious activity; he's making a Zen garden. I take a raincheck on lunch (they're eating out on Simpson *mère*'s credit card as a solution to having run out of ready money) and wander up towards the church, where I'm urged by the rest of the mob – all the familiar faces – to pull up a chair in Lukas's place. As the drinks arrive I feel relieved to have left the fag-smoke and dysfunction behind. I look around, and I do feel, at some level, that it has been a genuine pilgrimage in this sense: that we've searched for some kind of truth together, all of us, here at these tables, over tea and cakes and ices: now it's time to see if we can push the moment to a crisis.

Discussion is bitty at first. Mary-Ann becomes revelatory, quiet in my corner, away from the older folks: 'I've been thinking about a lot of things. I was quite promiscuous in college, you know, and Dick and I had a healthy sex-life. Did you know that we spent our last weekend together in bed? The whole weekend? I'm increasingly taken with the idea that maybe I fucked him to death.' Nora Batty, arriving late, shows off her purchases. She's been shopping again, for the third time this week, and arrives with a 120-dollar gold cross on a chain. Cecilia corners me and awards me the set of rosaries she promised, and urges me to keep them with me wherever I go. 'If you're in trouble,' she says, 'just touch them; will you do that? They keep you from evil, and we all need that.' We do. Lawrence sips his orange juice and smiles inwardly. James, who has been banned by his mother from going to Sarajevo, or Split, for a night away, as he'd hoped – Mostar was the mostest, as far as he is concerned – scowls inwardly and tries to make the best of it.

After a bit we get to talking about the place, and how it's going to develop. This involves a fair helping of the Medjugorje

241

mumbo-jumbo: for after the last message to the visionaries, Cecilia says, it's said that a permanent sign, directed at non-believers will be passed on and then spread via priests worldwide. Cecilia says that she doesn't know why, but she just has a sense that that will be *soon*, that things will be winding down here. I ask whether it's thought that Mary will reappear somewhere else where there's trouble or war or strife, but they think not; Lawrence says that the Virgin of Medjugorje has told people that this will be her last appearance on earth. Nora Batty half-corrects him: 'On *this* earth,' she says, and although I've no idea what she's saying I kind of know what she means.

Lawrence is interesting on the visions and the visionaries. He says that what strikes him about the Virgin's appearances, wherever in the world they happen, is that they all happen in front of people who have what he calls 'nascent' intelligence; people who are not very well educated. It's both an advantage – 'the message can be relayed with absolute exactness, without interpretation' – and a disadvantage – 'it prejudices more intelligent people against the message'. He thinks that what is going to happen is that the Virgin will stop appearing in the next millennium, but that someone 'more intelligent' will appear, such as the Baptist, and that the announcements will take on perhaps a little more in the way of meat. But it's clear he takes the content of the messages with a pinch of something not unlike a pinch of salt: 'I'm trying to believe – I'm willing to believe – that's my job – but there are certain things I won't accept.'

Encouraged, I finally decide to go boldly where no man has ever gone before, and I put on record with Cecilia some of my objections to apparitions. I mention hysteria, and other psychological syndromes of teenagers under collective stress. I describe, in some detail, the precise objections to Medjugorje made by the local bishop. I describe some of the trials of the week; my disappointment at what I feel is the limited range of the Virgin's message-making, especially when held up against the pain of political transition. And I ask, genuinely seeking, what she will do if the bishop's objections get meat on the bone. It's possible, I say, that the next Pope will not be like the present one, and a liberal regime might make its mark by coming down on Marianism. What if a future Pope decided against Medjugorje, I ask? What if it was suggested that doctrinally these ideas that were being expressed were not sound? Would she still believe in the visions? Would she be prepared to stand up for what was said here if standing up was disobedience under a future Vatican culture?

She flummoxes for a little bit. 'Are you asking me what I believe?'

'I'm asking you what you would do.'

'Because I believe in the One True Church,' she says.

'That's not the same thing,' says James.

With more patience, I repeat: 'But what if the Church spoke against these things here?'

'And there is no way on God's earth that the One True Church can say a word against what's happening here.'

James says, impatiently: 'Mum, you're not answering the question –'

'Do you hear me! Anyone who speaks against this place is doing the devil's work!'

She turns on James first. For a second she appears to be almost fighting for breath; she accuses him of being a cynic. Then she goes for me in the same vein, but she's not allowed. For Nora Batty, in a way that rolls the years back to my schooldays, in turn gets cross with me: 'Why are you always asking questions?'

I say, obtusely, that I think that asking questions is what going on pilgrimage is all about. Cecilia grabs her bag. She almost goes without a word, but stops: 'You', she says to me, 'are like those priests that take the statue of Mary out of the church: you're doing the devil's work.' And off she goes: to shop, she says, to stew, I think.

Lawrence sits and cradles his drink, and shakes his head. I can see he's tempted to come along with me, but something calls him otherwise; there's no way that I can be left with the idea that his disagreement with her means he agrees with me. 'Listen,' he says, patiently, 'I have faith. So the problems of a place like this don't bother me. I see inconsistencies and they pain me, but it's my view that without doubt there's no faith: if I don't examine everything I think and feel then it means nothing to me. I understand what you've been saying, that love thy neighbour is what your belief comes down to,' he says, 'and what you've been trying to show us is that these Croats don't. It's disappointing, I agree. The visionaries, too, disappointed me. They were repetitive. The priests disappointed me: I found them turgid and mundane.' He is solemn when he says these things. 'But what you must understand is that my *faith* is not affected. For me, these matters only work if I know and question. It's a dialectic thing, not an instinctive one. Faith is not faith which alters when it alteration finds, of course not, and on the journey you have a *duty* to enquire.'

He tells me that he has found a rhythm since our morning up the mountain; that he has been rising at four, and walking there each day, and that this morning, though it thundered and lightninged, he still made it to the top, the man of pure heart, and considerable affirming doubt, who can climb the Mountain of the Lord.

In the evening there's a heady, bright atmosphere back at the Pansion. Some, I suppose, glad to be going home; for others, jobs well done, stones laid, souls laid to rest. Some of course, disappear to say their prayers; others give the impression that their pilgrimage is done and that there's no reason not to crack open what's left of the Herzegovinian in Tomas's cellar.

I take a look around at those with whom I have passed on this journey from understanding to knowledge. Cecilia is not speaking to me, except to say that she'll be back; but that she doesn't expect me to be there. There are some whose paths and mine have hardly crossed – an old publican couple from the south coast invite me to come and have a pint at their place, and a brother from Ampleforth retires with the quiet, pompous dignity he came with. Errin and her daughter and the Petit Prince are staying another week; their eyes are bright. Valerie kisses me on the cheek and wishes me well. Mary-Ann tells me about leaving her prayer-stones up on the mountain. They mean, she says, that she has left her grief behind in this place, a 'noxious beast', without which she can more easily carry Electric Dick with her in her heart. It's clear she'll be okay; as if she's done the grief without the establishing shots. The Simpsons I don't see but after I take an early bed at eleven I hear them shouting on the patio at half-past one. I think they'll be okay too.

And, of course, so will Nora Batty and Angela and Cecilia. As, next morning, we descend the mountain and drive along the coastline of the ungodly ones, they sing some happy-clappy numbers and say the rosary. They will be back, in spite of the ice-cool courier telling us we should be building our own Krizevacs in the gardens of our houses, not troubling ourselves with returning. So everything can be put away, put behind me safely, including my own brush with speaking out. Except one thing: on the flight home Lynda, the sassy, young, hip black girl with the teaching job in Hackney and the family in Nigeria and the boyfriend in Chicago tells me a tale of being up on top of the mountain. And she tells me that up there, as clear as day, and without any possibility of contradiction, she saw the sun dance: saw it fill with a black disc and then watched as the red rim began to spin and spin and spin and promise the end of the world. What of that, her expression seems to say: it was a surprise, a pleasure, but no big deal. Her faith, her expression says, has deeper mysteries.

St Denis (Dionysius)
Feast: October 9
Invoked Against Demoniac Possession and Internal Strife
Denis, first Bishop of Paris, was martyred in 258. His beheaded body was seen to carry his severed head some distance from the axeman's block at Montmartre, so his killers threw his body in the Seine.

Sunday, 6.22 p.m. 'Let Our Ordered Lives Confess the Beauty of Thy Peace', or so they're singing as, on our way from Knock, we come to be passing, again, that place where I was conceived before my parents made their boat journey, like so many others of my ilk, to England and Scotland; we are back in Joycean lands, as we drift down the coast from the centre of the city out to the hinterland; it's the opposite journey from Joyce, in fact, whose impoverished family moved in, out of the salubrious sea air of the south and into the squalor of the place where he lost his virginity so memorably. The Martello Tower passes, and the forty-foot pool, and the sort of beaches where Stephen Dedalus and Leopold Bloom both gazed impurely on the girls bathing, and a hundred sites of *Dubliners*, before we come to Bray and our hotel.

I guess we should have known that we were being sent so far out only to save money, and the hotel where we end up is Fawlty Towers enough already without Sister Pius leading us on our merry way, without Luisa reminding her of her promise to get her a single room, or was it a pint pot? We stand in the lobby, in damp, dank air, on tacked-together mismatched Axminster, for what seems like hours, while Sister Pius is told there are no singles, that the phone system won't bear the weight of all those wake-up calls, that they were really expecting us very much earlier; I am chatting and smoking with a Burmese woman, who says she took up smoking under stress, which I'm inclined in my usual way to discount until she tells me the stress arrived when, at thirty-nine, her husband died, leaving her with eleven children to look after. By the time we're all sorted, everyone's tense; and that's without dinner, at which a Spanish waiter who doesn't speak English runs around under the eye of an eccentric proprietor, bringing as many wrong things as it's possible to bring.

Yes, of course, it's Manuel: everyone who asks for fish gets chicken, and everyone who asks for chicken gets fish; if you ask for nothing then you do get what you asked for, but to judge from appearances, this is of scant consolation. Mac and Nancy want water: he brings a single glass of water, then, when asked for more so that drink can be shared amongst the table ('We are travellers', Mac tries his verbal nobility again, 'tired from the road') he brings a perfectly miniature, and perfectly silver, pot of boiling stuff for tea. As for the brown sauce Edmund wants; well, it's a saga, not a story, and an unfinished saga at that. As Manuel's assistants, five big-titted bucolic-looking girls, carry plates of boiled-to-death vegetables to supplement our mismatched meals, one or two words start to fly, and one or two of the party are a little ungenerous in their attitudes; I, meanwhile, am saddled with Luisa, who sits at my table, having claimed me as her only friend, talking loudly about how there are no Christians in this party, which is – on a Kafflik pilgrimage – perhaps not the most tactful of ways of expressing displeasure at not being roomed according to her station.

Her meal becomes a rant, her rage her bread. She claims that everyone has been *staring* at her for demanding a single room, which was why she waited for me, and then she wants a *cigarette*, although she doesn't smoke, and all the time she utters, in her all-too-audible voice, notions that I really don't want anyone else to hear. No: she's *not* going to take it lying down, any of it, and she says so in garish estuary, in Mike Leigh-woman tones. 'That MAN!' she exclaims. (As she does she looks at some hapless individual, who smiles back beneficently.) 'That WOMAN,' she yaps. (As she does some eighty-six-year-old smiler passes by, handbag to hand, barely keeping the motor running.) 'I said to Sister Pius, Sister, don't PATRONIZE ME!' (Even Sister Pius, overhearing, manages a wan smile from the other side of the room.) 'I'm going to have a CIGARETTE!' Everyone who faces her seems to treat her warmly; yet she keeps up the chorus, the relentless barrage of insults at all and sundry and no one. 'They're LAUGHING at me!' Who? 'Your *friend* Edmund.' Edmund is not here yet; he comes in, and he's nice to her, calms her, talks to her. Only the woman from Stamford Hill, who perhaps justifiably feels her reputation has been a little impugned, seems to show any hostility at all, and she's weird; she couldn't hit a cow's backside with an emotional banjo. But, regardless, Luisa carries on: 'That's not RIGHT!' 'I'm SORRY, but that's not RIGHT!' 'I need to get angry and I WILL GET ANGRY!' 'It's my FAITH! I won't let THEM tell me what to do!' Slogans of self-counselled self-realization trip off her tongue; there's a new ritual there, I think, howsoever she's tied to the old one by upbringing and belief.

Later, at 9.15, there's Sunday mass, with bulbs in sockets hanging across between two chandeliers that don't work, in what is laughably called the Conference Suite. The sea is calm outside, and the last beachcombers are making their way along in the dim half-light as we all come together – Mac's tired travellers. Jude the Obscure is anything but: rising to an occasion

248

that needs a little direction, he takes responsibility, is perceptive; clearly feels we should be growing together, not falling apart, if this journey is to mean anything, and he has a message to give before it's too late. 'We thank God that our journey has come to an end here, and that we can celebrate the Eucharist together. At the end of a tiring journey we can feel stressed and weary, and when stressed and weary it is possible to hurt people, to say and do hurtful things. We ask God to help us in easing some of these wounds: if we are the hurter, we pray that we may be reconciled; if we are the hurt, we pray that we may find the strength to forgive.'

Luisa is beside me as he says this, and for the moment she is satisfied with an loud exhale; the disdain is pretty clear, but my inner embarrassmentometer reads only about two or three out of ten. Fr. Jude has the Chinese man read from Exodus – something about a long walk and holding fast, though it's not easy to make sense of – and the Nigerian woman read from Romans – something about how we are to be reconciled in the holy spirit, forcefully done. It's cosy, nice, uncontroversial, but somehow not without challenge as the tensions seethe and mutter under the surface of the gathering. The Gospel has the apostles giving without charge, and receiving without charge, and Jude's sermon describes the Israelites on their journey, waiting desperately to settle somewhere as they must go on to wherever they're going.

True to his word of the night before, when he talked of a commitment to narrative, he uses a story to illustrate: a man whose horse is his livelihood finds his horse has run away – his neighbours tut, bad luck, he says, good luck, bad luck, trust in God, the horse comes back with ponies, the neighbours cheer, good luck, the man says, good luck, bad luck, trust in God. One pony is wild, his son rides it, falls off and breaks his leg; the neighbours tut, bad luck, the father says, good luck, bad luck, trust in God. A war breaks out and all the young men of the place go off to fight and are killed – all except the man's son, stuck at home with the broken leg. The neighbours cheer, good luck, the father says good luck, bad luck, trust in God. 'When you have faith,' Jude says, concluding, 'then you can accept anything.' It seems obvious, clear, almost glib in its attempt to embrace and draw everyone together, but Luisa, with a Ph.D. in the science of self-realization, is not having any of it. First there's another exhale, then a *hiss*, then a HISS! with an exclamation mark, then: 'RUBBISH!' she says. 'That's just not TRUE!'

'We need,' says Jude, calm, looking at her, 'to grow in the attitude that says, "Thy will be done."'

Luisa puffs, then PUFFS, then tuts again. 'NO! That's NOT what we have to do,' she says, almost quietly; though meant just for me, it's louder than any other voice in the room. 'What we've got to do is look after OURSELVES!'

'It's easy,' says Jude, not flapping at the murmur, 'to say a lot of prayers, to go on a pilgrimage. What it isn't easy to do is to love others. But we must try. We must try.'

'Oh this just isn't RIGHT,' says Luisa. 'This is all OLD WORLD stuff! This could have come from the JESUITS! It's all changed! What you've got to do is to love YOURSELF!' And so saying – loudly and blush-worthily, she walks – nay storms – out of the makeshift church – nay the Conference suite – into the dark beach-windy night. 'I need to WALK!' she says, 'see the SEA!' And she goes, taking her therapy culture with her, out into the night.

I look around after she's gone. The rest seem relatively undisturbed, and are standing around in various postures of togetherness, displaying different aspects of piety. The eyes around the room are raised or lowered, rarely out ahead; the knees around the room are crooked, genuflected. Breasts are beaten, but few seem bothered about her, out in the night; for a moment I am torn, I am moved by the personal journey of the person in need, the person who is out there. And yet, there's something else: inside, here, those left make a big circle, encouraged by Jude, and circumnavigate the whole room while they make their signs of peace; each walks around the whole circle, wishing well to others. It's visible that I cannot find, as I look at faces, a single person who has attempted to convert me this weekend, and as a result I can do it with a clear conscience, can offer thanks and praise. Good luck, bad luck: trust in whatever is your God. These people have taught me much about togetherness.

At communion, the priest has to eat the extra wafers that someone has put aside; presumably for me, presumably for Luisa. We are bonded in one way, though I'm not sure whether Mac and Nancy obey the rules so finely as to be also stuck outside the charmed circle. Outside, I look for Luisa, wanting to encourage her to take her own path, but also wanting to lure her back in, to ask her to see that there's a commonwealth in, but also another commonwealth out that she can join if this is all getting too much for her, but she's gone, has, God-like, made herself invisible to the rest of us. I make my call home, the call that makes me secure, and know that Luisa, ten years divorced, on her own, can't make that call, no matter how many solicitors or popes she can call in to take on Sister Pius and the travel company – and she has mentioned contacting both of these – can no more get up and walk than the cripples of Lourdes.

Everyone but Luisa gathers in the bar later, where the Irishmen put back a few whiskies, where Mac and Nancy down some pints, where Edmund once again samples the taste of the wine that has cost him his driving licence. Mac and Nancy hold forth – Mac about the 'blessing' of getting a drink in the pub, Nancy about doing nothing wrong. Mac says another quiet thank-you for making sure that he and Nancy were not roomed separately, and he tells a tale of a parish priest who tried to have them blacked out of a party going to Lourdes; how he had to fight the absurdity of a seventy-five-year-old couple of fifteen years' standing not only being asked to sleep apart but being lectured when they explain that they have other rights. I go to bed late, see the Bible by it, and I don't look at it. But here I don't feel like an outsider. I suspect Luisa needs, above all, a touch of that same resistant therapy, if she's really to look after herself.

Monday, 7.29 a.m. *Now The Green Blade Riseth* – or not, in fact. I have been up for twelve minutes, having used all but one of the thirteen the hotel made available when their alarm system broke down, not because of the weight of calls but because, apparently, Manuel had put me in the wrong room. Luisa has been back from the beach – she has gone for a morning walk rather than risking spending any time with the jeerers and the mockers at the breakfast table   for precisely twenty seconds, with sixty seconds to spare. (The sixty seconds represent a sort of paranoia: she couldn't be sure we wouldn't take the excuse of her lateness as a chance to go without her.) Paul is trying to load us on to the bus: our luggage dematerializes, Mac collects his little Fatima hat from the floor, and Sister Pius is lifted physically on. Within two minutes of leaving Jude has wished us a good and holy morning and the Chinaman is singing over the mike: *But you are alwaysh / Closh to me . . .* And of course, whatever propaganda he might have put out the night before, we make the boat all right – Paul the driver knows his business, and knows this business with Sister Pius well.

Once aboard, the rest go off to mass in the chapel, while I sit on the deck watching the container base fade off into the distance. I fall asleep for a while, then talk to a Canadian on her way back from spreading her mother's ashes back in the home country. I only just make the duty-free before it's closed; when I see Mac and Nancy still way behind, I think they're going to miss the coach; but lo and behold, as I'm stuck behind four VISA card users, another till opens up for them just as they arrive and they're spirited straight through and back to the bus before I am. (On the way down the bus he hits me when I suggest he could just have commanded the waves to part and let Paul drive us across.)

On the bus from Holyhead there's another bit of kerfuffle when Luisa calls me forward to let me know that her video-tapes (particularly the epic of Padre Pio, but she is also worried about Christina Gallagher) have been 'stolen' by Sister Pius. 'I'm going to get the Pope and the *Universe* on to this!' she says. 'Those tapes are IRREPLACEABLE! They have sentimental value! She's just trying to WIND ME UP!' says Luisa, and she then practically has a fistfight with one of the African women when the latter takes exception to Luisa shouting out, 'The people on this bus are not CHRISTIANS!' She makes several passes by my seat. The first time she just wants to explain the conspiracy against her; the second time she wants to tell me that the old woman next to her fully supports her and is disgusted too, the third time she asks for a cigarette which she apparently wants to smoke in the bus's minuscule cludgie. A general search – a replica of the unsuccessful one for the video camera, which kicked off this shebang – is carried out, with an equal lack of success; a thousand chiefs, no Indians; lots of words, very little action. The one quiet person throughout is Paul; he waits until we all get off for our service station burgers then finds the tapes snuggled absent-mindedly in Sister Pius's bag. It's clear she's just demented (she turned the bus upside down looking for them) but it doesn't matter to anyone except Luisa, for whom cock-ups do not exist. 'It's a CONSPIRACY! I've a friend who's a SOLICITOR! I'm going to take legal action! . . .'

Paul puts on Bonnie Stewart, searching for an atmosphere that seems to have evaporated somewhere on our long and winding road (we're close to a new entity, Pilgrimage Rage). To distract myself from endless hours of this and of Paul's Irish Joke tapes, I talk to the Sri Lankan woman; her daughter (six) has already been to Lourdes four times. 'It's nice,' says Edmund, 'they're growing into religion'; but I can't help remembering that for three days the mother has fed the baby with a spoon. I say goodbye to them first. Luisa, too, I say goodbye to early, somewhere near a full-width half-sphere rainbow by the lift-shaft training tower in Northampton. Sister Pius has long stopped coming up and down the bus – these recent events seem to have bated her energies – but she does sum up, emotionally myopic: 'Thanks to everyone, including God for the weather . . . you've been good pilgrims – very well behaved and very prayerful. That's the main thing.' The burning sun with golden beam has transformed into a silver moon with a softer gleam, and the lights of evening have found a voice when I leap off to make the homeward journey.

And how can one not think, in the solitude of steps retraced, of St Christopher, the patron of travellers? Who wandered the world in search of novelty and adventure as a young man, and finally – coming upon an ailing hermit whose life's work was to show voyagers the safe place to cross a certain river – found a life's work of his own? And who should come to cross one day, but the child Christ, who, in addition to carrying a few pounds of natural weight, also bore the weight of the world on his shoulders? Opening my own front door I have an opposite sensation – a feeling of lightsomeness, of completeness, a feeling of perfection. A feeling that I've reached the end.

'I tried to love God, he said at length. It seems now I failed.'

So how does it happen that the game comes to be up? How does it happen that this Stephen leaps from the exultant exit from the informal confessional in Liverpool to the turgid, spiritless, faithless end that seems to run from here to eternity? The inwit he feels there proves to have no capacity to enlighten his life, since he still lacks that crucial conviction, that faith that he knows, and will know better later, from his life of love. So he releases himself from the oil-lamp-filling guitar-strumming, and opts instead for a life of going through the motions, as most of his friends do; life (on Sundays, at least) is a series of cowardices, a series of slimy deceptions that darken his inner doors with their hypocrisy. If the story starts with the small boy travelling alone but obedient to serve the Canon's mass, it ends with the big boy sitting surrounded by disobedient friends in the café, drinking coffee and smoking in six o'clock, Sunday evening, sullen silence. At seven each returns home with Polo-mint breath, answering with confident creativity enquiries about who said the mass and what the sermon was about.

The rest of life becomes equally void of strength, of resolution, of example. The relationship with the girl descends into typically late-adolescent stuff – betrayal, non-communication, desultory sexual activity. (There is some anorexia at a later stage: the joke is that it becomes a cautionary tale a devout Kafflik could use to warn young people off early sex.) The tiny world that surrounds his school and church is rocked by a series of scandals that only the Kafflik world could find scandalous. (Dr So-And-So, pillar of the Papes, is found to have had a twenty-year affair with his secretary; Mr So-And-So, lawyer and fellow-pillar, has another home, another child to add to the three born in wedlock; bog-standard Harper Valley business.) He needs out, but struggles for the strength, doesn't have that epiphanic moment on the beach that Joyce's Stephen has. The story that begins with a bright-eyed infant clutching 'Our Mother Mary' ends with narrow-eyed adolescent contempt for self, for others, for the workaday world.

His school career is fine; he is well taught in many things, does well, plans his escape. Fr. F, hanging on grimly, takes the Sixth Year R.E.

255

himself, and, in his blindness and bigotry, unintentionally trains his students in dialectic inventiveness: in these heady heights at the top of the school, discussion is at last permitted, and his classmates, full in the knowledge of things, spend endless weeks framing intellectual traps for Fr. F to fall into. So, when Fr. F has set out the Church's position on contraception, outlining the Vatican's pro-sanctity of life position, Boy X is primed to ask, formally and disquisitionally: 'Father. If contraception is frowned upon by the Church, is it then considered acceptable for Kafflik dog-owners to sterilize dogs?' When flummoxed (there being no Vatican position on this question) Fr. F has a catch-all answer: 'Faith is a gift of God.' And so, Boy Y: 'If natural birth control is a deliberate avoiding of pregnancy, is it not in effect of intention, the same as using a barrier method?' Fr. F: 'Faith is a gift of God.'

And of course, there is that subject close to the heart of all aspiring freedom seekers, the issue of free will and determinism. Remember the background – God sees everything and knows everything, drummed in from day one. But, Fr. F reveals to us at this late stage in the proceedings, God has been so good as to give us free will; 'not free will entirely', says Fr. F, 'but the freedom to choose right'. 'But father,' says Boy Z, 'if God knows everything, does not that mean that he knows what we are going to do in the future?' Fr. F: 'Of course.' Boy Z: 'How, then, can we be said to have free will if God already knows what we will do?' Fr. F: 'God allows you to choose whether you will do what he already knows that you will do.' Boy Z: 'But if he knows that we will do it, how is any other outcome but that we do it possible?' Fr. F: 'Faith is a gift of God.'

So, it seems, like Joyce's Stephen, this Stephen has an unpleasant puppiness, a pompous pseudo-intellectualism, to add to his deceitful double-dealing. But he does make an attempt at honesty, at coming clean, at some kind of redemption within the family. In the end, faced with the multiple truths of his existence – and truth is important – he resolves that something must be said. He does not know yet that this is the screw-up event to defeat all comers, the occasion of informing those at the bosom of the family that you no longer reside there, letting them know not only that you do not share their beliefs, but that (in their eyes) you happily embrace the journey to eternal damnation. He knows he has been always told to tell the truth, to be like George Washington by the cherry tree, to be like so many of the saints and martyrs who have not denied their faith, even when the pyre or the scaffold awaits. And so he tries to do so, unaware of how it's a dagger to the heart in this world where the gifts of God appear to have been unequally distributed.

Stephen sees the way forward when he hears his parents talk to their friends about his older brother, about their long-held disappointment that he has slipped away, and that he no longer attends mass. They say it is not the non-belief and the non-attendance that bothers them; it is the fact that he seems to have acquired non-belief and non-attendance without any tremor of inner perturbation, without any sense that he has thought about the importance of these things before departing from the Way, the Truth and the Life. They blame themselves: he did not get to study under the Jesuits, so perhaps things might have been different; nothing they can do now, of course; but would it be too much, in response to the openness in which their children have been brought up, to ask for a decision well made, carefully thought-out? For what stings like endless death is the apparent laziness of the way his decision has come about; the way the faith seems to have been conquered by thoughtless sloth . . .

Being the truthful sort, and the respectful one, Stephen resolves to make sure the same cannot be said of him. So when – finally, at seventeen or thereabouts – he acquires the composure to find his position untenable, when he begins to long to be like a George Eliot, or like a Joyce's Stephen, in the clarity and simplicity with which they find religion a transparent irrationality, and wishes to speak in a voice that is as clear as theirs, he takes a breath and opens a long summer's debate with his father, with the intention of finding a conclusion at which, unlazily, sensitively, truthfully, triumphantly, he brings to an end this tension between the desire for truth and the practice of it; without blushing or embarrassment or shame, he will announce, and have accepted for its distilled poise, his departure from the Kafflik Church. And so he sets about the task with gusto, raising issues great and small: the conflict of the human and the divine, the problems of ecumenism, the search for a more vibrant truth in the modern world.

But the moment of the final declaration never quite seems to come. His father rises to the debate with equal – and sincere – gusto, behaves not at all as if there is only one end to all this, and sets out unwittingly to combat the declaration that he does not know is on its way. He is not at all irrational, not at all dogmatic. In different words Stephen is told to look up and not straight ahead now and again. In different words he is told that God does not damn those who flirt with the other side, if it's another side that is the question. In different words he is told that faith is a gift of God. Painfully, particularly for him, his father retells his stories of the occasional (and temporary) disappearance of his own faith; of the books he reads when he is troubled by what he sees in Stephen, when he endures a dark night of the soul; he piles them on the table like a source of providence.

This moves Stephen for a while, as it must do – he has no idea that his father has ever wavered in this way, has no idea of the element of fear that lives in the doubt that is the essence of faith, and in such searing honesty lies a tempting pathway forward, a way away from the lazy rebellion of those Sunday evenings in the café. It makes him stop for thought, bring back to mind the whole tale, the whole pilgrimage-like journey from the small beginning to this likely end. But in the end there is only one end, for Stephen has called, one way or another, and no voice has come back to answer; if it is indeed a gift of God that is the key ingredient in this whole shooting-match then he has to declare that he has not received it.

So he decides that tonight is the night, and that he must come out once and for all. He makes an opportunity, a time and a place, a chance for a face-to-face every bit as profoundly honest as that which took place in the retreat-house; he decides what the right note is, one that fulfils *and completes the process of the debate that the summer has brought. And that night, more or less as he opens his mouth to make this momentous statement, with a huge weight hanging on his lips and his tongue, his younger brother announces, abruptly and without preamble, his own unilateral decision not to go to mass any more. In the fallout, the words dry up in Stephen's mouth and condemn him to a silence of almost Trappist proportions on the subject; a silence which lasts long beyond the point at which the truth was plain to one and all.*

These will be painful things long into the future. At seventeen, he has no real sense of their significance, their centrality, to those one deals with; he has no sense of the complexities of the adult world, of the disappointments that your children can bring. And Kafflik adults, very likely, have – or did have – little sense of the changed world of which one is trying to make sense. So Stephen offers to those people who are most hurt by decisions made long ago this account of what happened: the story of a happy childhood, of difficult times, of a moment of pure faith, of its failure to sustain and grow and develop and offer resonance often enough or regularly enough; along with an assurance that their own beg-to-difference on these questions is deeply respected; and that even after the canon-shouting and the vestment-learning and the irreverent climbing up the Mount of Venus they should know that he did – that he does – take seriously the question of belonging to a family such as this.

Seriously enough to make a journey such as this one is, and to find, in spite of flippancy, deep sources of respect there; and seriously enough to say that because he was so well taught to tell the truth, he does not want to lie any more.

Recessional

There's not a Kafflik in sight, I'm sort of pleased to say. No silly sisters, no bumptious brancardiers, no Virgin's volunteers, as I set off on one of all the roads that lead to you know where. At the end of this thing, I am off to the middle of the thing; to the panting heart of Rome beneath the apostles' crowning dome. It's not that I'm alone far from home; my true love, the tree on which my fruit hangs, is with me. Our child born out of marriedment stays at home with the children of no-longer-marriedment, looked after by the grandparents-of-one-but-not-the-other-two; maybe a non-Kafflik sense and sensibility is required to pick your way through this kind of post-marital mush, but we get to Gatwick in good time and spirits.

It's Good Friday when we set off, and feeling the blasphemy of flying at three o'clock (kick-off time for the crucifixion, of course) I half expect to fly through thunder and lightning. In general, and in memory, Good Friday for me is dark churches full of feet-of-the-cross-kissers and passion-hymn-crooners, not the Channel and the Alps and the fine afternoon I see as we fly in over Ostia. From Fiumicino it's a neat run by local train (through suburbs where allotment patches punctuate apartment blocks stacked with Chinese alphabet aerials) to our hotel. The concierge has a sharp black suit and a dazzling white shirt, and is framed by a behind-desk-wall of sparkling mirror. Up in our room the walls are moiré, the furniture is gilt-bronzed, the taps are gold, even the lavatory brush has a gilt finish. But the stench from the drains is rising fast from a toilet made in Hull, and, on the mini-television on the mini-bar, there's an Italian game-show whereon a woman with lilac lipstick and a silver wig like a pineapple top is showing planet cards to a mini-skirted mother and daughter team.

We're in the City of the Saints now, that's for sure, and Disney eggs in bright foil sit atop the café counters all the way along the road into town. At six in the evening, over a cup of coffee you could cut with a knife, I cut a deal with my fellow traveller, my heathen honcho. Friday, Good Friday, will be mine and the Kafflik Church's, and so will Sunday, Bloody (Easter) Sunday. In fair exchange, the programme for Saturday and Monday will remain devoutly secular. The evening, therefore, finds us following a tale that every Good Friday evening the Pope makes an appearance at the Colosseum walls to say the Stations of the Cross. Somewhat travel-lagged, we negotiate our way into the centre; we find our way by following a crowd of nuns. There are white nuns and black nuns and Chinese nuns; nuns in white and brown and black and blue; European nuns in trainers and African nuns in flat black shoes; and a single Italian nun, southernly brown, smartly sartorial in grey slip and white bobby-sox, who waits for her colleagues at Trajan's Column.

Another blast from the past: I notice all the non-nun women I see have their heads covered, as all women did up to about 1970. I am tempted to mark it down to atavism, to primitivism, until I notice that the sky has suddenly blackened in sensational style; that it's a real Good Friday after all, and they're just protecting their blue rinses. When the first downpour comes we duck into a bar, and sit underneath a Botticelli print sipping dark French beer until it dries out. As the hour approaches nine we make our way down to the lee of the arena. There are mobs and mobs standing, sitting, perched on every high spot and vantage-point; the Kafflik and Apostolic Church is out to play – grannies and schoolchildren, Italians and *estranieri*. Piped music

261

from less than heavenly-sounding choirs enfolds us, and there are flaming torches lit up high along the wall that divides us from the Forum.

So what if people are facing in several different directions, as if none is quite sure where the centre of the action will be? People travel for all sorts of reasons. For Queen, Buck House and the Horse Guards read Pope, Saint Pete's and the Swiss Guards, and some of those who come to gape carry candles in one hand and video cameras in the other. But if they expect to take back pictures of Papa they are disappointed, because what arrives to fill that space up by the torches is not a single Pope but a great squall of rain. We stand there for a bit, in the teeth of the deluge, but nothing happens, and in the end, half an hour of water later, we give up on the not-yet-appeared John Paul II, buy from a Sri Lankan vendor an umbrella that, at the first gust of wind, folds entirely inside itself and, diluvially damp, retire to a neighbourhood trattoria where a group of deaf men are sitting and (like Robert de Niro waiting, though in sign language) talking Italian.

Well, I reflect, there's always Easter Sunday to take a peek at the Pontiff. Late in the night, the toilet door shut fast against the Roman drains, I lie in the dark and dream of Gladiators, Fishers of Men throwing out a net, and the sky rent in twain. Above all I am thanking whatever stars have brought me to the point at which I write my own programme. For the last time I was here, circa 1976, there was no option on backing out, no possibility of disappearing from the sight of the Papa on a whim such as ours; like much of the rest of my childhood, the school pilgrimage to Rome was not something for which one organized one's own itinerary. Things were proscribed, circumscribed, inscribed in the ad passed round our classes. The offer, as blunt as those I have more recently answered for Lourdes or

Medjugorje or Knock, was for six days and five nights of pilgrimage in Rome, full-board, with all excursions including a full religious programme included; and, as an extra, the particular and special chance of ringside seats in St Peter's for the canonization of a saint.

True to the Ignatian principle of giving without counting the cost, my parents, sold, paid up. We flew from Glasgow back then, I among half a planeload of tartan-clad schoolmates. We were patriotic for all sorts of reasons. If we'd been allowed we'd have followed Scotland to Wembley and, of course, at this time and this place, the Bay City Rollers were shang-a-langing their way up the pop charts. More significant now was the sudden merging of the nationalistic with the religious, for the central event of our week away was to be not just *any* canonization, but the canonization of Blessed John Ogilvie, wee Glasgow's own wee saint, a model Pape whom the Proddies martyred at Glasgow Cross in 1614. Not since Celtic, the Glasgow Kafflik standard-bearers, had made the European Cup final in Lisbon in 1967 had so many left-footers been found boarding charter flights from Abbotsinch.

For my schoolmates Blessed John was not just a Scot (the first to enter the calendar since Margaret, Queen of Scotland, sanctified 700 years before) and not just a Glasgow boy (martyred just a hop, skip and a jump from the Celtic stadium), but also a Jesuit (and consequently the protector of the junior school, where two of my brothers were enrolled). On whatever date his feast fell, that day a gladsome anthem would ring out at our normally moribund school mass. It was our 'Jerusalem'; one of those big belted numbers that the big-boy bass-section at the back gives its heart and soul to:

> Blessed martyr, thy example,
> Will our strength in weakness be,

Hear our cry in times of peril –
Ogilvie! An Ogilvie!

On that same feast-day, once a year, some Jesuit preacher would tell the life story we'd all heard before. Of BJO's birth, in 1579, to noble stock in Banffshire; of his being sent, at twelve, on a Grand Tour which would end in Germany, at a Protestant academy, but ended instead at Louvain, where, one understands, the school team kicked with the left. Of his 1599 application to join the Jesuits, his 1601 vows of poverty, chastity and obedience, and his full-blown ordination in Paris in 1610. Of his first request as a priest, that he be sent back to a Scotland in the tight grip of reforming Protestant rulers, among them his own father, who (unknown to him) had in his absence become a commissioner – with splendid aptness – for the capture of itinerant Jesuits.

Ogilvie sails into Leith around about 1613; off goes the dog-collar, on goes the disguise (no Big Boys, we assume, will ask a horse-trader named John Watson if he's a Kafflik); he utters stirring words about 'the Church's antiquity', its 'unbroken succession', its members' 'sincere and perfect virtues shown in despising the world'. In Glasgow he is inevitably tricked, arrested, and tortured. It's good old thrilling priest-hole stuff: kept awake for eight days and nine nights by a round of jailers prodding him with pins, rods and knives, he nonetheless refuses to recant. Deals, plea-bargains, even escapes are desperately offered by authorities desperate not to make a martyr. As he goes to the gallows a minister is despatched to offer marriage to the Episcopalian Archbishop's daughter, with the richest prebend in the diocese as a dowry . . .

But she was only the Archbishop's daughter, and Ogilvie chooses hanging, drawing and quartering ahead of a lifetime with her. In truth he is only hanged, but his smuggled-out prison memoirs become a little local bestseller, and something like a cult (or what might have been a cult, if it had started somewhere less black-roofed, somewhere more Mediterranean) started and made a link which involved BJO becoming by arcane process SJO, worthy of a place on the painted list of saintly initials on the walls of St Aloysius's Church, and the real centre of this tartan-clad pilgrimage of 1976, which, of course, also touched down at Fiumicino, and which, of course, also featured a ride through the suburbs and the apartment blocks, albeit to a rather less gilt-ridden hotel.

Our programme back then was constructed on the principle of when in Rome, do as good Kaffliks on holiday do, and our days were entirely devoted to worship of a highly ordered fashion. We were bussed to the Gesù, the Jesuit HQ, where we had a mass and were encouraged to gaze at the frescoes above. (Shown officiously to our seats, we did not get to see Bernini's gorgeous statue of St Robert Bellarmine.) We were bussed to the Church of San Ignazio di Loyola, where we had a mass, having found ourselves conveniently positioned to see the illusionistic painted cupola. (Nobody took the trouble to explain the meaning of the fantastic ceiling behind us, however.) And we were bussed to San Paolo fuori Le Mura, where we had a mass and, in our ordered rows, could gaze at the stupendous marble altar-canopy. (The mosaics of Pietro Cavallini, just around the other side of the columns, we were not able to see.)

And so on, and so forth; memories are vague, of course, and spiritual memories are the vaguest of all. What is really most clear to me is that in that series of regimented expeditions, I discovered two things about myself. One was that I was short-sighted; I suddenly found that I could not discern the features of one of the familiar Jesuit priests up there in front. The other was that I was hearing mass in some of the most beautiful, resonant churches on earth, but that I could find no resonance there. Going to mass again and again and again in that week did not deepen my sense of belief. In fact it did the opposite; it offered an intensive opportunity to understand how deep was my numb unthrilledness, even there at the centre of things. I suppose that what it means is that, there and then, ordered from pillar to post, sat in neat rows and made to hear mass after mass, I first understood clearly that I had no faith.

Maybe that is why the excitements of the night seem clearer in the memory; less painful that way. And we did behave painfully. After *antipasto* and pasta and *carne* we were set free to wander for an hour in our school uniforms, and, wearing ties tied big enough to fill the V of our V-necked jumpers, we searched desperately for the debauchery of *una birra* bars that would serve us. We ran around the town, I remember, telling uncomprehending Romans they were cocksuckers (such was our pre-Euro education, our sense of Kafflik solidarity) before slipping back into our cheap hotel invisibly (for the Jesuit crew were of course watchful, as they cradled their post-prandial whiskies and sambucas) the worse for wear. Good Kafflik boys, we were, all of us.

Sincere and perfect virtues shown in despising the world? Something like that.

No doubt we were up and about next morning, bright and early, dressed and ready for the next mass. We certainly never got to sleep in, back then, as we do now, on this secular Saturday in the Rome of the present day. Eventually the drains drive us to get up, to breakfast among gold and mirrors, to talk some sights. Herself sets the itinerary, and it stuns me as she lists where we will be going. On the basis of my previous journey, I have long been in the habit of thinking of Rome as a place I know. But I realize now that on the previous visit we saw nothing of the glory that was Rome; our programme took in only glory that was Roman Kafflikism. Back then we saw only churches, monasteries, papal residences. (We were even taken to visit a seminary, the Scots College, presumably in case any of us should feel a vacational-vocational urge.) Everywhere we went the adults who were with us showed piety and respect and allegiance, but they did not show us the Empire.

So today my heart thrills with a profound sense of joyful release as we do the obvious, the glaring, the basic. We take a bus downtown and walk the Forum, kicking up the dust as we frolic through the Temples of Saturn and of Castor and Pollux, and joyously puzzle with the Latin on the Arch of Septimius Severus, on Titus's Arch, on Phocas's Column. It becomes an orgy for me, this Roman world; I become randy for non-Kafflik ruin. Vesta's temple, Antoninus and Faustina's, that of Saturn. The House of the Vestal Virgins. The Rostra. The Curia. Augustus's Forum, Caesar's Forum, Nerva's Forum. Caesar's Basilica, Aemilia's Basilica, even Constantine's Basilica. (I liked Constantine as a boy; remember that cross he saw in the sky when imperially hunting deer? An empire turned Christian that day.)

In front of us, as we pass through, a group walks with their guide in charge. They look up at the Church of San Lorenzo, which sits smack dab in the middle of the Roman ruins. They seem to stop specially. There was, it seems, originally a Roman temple on the spot, upon which was imposed a Doric front of sorts to make a place of Christian worship. The tourists, Kaffliks all, receive instruction, and learn to think of the prefixing of 'Roman' with 'Holy' as progress. The guide stands for a second, pointing at something floating high in the space of the façade, abandoned by the disappearance of some steps, or a plinth. Who knows? He does. 'Notice where the door is,' he says, authoritative, clipped. They notice.

We lunch nicely, drink a beer, smoke half a fag, but we're anxious to return to what we were doing. Later in the day we wander down to the Colosseum. We wander and climb, and as we turn a corner, we find the same pious party are there. This time they are on their own, chatting among themselves, filling the spaces their knowledge lacks with half-remembered imaginations. 'Was there a roof there? I think there was a roof there,' someone says, and another agrees. It seems a hopeful sort of behaviour. Watching them feels like watching myself back then, as I sought to hold on to something slipping away, as, faithless, I tried to fill the empty space in exactly the same kind of way, hoping that something might come along to supply that which we were assured would come but which simply never bothered to turn up; which therefore filled my later childhood with a permanent sense of something missing.

If faith is a gift of God and you don't have faith then it takes courage, as a child, to avoid feeling ungifted. I don't think I ever had that courage. I think, having looked up clear at this thing in the course of these journeys, that is the one thing I can see now. For this travelling has been a seeing, has been a cure for the strange myopia that developed in that week in Rome way back then; and I am not talking about the one for which I now need glasses. For like many of my fellow-sufferers of Post-Traumatic Kafflik Syndrome I responded to the discovery of a void not by filling it with good humanistic concerns but by spending years in a wilderness of semi-pretence, hiding the true condition my condition was in, ashamed to come clean for feeling dirty.

So when I married first, familially apprehensive of the consequences of otherwise, I married in a church. I stuck with it, even though the preparation included compulsory attendance at a preposterous Marriage Counselling course which featured an Irish canon barking out 'no primrose path' warnings and a sweaty doctor telling anti-contraception tales of babies born holding IUDs in their hands. Undisturbed by this lunacy – or at least prepared to pretend for other reasons – I had baptisms done on my first children when I had them. Primarily for the sake of others – though ultra-selfishly in doing it to avoid a strife I couldn't face up to – I stood up and made promises to renounce the Devil and all his works, vowed to help my infants to grow in the love of the Lord.

It is possible just to carry on that way for a lifetime, of course; maybe as you grow old you drift back, you find something that suits your middle age, your search for belonging; it reinforces your culture, and you stay, and you tell your grandchildren that on the long and winding road of the world you lost, but found again, your faith. It did not happen that way for me; the collapse of my first marriage and my simple assertion to my family that I had no interest in spending the rest of my life in the Kafflik way of divorce – lifetime celibacy and truth to the original vows – brought with it a kind of openness to my relationship that I had never known before. A range of issues had to be faced in my dealings with myself, and the knowledge of that numb unthrilledness was one.

So it has been on this journey. Looking up clear, I have felt that numb unthrilledness again. I have felt other things, too, other echoes of something deeper, more profound. I have felt able to take or leave, and to reject the old propaganda that you must be in or you are out. I have begun to see that when you deal with any family, particular or universal, the key thing you need to show is honesty, or else it cannot be your family at all. The knowledge of these things, learned on this journey, and their combination with other things, learned in life-lessons on a harder road than that just travelled, I feel have made me a whole person at last; has restored my sight; has shown me where the door was. I suppose I feel that this travel has been a religious experience – that it has redeemed my soul.

What of that? Back there in 1976, the programme of masses

culminated in a real religious experience such as the hardest-lining Medjugorje-goer would have to acknowledge – the Big One, the Canonization itself. Again, we were wheeled in, parked in seats near the front, gazed on by tourists imprisoned behind wooden walls. (This only after a funny thing on the way in, something that only my home town could throw up – Pastor Jack Glass, Glasgow's own tub-thumping Ian Paisley-type Protestant fundamentalist, seen being bundled away, apparently for unfurling, in the middle of St Peter's Square, an Orange-march-type banner saying NO POPERY HERE.)

We were made to know what a privilege we had to be where Popery unquestionably was. We even had what was dubbed a 'private audience' with the Pope the night before. (Old hands will know that this means that you sit in a specially built stadium-barn, while adults sit and gape reverently, while children such as I was doze at the dreary drone of a translated text.) On the morning itself the baroque complexity of St Peter's seemed ordinary, however over-wrought; I was born to baroque 'n' roll, and had lived endless hours of my life in fancy churches. This – what with the dirty off-brown mosaicing around the interior of the dome, and those horrible green marble twists holding up the altar-canopy – just seemed a bit bigger and a bit more horrible than the average.

Much more eye-opening was the behaviour of the congregation. There were bagpipes in the Basilica, and kilts in the Curia; and there was a throng of dizzy Scottish nuns, excited to distraction by making it to the heart of things at last. Plonked in our rows long before the kick-off – such an orderly life we lived – we had a chance to watch the bigwigs arrive, and to watch the punters do suitable respect to hierarchy. All around us people, especially nuns, and predominantly women, did reverence to the leaders of the operation who were exclusively men. This reverence was shown by gradually, and growingly, increasing the level of applause proportionate to the level on the religious-evolutionary pyramid to which the bigwig belonged.

Mild applause and clapping: the humble features of John Fagan, the Easterhouse man, the spontaneous regression of whose terminal cancer had supplied BJO with the miracle he needed to become SJO. Less mild applause – the Scottish bishops, in strict order of importance. Aberdeen (applause), the Auxiliary of Edinburgh (more applause), the smoothie anti-abortionist (then Auxiliary of Glasgow) Winning (applause and cheering, received with that slightly smug smile), the tub-thumping Archbishop Scanlan of Glasgow (applause and cheering, barely acknowledged), and (whoops and cheers) Cardinal Gordon Joseph Gray of Edinburgh and Saint Andrews. But however well-received he is, his reception is mild compared to that which the superstars of the operation receive when they make their way up the aisle. A whole raft of purple-clad Curia-ites emerge, to wild nunly celebration, heading a procession which finally features Bafile, the Cardinal in charge of the Congregation of Saints, Arrupe, the Head Honcho of the Jesuits; and the Papa himself. Leaping to their nimble feet, the nuns raise the already precipitous roof as soon as the frail old man comes into view, as soon as they see him carried in (as in 'I'll have two pints of what the Pope drinks') the Sedia Gestatoriat. I myself do not leap up; oh, of course, I kneel and stand like all the rest, and generally offer lip-service to the service. I know the ball's on the slates and the game's a bogey, however much they shriek and scream in the rows behind. And when I return home at the end of the week I slip easily into a practised routine of that amused but semi-reverent summary that has always been the tone of my Kafflik travelling.

There's nothing to stir a nun's blood this Sunday morning in Rome, twenty-odd years on. The Pope has changed, of course, several times; Paul VI went soon after the Ogilvie day, and then we had the murdered one – *not!* – and then the nice Polish one who promised so much, who used to ride a motorcycle pursued by the fascistic Polish cops, but who turned out to be a rod of iron, a moral Mussolini himself.

Easter Sunday is of course an *Urbi Et Orbi* day; is the day when, out there in the Square in the Roman springtime, the Papa speaks to the city and the world. And of course I do intend to be there, do intend to pay my proper respects to the Big Man. Before I go to bed on Saturday at twelve, warm with wine, I check with the sharp-suited concierges, and they tell me that Papa won't preach before eleven. I am a little late in waking at ten, but it's OK. My head's a bit heavy, and the room has a certain heavy-curtained blackness, but I rise full of purpose, and start to shave, and shower. As I dress, of course I switch on the television, as you must do, whatever the time of day it is, if you are in a hotel room in another country; and what I see on RAIUNO is that the pill-prohibiting Pontiff has already staggered, last-leggy, to his chair, and that the Easter Sunday mass is already well under way. It seems only too appropriate, somehow, to the general weakness of my spiritual fibre, that I end up making my final observances – the last act in this process of closure – sitting downstairs in the hotel restaurant watching from five miles away with a croissant and a cup of sweet chocolate.

The screen doesn't suggest that much is missed. The supreme one sits slumped in his chair for most of the time; he remains sitting to preach. There's a bright sun, goldware, an altarful of flowers, the usual hysterotechnics of the Sistine Choir. The sick are Lourdes-like up at the front, ahead even of the cardinals and archbishops; beyond them, the façade of the Basilica is entirely covered in a builder's tarpaulin. Nothing much, then, to draw the eye away from that frail old man preaching about *risorgimento*, about resurrection, and I know what I've always known really, that there's no such thing for me and for that thing that did a runner in the same place some twenty years ago. Something else, maybe, something like *reconciliazione*. But not faith.

And of course, there is Monday – there is pagan day. Before we fly out we take a tram out to the Villa Borghese. Ironically, the place has a Kafflik origin; one of the Cardinals Borghese, having presumably plundered the Vatican cellars, had it built in 1605, in the days when Kafflik priests of a certain seniority required a property to match. Now this spot amidst the gardens is more profane than sacred; so it proves for me.

Herself says she came there while Interrailing ten or twelve years before, and remembers it brown and shabby, a ruin, if fabulous. Like the façade of St Peter's at the panting heart, it turns out it's been undergoing change; unlike it, it's finished, complete, perfected. With help from IBM and the Banco di Lavoro the villa is now a pristine place, full of grace. Inside, in each gorgeous room there is a statue of Bernini's. The Cardinal, hedonist and patron, commissioned them from the young sculptor, so these too have holy origin, but they are primarily pagan, are mostly mythical in subject-matter. And how much finer are they than the Bellarmine, which I never saw, or the interior of St Peter's? There is a David, on which Bernini's own features sit hard in the moment before the stone is thrown; and Persephone with Pluto, whose thick male fingers seem to make indentation into the marble, seem to bend it and shape it like a sculptor working in something much more malleable.

Before Apollo and Daphne we stand in wonder, together, for half an hour, watching the cloth swathe and body arch as the beautiful half-boy god Grecian Urn-like almost catches the lovely girl before she turns tree; watching her leg between the groin and the toes merge gorgeously into the marble trunk, and the bark reach luxuriously towards her groin and fuse into

273

loin-cloth as, absolutely rooted, she nonetheless seems to be ready for take-off. We walk around and around, and see it front and back and sides. It gives the clearest of messages in its deep, profound pleasure: it's pagan travel for me from now on.

(As St Paul said, as he packed his suitcase and headed off for Damascus . . .)